London School of Economics
Monographs on Social Anthropology

Managing Editor: James Woodburn

The Monographs on Social Anthropology were established in 1940 and aim to publish results of modern anthropological research of primary interest to specialists.

The continuation of the series was made possible by a grant in aid from the Wenner-Gren Foundation for Anthropological Research, and more recently by a further grant from the Governors of the London School of Economics and Political Science. Income from sales is returned to a revolving fund to assist further publications.

The Monographs are under the direction of an Editorial Board associated with the Department of Anthropology of the London School of Economics and Political Science.

London School of Economics
Monographs on Social Anthropology
No 57

Sacrifice and Sharing
in the Philippine Highlands

Religion and Society
among the Buid of Mindoro

THOMAS GIBSON

THE ATHLONE PRESS
LONDON and DOVER, NEW HAMPSHIRE

First published in 1986 by The Athlone Press
44 Bedford Row, London WC1R 4LY and
51 Washington Street, Dover, NH 03820

British Library Cataloguing in Publication Data

Gibson, Thomas
    Sacrifice and sharing in the Philippine Highlands:
    religion and society among the Buid of Mindoro.——
    (London School of Economics monographs on social
    anthropology, ISSN 0077–1704; no. 57)
    1. Buhid (Philippine people)   2. Mindoro
    (Philippines)——Social life and customs
    I. Title   II. Series
    305.8'9921   DS666.B7/

    ISBN 0–485–19559–3

Library of Congress Cataloging in Publication Data
Gibson, Thomas, 1956–
    Sacrifice and sharing in the Philippine Highlands.

    Bibliography: p.
    Includes index.
    1. Buhid (Philippine people)   2. Buhid (Philippine
people)——Religion.   I. Title.
DS666.B78G53   1986   305.8'9921   85–15771
ISBN 0–485–19559–3

Typeset by The Word Factory, Rossendale, Lancashire
Printed in Great Britain at the University Press, Cambridge.

Contents

Maps

Figures

Acknowledgments

The author would like to thank the following for permission to
reproduce copyright material:

Professor David Steinberg and his co-authors of *In Search of Southeast
Asia* for Map VII.

The editor of *Anthropological Linguistics* for Map III, which appeared in
Volume 12, 1970.

The American Anthropological Association and Harold Conklin for
Map II, which appeared in *American Anthropologist* 52 (2), 1949. It is
not for further reproduction.

The University of California Press for Map VI which appeared in
Colonial Manila, by Robert Reed.

Preface

This book is a revised version of my doctoral dissertation, *Religion, Kinship and Society among the Buid of Mindoro, Philippines*. My understanding of Buid religion and society, such as it is, derives in equal measure from the instruction and moral support I have received over the years from two groups of people: from the Buid themselves and from those who taught me social anthropology at the London School of Economics. Among the former, I should like to thank, in particular, Gaynu, Agaw, Lifus and Yaum. Among the latter, I should like to thank, in particular, Maurice Bloch and James Woodburn. My wife, Ruhi Maker, and my parents, Count and Katherine Gibson, have provided me with unfailing moral and material support when it was most needed.

Many friends in the Philippines provided me with a warm hospitality. I feel an especially deep sense of obligation toward Benita and Pedro Magannon of Lubu, to Genoveva and Frank Rivera of Roxas, and to Gloria and Antonio Gayus of Lisap. Father Antoon Postma, Professor Ponciano Bennagen and Dr Estaban Magannon provided me with many stimulating discussions concerning my research and taught me that commitment to the peoples one seeks to understand in anthropology is a prerequisite to any scientific research.

Fieldwork was made possible largely by a postgraduate studentship from the London School of Economics. Funds for the purchase of equipment and for travel to and from the Philippines were provided by the Central Research Fund of the University of London. The Ethnography Department of the British Museum supplied an additional grant for the collection of Buid material culture. A grant from the Radcliffe-Brown Memorial Fund of the Royal Anthropological Institute aided in the final stages of preparation of my thesis. Within the Philippines, I enjoyed the institutional support of the National Museum, the Department of Anthropology of the University of the Philippines, Diliman, and the Institute of Philippine Culture at the Ateneo de Manila University.

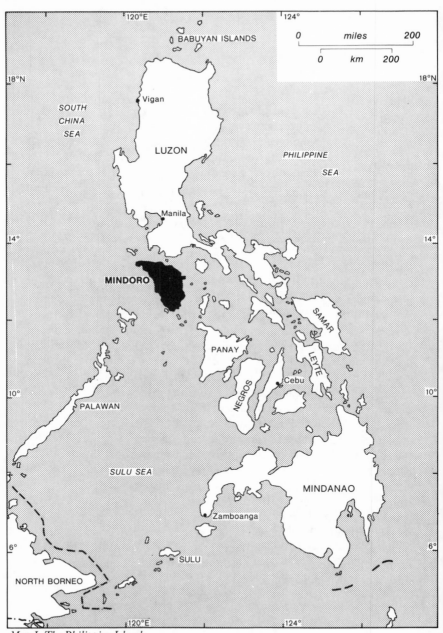

Map I The Philippine Islands

1   Introduction

The plan of this book follows the development of my understanding of Buid culture and society in the following way. I found, and
I believe it is a common finding among anthropological fieldworkers,
that certain domains of Buid experience were more immediately
accessible to me than others. Those aspects of Buid life which related
to the immediate social and physical environment; to basic somatic and
emotional experiences; and to the simpler forms of social interaction
such as conversations about the foregoing, were not, on the whole,
completely unintelligible to me at the beginning of my initiation into
Buid culture. These aspects are treated in the first part of the book.
But the underlying intellectual and moral assumptions about the way
life is and ought to be are still not entirely clear to me and, perhaps,
never will be. Nevertheless, I believe that I was able to achieve some
degree of comprehension of these after two years, and hope I will be
able to return to the Buid in future and acquire even more. What I call
the idioms of Buid social organisation are treated in the second part of
the book. The Buid also claimed to have sense experience of a whole
realm which will forever remain closed to me: that of the invisible spirit
world, a world of great concern to the Buid, interaction with which
occupies a great deal of their time and energy. Even here, I feel I was
able to achieve some understanding. This world is covered in the third
part of the book. Now, one of the basic theoretical assumptions made
in this book is that those domains of experience which are most
accessible to an outsider also provide the raw material on which the
members of a society draw for images, symbols, metaphors, or idioms,
call them what one will, in constructing their more abstract concepts,
and that the way to go about understanding religious, moral and
cosmological beliefs and practices is to link them to the varieties of
mundane experience with which they are associated by the people who
hold them and carry them out. I try, then, to link the first, second and
third parts of the book together in the final part.

The problems which were to dominate my field research and subsequent analysis were set for me from the very beginning of my contact
with the Buid. Mine was not a carefully planned investigation of a

1

limited domain of Buid life, plotted out in advance of immersion in their social and physical environment, with little prior knowledge of them, but a continuing struggle to come to terms with their fear of outsiders, and my fear of rejection by a group into whose care I had committed myself for longer than I had at first supposed. The problems I met with may best be summarised by presenting an account of my field experience.

My first trip to Mindoro took place in July 1979. Mindoro is the seventh largest island in the Philippines, lying just south of Luzon. It has a total area of some 10,000 square kilometres, and a population of fewer than 700,000. Geologically, it is part of the Sunda shelf which forms the base of the land masses of the Malay peninsula, Borneo and Palawan. According to Wernstedt and Spencer, its flora and fauna also exhibit closer affinities to those of Borneo than to those of the rest of the Philippines (Wernstedt and Spencer, 1967; but see Conklin, 1957: 27). The island is reached from Manila by a two-and-a-half-hour bus journey to the city of Batangas, followed by a further two-and-a-half-hour boat trip to the provincial capital of Oriental Mindoro, Calapan. Upon reaching Calapan, a host of *cargadores* descend on the ship and compete to carry one's bags to the waiting buses, which set off as soon as they are loaded for points south, following the erratically paved 'national highway' along the coast. To the passengers' right the mountains of the interior rise sharply up from the irrigated rice terraces of the coastal littoral, culminating in the towering peak of Mount Halcon, which rises over 2,500 metres from the plain in just ten kilometres. On the densely forested slopes of this mountain live the still little-known Alangan tribe. Proceeding down the narrow coastal plain, the bus stops in a series of market towns, before following the highway inland to cross the Bongabon river by means of the reinforced cement bridge at Lisap. It is often said and, I think, firmly believed by local Buid and lowland Christians, that the construction workers brought in to build this bridge reinforced its huge cement piles with the bodies of small children abducted from the area so that it could withstand the force of the river in full flood.

It was at the Lisap bridge that I dismounted, having a letter of introduction to one of the tenants of a local landowner, Severino Luna, who had a ranch on the Siangi river just above the bridge. Luna had published a book about the life of a Buid youth, known as Bag-itan, with whom he had become friends during visits by the youth to his ranch in the foothills (Luna, 1975, see Map V). Telling the group of

Christians standing around the shops precariously perched on the cliff next to the bridge that I was looking for the 'Mangyan', they pointed two Buid out to me. While the Christians were all dressed in what is best described as American-style clothing adapted to the tropics, the two Buid youths (who had come, perhaps, to buy some rice or cakes) were dressed only in filthy loincloths and had masses of matted hair roughly tied up with cloths. Even more striking was the contrast between the assertive manner of the Christians, who immediately approached and engaged me in conversation, and the manner of the Buid, who stood cowering beside the trail, and who became even more agitated when I approached them. They fixed their eyes on the ground, and refused to acknowledge the fact that I was asking them in Tagalog the whereabouts of Luna's friend, Bag-itan. I later came to learn that it was impossible for me to engage even my best Buid friends in conversation while at this place of the *luktanun* (Christian lowlanders), for most Buid are in a state approaching panic when they venture into the lowlands. This is the image most lowlanders have of the Buid: an image of dirty, terrified creatures of the forest. The image the Buid have of the Christians is one of the central themes of this book, and I shall not go into it here except to say that it is equally negative, so much so that it is difficult for one having been closely involved with the Buid to write objectively about the Christians. In this book, I shall be dealing with the lowland Christians only as seen through Buid eyes. This will leave the reader with an extremely biased image of the lowlanders, I fear, but this book is, after all, about the Buid, and I can only apologise to the many Christians who showed me kindness when the Buid were still wary of my identity and motives.

My initial plan was to learn the local form of Tagalog, used as a *lingua franca* by both the Christians from different parts of the Bisayan islands and by the Buid, as a preliminary to learning the unrecorded Buid language. I planned to do this living among the Bisayan settlers in Siangi before moving on to live with the Siangi Buid. I soon realised, however, that the Siangi Buid are under intense pressure from the large and often violent Christian population which has taken over the flat land in their valley. The Christians in the mountains tend to be a rather lawless population and, indeed, many of them are there due to their record in the lowlands. Nevertheless, I spent three months among them, learning enough Tagalog from them to get by, and also acquiring some idea of their social organisation and values, which was clearly necessary for an understanding of the social environment in which the Buid lived. At that point, I felt that my association with the Siangi Christians had so compromised my standing among the Buid that I would have to work in another area. I persuaded a leader of the Buid in Fanuban to guide me to Ugun Liguma, where I found a youth from Fawa to guide me up-river to the mouth of the Ginyang (see Map IV). The confluence of the Ginyang and the Bongabon (known in Buid as Binagaw) rivers represents the extreme limit of Buid territory in the north. Only by chance was I allowed to spend the night in Ginyang, and the next morning I was brought back to Ugun Liguma and abandoned to my own devices. I made my way back to Siangi. From this trip, I decided that the best situation for fieldwork was to be found in Ugun Liguma. Ginyang, while constituting a more traditional region, is completely cut off from the lowlands whenever it rains, for it can only be reached by crossing the Bongabon river several times. The river can rise from a depth of one metre to well over two in a matter of hours, with a current so strong that it is uncrossable by even the most experienced Buid. They maintain rattan bridges on the upper reaches of the river where the banks narrow into sheer cliffs, in order to maintain communications during the rainy season. Ugun Liguma, on the other hand, can be reached, if by a rather circuitous route, without crossing the Bongabon, and is fairly easily reached when the river is fordable. Furthermore, the Buid up-river from Ugun Liguma continue to dwell in dispersed settlements each containing no more than two or three house-holds, making the study of such exceptional events as births, marriages and deaths difficult. As a prominent geographer has noted: 'the interior of Mindoro is densely forested and accessible only by a network of rough mountain trails, which instead of paralleling the ridges or valleys, persists across the grain of the topography' (Wernstedt and Spencer, 1967: 429). Movement from one settlement to another is extremely difficult, especially in the rain, which turns the steep trails to mud, and can only be accomplished barefoot or with ice cleats strapped on to one's shoes (Postma, personal communication). I decided that Ugun Liguma pre-sented the best compromise between the more acculturated Buid settlements down-river and the more 'pristine' dispersed settlements up-river since the population of the Ayufay river valley was still in the process of aggregating into the large settlement of Ugun Liguma when I arrived. This had the added advantage of providing me with an opportunity to observe the process of population concentration as it occurred. Whether or not the new 'barrio' of Ugun Liguma would survive was still an open question when I left the field in September 1981.

I returned to Ugun Liguma in October 1979 only to find that it was empty, the inhabitants all having returned to their swidden houses. The leader of the settlement, Agaw, had formed a smaller settlement some years earlier on the banks of the Ayufay and it was there that the greater part of the Ayufay Buid were now staying. I continued on to Ayufay, and Agaw let me sleep in his house, but while I was out for a walk on the third day, he and his family quietly disappeared. My situation was saved only by the fact that there was one Christian family in the settlement which had come to sell salt, sugar and other items to the Buid, who had just been paid for their maize harvest. This family knew of me through relatives in Siangi. They agreed to look after me and gave me a small hut of my own to sleep in. This arrangement took the immediate pressure of my presence off the Buid. It would probably not have been tolerated had I been directly dependent on them at the beginning.

The first few months were difficult. Not only did I contract malaria and dysentery from inexperience, but the Buid are highly suspicious of outsiders, particularly tall white ones. I had been prepared for this by a previous fieldworker, Pennoyer, who had been 'evicted' by one Taubuid community (see Appendix I). It was not until a year later that I learned that I had been regarded as a witch (*aswang*) when I first arrived. *Aswang* beliefs are current among the Christians as well as among the Buid. They are inherently evil human beings capable of taking on animal forms in order to prey on the flesh of other humans (cf. Lieban, 1967: 66 ff.). It appears that the Buid had associated me with the American Protestant missionaries who had been working out of the settlement of Batangan for many years, and who were the only whites the Buid had ever encountered. These missionaries subscribe to a fundamentalist version of Christianity and make a point of suppressing all manifestations of the traditional religion as soon as it is in their power to do so. Above all, this involves the suppression of animal sacrifice, which, as I shall show later in this book, is the primary means by which the community of the living maintains its internal unity and defends itself against spirit attack. The Buid interpreted the missionary attack on animal sacrifice as an indication of their alliance with, or at least similarity to, the evil spirits. As I interpret it, the Buid identified the missionaries (and myself) as *aswang* because it is the only category which covers both humans and spirits. It is actually quite peripheral to their central concerns with the spirit world, and may in fact be a borrowing from the Bisayans, as I never heard it raised in any other context.

Gradually, beginning with Agaw and with Gaynu, who was to become my best friend and informant, these suspicions began to break down as I persisted in my attempts to learn the Buid language and culture, and to participate in their rituals. What my actual purpose was never became clear to many, and was perhaps only fully understood by Gaynu, who accompanied me to Manila a year later. There I showed him the National Museum with its carefully labelled artefacts from mountain groups all over the Philippines. It was not until some six months had passed that I began to collect any real information, or even to make a proper start at learning the language. It was only after a year that I made the final step toward full acceptance by the Buid, when Agaw himself decided that as I spoke their language and supported them in all their dealings with the Christians, it was no longer right for me to go on eating with the Christians. He suggested that I take my meals with his family, and I did so until my departure fourteen months later. By this time, I was told, I was no longer a *luktanun* 'alien', but *Buid yadi*, 'also a Buid'.

Several factors were decisive in my eventual acceptance by the Buid. The first was the presence of the Bisayan family who had exceptionally good relations with the Buid, and who were willing to look after me during the first months. Without them, I think I would have been boycotted into defeat. The second was the determination by Agaw to hold his community together and open it to contact with the outside world. The third was Gaynu, whose intellectual curiosity overcame his suspicion from the first, and who accepted me as fully human during the most difficult period. Finally, the arrival of my wife Ruhi in July 1980 served to humanise me even to the most conservative. Not only was she close to the Buid in physical appearance, being Pakistani, but she established an immediate rapport with the spirit mediums. She stayed with me in the field for more than six months, and her success in gaining the confidence of the Buid could later be measured by the enthusiasm with which the Buid greeted several other visitors I brought them. These included Dr Harold Conklin, Dr Maurice Bloch and my brother, George.

I have covered these details of my field experience at such length because they help to place the sort of data I gathered and the sort of issues I address in this book in the proper light. I was given only the vaguest accounts of what I did not observe and question as it happened. The Buid are not given to theorising about their social system, nor even to contemplating hypothetical social situations. Some of them, such as Gaynu, are a good deal more interested in metaphysical speculation than others. While of interest in itself, this propensity does not aid the researcher in elucidating the actual principles of social behaviour in concrete situations. I hope that I was able to observe enough particular events during my two-year stay in order to construct a general model of Buid society. The Buid have no such model themselves.

A central concern of both the Buid and of this book is their relationship with the outside world. The questions to which this book is intended to supply some answers were posed for me at the very beginning of my fieldwork: the Buid live within one day's journey from Manila, yet seem to have persisted as an autonomous culture and society into the latter part of the twentieth century; they are extremely suspicious of outsiders, yet never show any signs of aggression or violence towards them; they would normally be classified as a society at the 'tribal' stage of social evolution, yet my attempts at applying the 'genealogical method' as a key to understanding their social organisation led nowhere; they are continually meeting in large groups to discuss serious matters, but seem never to quarrel; and they seemed to be completely obsessed with the invisible world, many of the men spending night after night chanting quietly in the darkness.

In Chapter 2 I describe the general historical context in which Buid society has developed over the past few centuries, although we know nothing of the Buid themselves before the Second World War. This history accounts for their survival and enclavement within the larger Philippine nation, for the existence of parallel, distinct, yet interdependent societies in the highlands and lowlands of Mindoro. In Chapter 3 I describe the traditional Buid environment and economy, showing how they contrast with those of the lowlands, and how they are currently being transformed as a result of Christian penetration and cash cropping.

In Chapter 4 I describe the lack of importance of the idiom of kinship in Buid social life, and the idioms of companionship which take their place. The marital relationship, its initiation and dissolution, constitutes the key to Buid organisation, as the most important type of companionship. In Chapter 5 I describe the emergence of corporate groupings, based on residence in large-scale settlements, and the consequent transformation of the traditional system of social organisation.

In Chapter 6 I describe Buid spirit mediumship, with its peculiar emphasis on the collective apprehension of the spirit world, and on the need for cooperation in driving off the predatory spirits. In Chapter 7 I describe the various forms of animal sacrifice practised by the Buid, culminating in the sharing of meat with the spirits of the earth, the source of all human and crop fertility.

In Chapter 8 I draw out the parallels between the human and spirit worlds, and between collective participation in social and religious activities. I show that collective ritual has provided a model for the conduct of the corporate affairs of the new settled communities, and that the mystical dangers which stem from communal division serve as an effective incentive for the maintenance of social solidarity now as in the past. Finally, in Chapter 9, I venture some speculations concerning the way in which Buid society and religion have developed as a result of enclavement within vastly more powerful societies for the past four hundred years.

1

The Historical and Economic Context

2   History

An understanding of the early history of the Philippines before the American occupation in 1898 is essential for explaining the survival into the twentieth century of the various highland groups in Mindoro as autonomous societies. This period is covered in a summary fashion below. In the second part, the policies of the American and Republican governments of the Philippines towards the 'non-Christian' tribes are reviewed, and the post-war histories of Mindoro as a whole, of the municipality of Bongabon, of the Buid within that municipality, and of the Ayufay Buid are briefly recounted.

The Pre-American Period

> . . . the first actual mention of the Philippines seems [. . .] to date from the tenth century, when certain traders from Ma-i, the present island of Mindoro, brought valuable merchandise to Canton for sale, in the year 982 (Beyer, 1979: 26).

This suggestion was made by Beyer in 1921 and has been adopted by subsequent writers (cf. Majul, 1973: 39). The identification of Ma-i with Mindoro has been challenged, however, and it is now held by many to refer to the whole of the northern Philippines. There is a less debatable reference to Mindoro in a fourteenth-century Chinese source, which mentions an island of Min-to-lang (Wang, 1964, cited in Lopez, 1976: 12–13).

It appears certain, at any rate, that Muslim traders were using an eastern trade to China in addition to the western route following the coast of Indo-China from at least the tenth century. Mindoro would have provided a convenient stopping point on the way from Brunei to Canton (Majul, 1973: 39). When the Spanish attempted to establish their first colony in the islands in 1565, they discovered that the Sultan of Brunei had established outposts in Mindoro and around Manila bay. The first contact with the Mindoro settlements was made by two lieutenants of Legazpi, Juan de Salcedo and Martin de Goyti in 1570.

11

Salcedo landed at Mamburao on the west coast, where he found a 'very rich native town', and promptly sacked it. Continuing up the coast, he came to the small island of Lubang, where he discovered three fortified Muslim *kota* which he was unable to capture. The following month Goyti landed on the east coast at Baco, where he encountered a Chinese trading vessel (Lopez, 1976: 16–23). Three years after the foundation of Manila as the Spanish capital and the treaty with its Muslim ruler, Rajah Soliman, in 1571, the Spanish were concerned to learn that the Sultan of Brunei was continuing to extract tribute from the natives of Mindoro. In 1578 they decided to end this competition once and for all by installing their own protégé on the throne of Brunei. They defeated the Brunei fleet, captured the capital, and set up their own candidate as Sultan. He did not last long and the former ruler re-established control. After another abortive expedition, the Spanish abandoned their attempt to found a colony in Borneo (Majul, 1973: 110).

Early Muslim influences in Mindoro came, then, not from Mindanao but from Brunei (see Map VI). Brunei long retained control of Palawan and the Calamianes group of islands which lie between Mindoro and Borneo. When the Spanish arrived, Brunei had been gradually extending its sphere of influence along the Palawan-Mindoro axis, which points in a straight line toward Manila, and which, there is every reason to believe, constituted an established trade route to China. Further evidence of the integration of Mindoro into the economic life of the archipelago is provided by the retention of an ancient syllabic script among the Hanunoo and Buid in Mindoro and by the Tagbanuwa in Palawan. This script was once in use throughout the islands, from Ilocos in the north to Leyte in the south. There is no consensus of opinion as to its ultimate origins, but that it derives somehow from India, via either Sumatra or Sulawesi, seems most likely (Conklin, 1949b, 1953b; Francisco, 1966, 1973; Gardner and Maliwanag, 1939; Gardner, 1940, 1943; Postma, 1968, 1971).

Although the Spanish did manage to expel the Muslims from their established positions in Mindoro, they were never able effectively to assert their own authority over the island. A Muslim fleet attacked Mindoro and parts of Luzon in 1602, taking as many as 700 prisoners. They attacked again in 1636, taking more than 100 prisoners (Majul, 1973: 117, 133). In 1657 a Muslim chief seized two Chinese ships in Manila bay and retired to the old outpost of Mamburao to trade the captives and merchandise at his leisure (Lopez, 1976: 39). When the

Spanish made peace with the Dutch in 1648, and later withdrew their fort from Mindanao in 1663, a period of relative peace was inaugurated which lasted until 1718 when they returned to their positions in the south. This action sparked off a new series of raids and counter-raids. In 1726 the town of Manaol, just east of where Conklin did his fieldwork among the Hanunoo, was destroyed. By 1735 the population of the island was said to have declined from 3,169 families (presumably those paying tribute to the Spanish) to 2,034. This decrease was attributed to a mass migration to the neighbouring province of Batangas on the island of Luzon. The population of Batangas went from 3,151 families in 1753, less than that of Mindoro, to 15,000 in 1800. Migration from Mindoro to Batangas probably continued throughout the eighteenth century, accounting for the stagnation of the former province and the steep increase in the size of the population of the latter (Zuniga, 1973: 119). During this century the provincial capital, Calapan, was twice sacked and burnt to the ground by Muslim raiders, in 1753 and 1754. In the same year, 150 prisoners were taken between Bongabon and Bulalacao, the area in which I conducted my research (Lopez, 1976: 39). The Spanish were forced to send large expeditions against the Muslims, who continued to operate from Mamburao on the west coast of Mindoro, in 1762, 1772 and 1778; and later against the Muslims in Balete on the east coast, without achieving any lasting success. The Muslims were always able to retire into the mountains and bide their time. This must have had an effect on the Mangyan groups who were living there (Zuniga, 1973: 111).

What was in fact happening during this period was that the rising power of the Sulu Sultanate required an unending supply of slaves to serve as a labour force in the collection of exotic commodities such as birds' nests and sea slugs for its trade with China. Slaving expeditions ravaged the coastal areas of the entire central Philippines throughout the eighteenth and nineteenth centuries. The Spanish administration in Manila was either unable or unwilling to protect its subjects against this trade. Some Spanish officials were even involved in trading activities in Sulu themselves (Warren, 1981: 172).

In summary, then, Mindoro lay on the margins of the spheres of influence of the Spanish based in Manila and of the Muslims based in the south. Neither side had the will or the ability to defend the island as its own (see Map VII). The inhabitants of Mindoro suffered accordingly. From a relatively prosperous port of call, it was reduced to a backward and depopulated backwater. It was not until 1848, when the Spanish first deployed steamships against their rivals, that they were able to gain a decisive advantage over the Muslims. Previously, the light Muslim vessels had been able to outmanoeuvre the Spanish in the shallow rivers and estuaries of the islands. The last recorded raids on Mindoro occurred in 1870 and 1874 (Jordana, in Lopez, 1976: 41).

When the Spanish established themselves in Manila, they discovered that a lucrative trade could be carried on between the silks of China and the silver of the New World. In 1568 the first galleon sailed for Acapulco. The merchants of Seville and Cadiz reacted swiftly, for Asian textiles were undercutting their own products on the American market. In 1590 trade was restricted between Manila and New Spain, and prohibited entirely with the viceroyalty of Peru. Cargo with a value of 250,000 pesos a year was set as the maximum that could be traded, although due to a variety of subterfuges it usually reached 2,000,000 pesos. Even so, the colony remained dependent on a subsidy from Mexico, whence it was administered, until Mexican independence in 1821. Instead of creating an entrepôt in the Far East, the Spanish were content to limit trade to a level barely sufficient to provide an income for the Spanish residents of Manila. The original economic motives for acquiring the colony, i.e. control of the spice trade of the Moluccas and Sulawesi, and of the China trade, were abandoned one after the other. Domestic mercantile interests even lobbied the Spanish government to abandon the colony. That it was not abandoned was due to the influence of the religious orders which had come in search of souls, not profit (Phelan, 1959: 14, Cushner, 1971: 128–9).

Large numbers of Spaniards were never attracted to the Philippines, and most of those who came remained in Manila. Participants in the conquest were granted *encomiendas*, personal fiefs, in which they had the duty to promote the spiritual welfare of the inhabitants and the right to collect taxes. At the same time 120 grants were made of lands which were supposed to be unoccupied by natives. The beneficiaries of these grants soon sold them, as they had no intention of developing them and wanted to move into commerce. By one means or another, they soon found their way into the hands of the religious orders, who enjoyed more than two centuries of unmolested possession of these estates, all near Manila (Roth, 1977: 39–62). Not only did the religious orders become the most important landowners in the colony, but they provided much of the capital used in the Manila-Acapulco galleon trade as well (Cushner, 1971: 139). The combined income of the trust administered by the orders was more than 1,000,000 pesos in 1783 (ibid.: 151). Given such an enormous concentration of religious, political and economic power in the hands of the regular clergy, it is hardly surprising that their initial missionary enthusiasm should have turned into a conservative protection of vested interests.

Poor, isolated provinces like Mindoro received little attention from the missionaries, as they lacked the heroic attractions of the mountain province of Luzon with its gold mines, or of the rich Muslim areas in the south. In the first century of missionary activity, the Augustinian, Franciscan, Dominican and Jesuit orders replaced one another in quick succession on the island, with two gaps in which established parishes were entrusted to the secular clergy, a sure sign that there was little wealth to hold the regulars. The Recollects had charge of Mindoro for most of the eighteenth and nineteenth centuries, again with two gaps during which only seculars were present. Finally, in 1937, the island was put in the care of the Society of the Divine Word (Postma, 1977). An important factor in the frequent abandonment of missions was the activity of the Muslim raiders referred to above. It was all the clergy could do to hold on to lowland converts. Attempts at the conversion of the Mangyan were made by the Jesuits in 1636, 1645 and 1665, and by the Recollects in the years 1722–38 and 1750, but all their achievements were destroyed in subsequent raids. 'For the greater part of the 19th century and the early years of the 20th, there does not seem to be any record of missionary activity among the Mangyan' (Postma, 1977b: 262).

From the middle of the seventeenth century until the end of Spanish administration in 1898 a dichotomy developed between the hispanised Christians of the lowlands and the pagans of the highlands. This opposition originated in the inability of the Spanish to bring the highlanders under their control, but it soon became a structural feature of Philippine social life, in the perpetuation of which both highlanders and lowlanders had a vested interest. The highlands provided a refuge to which lowlanders could flee from Spanish abuses. During the period of the tobacco monopoly, which the Spanish used to support the colonial administration after the end of the Mexican subsidy, the Christians of the lowlands found it convenient to have an unadministered group of pagans in the highlands with whom to trade (Jesus, 1980: 167). Keesing identified a pattern in northern Luzon, 'of a Christian lowland community opposing Christianization of mountain groups to whom they supplied trade goods, through fear that their profitable commerce would be destroyed' (Keesing, 1962: 215). There are echoes of this in Mindoro:

From the side of the Christians themselves there was also opposition to the Christianization of the Mangyans. They feared that a Christian Mangyan would be harder to deal with when using him as a laborer or slave' (Postma, 1977b: 257, citing de la Costa, 1961: 473–4)

Postma is here writing of the seventeenth century. Over two hundred years later, Worcester attributed the failure of the American plan to settle the Mangyan to the hostility of the Tagalogs, who 'look with great disfavour on the gathering of Mangyans into settlements where they can be protected, as it renders it difficult to hold them in a state of peonage' (Worcester, 1930: 464). Clearly, there is a difference between the situation in northern Luzon and in Mindoro. The highland groups of northern Luzon often held the balance of power against the lowlands, periodically spreading a reign of terror through the Christian settlements of the foothills. They were able to trade on equal terms, if illegally, with the lowland merchants. In Mindoro, the highland groups were so weak that they always lost out in trade. In 1803 Zuniga was already reporting that lowlanders were lending seed rice and bolos to the Mangyan in return for half the harvest. Wax and honey were obtained from the latter for a nominal sum and then resold for exorbitant profits. Zuniga attributes the unwillingness of the Mangyan to convert to Christianity to this exploitation. The Mangyan did not wish to have any more to do with the lowlands than absolutely necessary (Zuniga, 1973: 120). Spanish sources are replete with descriptions of the 'natural naïvety', 'simplicity' and 'honesty' of the Mangyan, which made them easy prey to the wiles of unscrupulous lowlanders (Jordana, quoted in Lopez, 1976: 51). The attempted super-exploitation of the Mangyan by the Christian lowlanders continues to this day and serves as a powerful barrier to the cultural integration of the highland and lowland groups in Mindoro. It has been in operation for at least three centuries.

The integration of lowland Filipinos into the world economy was accomplished not by the Spanish, but by the British, Chinese and Chinese-Filipino mestizos. The breakdown of Spanish economic hegemony in the islands was a gradual process beginning with the British occupation of Manila in 1762. Thereafter, French, American and British traders began to appear in Manila, until in 1834 Manila was completely opened to foreign trade. The Spanish were quickly forced out of the competition. Sugar became a major export crop between 1850 and 1884, when France and Germany introduced bounty systems to encourage their domestic sugar beet industries. Land values began to rise, and by 1870 the native peasantry were rapidly being dispossessed by the Chinese mestizos who knew how to manipulate the newly implemented regulations concerning land surveying and registration. Land shortage was not a factor in the marginalisation of the peasantry. As late as 1920 there was still virgin land available in central Luzon, the most densely populated area in the country. It was, rather, the scarcity of the capital necessary to participate in commercial agriculture which drove independent producers into debt and eventual forfeiture of their lands (Fast and Richardson, 1979: 20–39).

It was not until 1880 that the changes which had been affecting agriculture in the rest of the country for the past thirty years reached Mindoro. In that year a religious order acquired a sugar estate of 23,000 hectares in the southwest of Mindoro, near Bulalacao. The last Muslim raid had been made on that town only six years previously (ibid.: 39). Mindoro thus lay outside the mainstream of economic life in the islands until virtually the end of Spanish rule.

I have dwelt on these early years at such length because they account for the relative depopulation of the island at the beginning of this century, for the lack of missionary interest in the inhabitants of the highlands, for the formation of a symbiotic antagonism between the Mangyan and the Christians, and because structural constraints on the economic development of the island were established at a very early date, despite its proximity to Manila. Taken together, these factors help to account for the persistence of traditional forms of social organisation in the highlands up to modern times. The highland groups have been under great pressure for many hundreds of years, from both their Christian and their Muslim neighbours. I shall return to the question of the effects of these pressures on Buid social organisation in the concluding chapter.

The American and Republican periods

The American administration was the first to establish full control over the highland pagan and southern Muslim groups in the Philippines. They brought with them the model of the Native Americans of their own country and attempted to apply it in the new colony. Operating with a crude sort of social evolution theory, the Americans classified the various groups in the Philippines on a scale of 'moral and social development'. They coined the term 'non-Christian' to cover all groups which had not been subject to hispanisation, and created in 1901 the Bureau of Non-Christian Tribes (BNCT) to conduct research into their social organisation in order to be able to recommend legislation to deal with them. This body was supplanted in 1903 by the Ethnological Survey which continued its work in a purely scientific capacity. Actual administration of the non-Christian groups remained in the hands of the Secretary of the Interior until 1916. Dean Worcester held this office until 1913. It was his opinion that lowland Filipinos could not be relied upon to govern the 'backward tribes' of the highlands. Authority over the non-Christians in each province was placed directly in the hands of its American governor. Christianity became a key factor in determining the political rights of Filipino citizens. A Supreme Court decision held that:

> Theoretically, all men are created free and equal. Practically we know that the axiom is not precisely accurate. The Mangyans, for instance, are not free, as civilised men are free, and they are not the equals of their more fortunate brothers. (Block and Lawrence, 1927: 3230, cited in Lopez, 1976: 88)

The Americans devoted most of their attention, as had the Spanish, to subduing the more aggressive societies of Mindanao and of northern Luzon. The Mangyan continued to remain almost invisible at the national level. In these early years the Americans made some half-hearted attempts to settle the Mangyan on 'reservations' where they could be 'protected' from Christians, but this programme met with resistance from both highlanders and lowlanders. In 1917, after four years of experimentation, the BNCT was reconstituted, endowed with administrative authority, and set the task of elevating the level of civilisation of the tribes to a point where they could be assimilated by the majority population. At that point, the territories of the tribes would take their place as regularly constituted provinces. Highland Mindoro, however, was not included under the jurisdiction of the new Bureau.

The Americans did succeed in encouraging immigration to the thinly populated coasts of Mindoro. Most of it derived from the islands adjacent to Mindoro, Tagalogs coming to dominate the northern regions and Bisayans the southern. This influx led to extensive land grabbing to the detriment of the Mangyan, and the administration was finally forced to recognise that a problem existed. In 1925 the BNCT was given jurisdiction over all the areas inhabited by non-Christians in the regular provinces, in addition to the control it already exercised over the special provinces. It had little effect, for the Mangyan were in no position to appeal against abuses. In 1935 the BNCT was abolished in one of the first acts of the new semi-autonomous Commonwealth government, and responsibility for the 'non-Christians' passed back into the hands of the Department of the Interior (Lopez, 1976: 106–17).

When the BNCT was abolished, President Quezon stated that: 'Considering the marked advance in the civilization and general progress of the special provinces, the so-called non-Christian problem has been reduced to one of solidification and development' (quoted in Lopez, 1976: 116). Following the Second World War, there was a massive influx of settlers and logging companies into the sparsely settled interiors of Mindoro and Mindanao. Armed resistance by the Muslims of Mindanao forced the government to concede that the 'problem' had not disappeared after all. In 1957 the government set up the Commission on National Integration, with the stated aim of continuing the old policy of the BNCT; that is, of effectuating the economic, social, moral and political advancement of the 'national cultural minorities', as they were now called (Lopez, 1976: 118). As with its predecessors, it concentrated its attention on the Mountain Province and on Mindanao. In 1975 it was supplanted by the office of the Presidential Assistant on National Minorities (PANAMIN), an organisation closely associated with its director, Manuel Elizalde, who belongs to one of the five wealthiest families in the Philippines. The aims of this organisation are often hard to distinguish from the business interests of its members (ICL, 1979).

Mindoro since the war

The American census of 1903 gave a population for the whole of Mindoro of 42,580, of which 7,286 were said to be Mangyan (Postma, 1977b: 262). This figure for the Mangyan is probably grossly underestimated, since the interior of Mindoro was almost wholly unexplored at that time. In 1947 the total population had grown to 167,705. By 1979 the population of Oriental Mindoro alone was 421,307, with an estimated 50,000 Mangyan (Provincial Development Staff, 1979). The figure for the Mangyan population is definitely exaggerated. Tweddell estimates the maximum Mangyan population for the whole of Mindoro at 29,000, although some of his figures have been questioned (Tweddell, 1970; Pennoyer, 1979; Lopez, 1976). Any estimation is more or less guesswork, but what is certain is that the Mangyan now constitute no more than 5 or 10 per cent of the total population.

Between 1903 and 1939 the population of the Philippines more than doubled, from seven million to sixteen million. The effects of this growth were especially severe in the old Tagalog provinces of central Luzon, because they were the most densely populated areas to begin with. Land scarcity, capitalist expansion and an efficient police force all contributed to the growth of large peasant unions agitating for a return to the old days of paternalistic landlords who would help out in times of crisis. When the Second world War broke out, these unions were so well organised that they were able to mount the only effective opposition to the Japanese occupation. They emerged from the war stronger than ever and well-armed. The landed interests, who had in many cases collaborated with the Japanese, viewed them as a communist-led threat to the newly independent nation and moved to liquidate them. After a protracted counter-insurgency operation they were crushed by the Magsaysay administration between 1952 and 1956 (Kerkvliet, 1977: 107–25).

One of the key elements in Magsaysay's 'pacification' programme was the resettlement of former insurgents on 'virgin' land in places like Mindoro and Mindanao. In 1955/56 the National Resettlement and Reconstruction Agency (NARRA) allotted 1,716 hectares of land to 606 pioneer Christian families from central Luzon in the municipality of Bongabon (NARRA, 1957). These official figures relate only to those resettled with official government assistance. The trickle of immigration which had begun during the American period now became a flood as land-hungry migrants took advantage of the opening up of government lands to private homesteading.

Real missionary work among the Mangyan also began after the war. In 1952 the Overseas Missionary Fellowship (OMF), an organisation most of whose members had been expelled from China by the communist government, began work in Mindoro. By 1956 it had evangelists working among all the tribal groups on the island (Lopez, 1976: 100). On the Catholic side, the Society of the Divine Word (SVD), which had been assigned the pastoral care of the whole of

Mindoro in 1937, established the first permanent mission among the Mangyan in 1958 (Postma, 1977b: 263; 1974: 21). One of the first objectives of both missionary groups has been to concentrate the nomadic shifting cultivators into large permanent settlements. So far their efforts have yielded only partial and highly localised results.

Bongabon since the war

The municipality of Bongabon comprises an area of 500 square kilometres at present, about half of which is inhabited by Buid (see Map IV). The Christian population has risen from under 15,000 in 1948 to over 40,000 today, resulting in a population density of 80 per square kilometre. As most of this population reside in the less mountainous area near the coast, the actual density of the Christian population is about double that figure. I would estimate the Buid population of Bongabon at 3,000, with an overall density of 15 per square kilometre. The substantial difference in population densities is related to the different types of agriculture practised by the two populations. The Christians primarily practise wet rice agriculture, producing two and sometimes three crops a year on the same land, while the Buid practise shifting cultivation on the steep mountain slopes of the interior, necessitating fallow periods of eight years or more before recropping the same land. Population pressure in the lowlands has led to a steady infiltration of Christians into Buid territory, following the courses of the major rivers and the logging trails constructed along them. These pioneer Christians practise a highly destructive form of shifting cultivation, planting the land with cash crops year after year until the land is exhausted. They then migrate elsewhere.

In the 1930s Bongabon was forested right down to the coast. The Bongabon river itself was swampy and infested with crocodiles. Just south of the market town was a large malarial swamp which gave the area an unhealthy reputation. Muslim traders from Mindanao used to come to trade brass gongs and glass beads with the Buid, and to hunt the crocodile, valued for their skins. Soon after the war, a Chinese entrepeneur constructed the first logging trails into the interior, reaching a point now occupied by the National Highway bridge at Lisap. He began systematically to log out the river valley. A sawmill was constructed in Morente to prepare the lumber for export (see Map IV). The river was transformed into a rocky stream periodically swollen by flash floods due to the erosion caused by these logging activities.

Then an irrigation project went awry in the mid-1950s when a diversionary dam was overwhelmed by the river following a typhoon, wiping out the partially constructed terraces below it and incidentally draining the coastal swamp. The mouth of the river shifted ten kilometres to the north. With the removal of a major breeding ground for malaria, a major obstacle to the growth of the municipality was eliminated.

The Chinese entrepreneur was replaced after a few years by a big operator working under contract to a transnational corporation. After he had taken out all the export-quality timber in the area, his concession was subdivided among three small-time local concerns. Starting in the 1950s the new logging roads began to open up possibilities for wealthy families in the coastal settlements to invest in the interior. Some of these families had come over before the war from Batangas in Luzon and from Aclan in Panay. They brought their tenants with them to clear the forest, often promising them a piece of their own land once the farms were established. Initially these landlords were only interested in the rice and maize lands of the littoral, but a few turned their attention to cattle breeding and tree farming in the foothills. There was a rush of applications for pasture and tree farm leases on government land in the mid-1950s under Magsaysay's policy of opening government land to commercial exploitation.

Obtaining a permit to raise cattle and tree crops entitled the holder to appoint up to three overseers and their families to live within the leased area. Each overseer had the right to farm five hectares for his family's subsistence. In most cases the permit holders soon found their projects to be uneconomic and lost interest in them, but the overseers stayed on. The now semi-independent overseers tended to regard the entire area of the lease as their own property and began selling rights to settle within its boundaries to other Christians. Payment could often be token, but the Christians did evolve an orderly system for the transfer of land rights among themselves which completely ignored the prior rights of the Mangyan and the technicalities of government regulations. Half of all the land in the province of Oriental Mindoro is classified as forest reserve and is in theory closed to settlement by non-Mangyan. Everywhere, it is fast filling up with Christian squatters (see Map VIII for the leases in the Ayufay area).

The Buid since the war
The Buid remember the pre-war period as a sort of golden age, when land and food were plentiful, population density was high, and there

was only a handful of Christians to deal with on the coast. The war brought an end to all this, as the Buid fled into the interior to escape from the Japanese. They returned to their homes after the war only to be devastated by a smallpox epidemic which wiped out between one third and one half of their numbers. One Buid gave me a vivid account of that period as he remembered it. He was born in about 1935.

> When he was a very small boy, the whole Bongabon watershed was so densely populated with Buid it looked like the market town looks now. There were only six Christian families in the whole area. There were Buid living right on the coast. Then a terrible illness came. Adults who were talking to one another in a lively way in the evening would be discovered dead in the morning by their children, who would think at first that they were still just asleep. In every house, where ten people had been living, only one child would survive. The sickness hit all the valleys from Fawa to Batangan [see Map IV]. The surviving children were so small they could not bury the dead, but had to leave the corpses where they lay in the houses. They could not make fires or shelters for themselves, but foraged for raw food just like pigs. Finally, Bangun came down from the mountains and took the children back with them into the interior. Only when these children grew up did they return to their homes.

This account has been influenced by themes from Buid mythology, which speaks of an age of dense population followed by some catastrophe, usually a flood; the consequent loss of fire; and the reduction of humans to an animal-like existence in which they must eat their food raw. But the epidemic and its severity can be independently confirmed from contemporary records. According to one account, 50 per cent of the Buid died in 1948/49 (Thiel, 1954).

When the Buid began filtering back to their homes in the 1950s and 1960s, they found much of their ancestral land already occupied by the Christian squatters discussed above. In most cases, the Buid only managed to reoccupy the upper slopes of their territory, leaving the Christians in control of the valleys. These lands are best suited for ploughing and wet rice cultivation, but are not particularly attractive for shifting cultivation. The present distribution of Christians and Buid thus resembles a contour map, the Christians having penetrated up the river valleys, and the Buid occupying the ridges.

Already in 1954 the southern Buid of the Batangan-Tawga area were complaining to an SVD missionary, Father Erwin Thiel, that the land on which they had planted banana, coconut and cacao trees was being stolen by Bisayan settlers. It is significant that their complaints were made in terms not of land but of standing tree crops (see Chapter 3 on land tenure concepts). The orphaned child of one of these complainants was called Yaum. He must have been about fifteen years old at the time (Thiel, 1954). Soon after Thiel's report, Yaum began working with the Bureau of Forest Development (BFD) as a guide, and travelled all over southern Mindoro (Lopez, 1981: 137). About this time, the Batangan Buid turned to the OMF for help in retaining their land. Around 1960 the central government appointed a 'Mangyan gobernador' from the lowlands. Yaum was quick to offer his services, and became his 'tinyente', leaving his job with the BFD. Drawing on his contacts with the BFD and the central government, Yaum dissociated himself from the Protestant missionaries, and managed to take most of the local Buid with him (ibid.: 114–16.) In 1963, the Commission on National Integration (CNI) began work in Batangan. It instituted an elected barrio council, and once again, Yaum was ready to take advantage of a new opportunity. He was elected 'barrio captain', and later, when the CNI set up a pan-Mangyan association, 'presidente' of all the Mangyan. This association did not last long, but it helped Yaum in widening his range of contacts (ibid.: 117).

During these early years, Yaum devoted much of his effort to concentrating the Buid population of Batangan, Nawa and Matanus into one large settlement on the Batangan river (see Map IV). This settlement contained no more than five households in 1960, but has since grown to over a hundred. At present it is divided into eight wards formed from the original local communities once scattered throughout the area. Yaum's persuasion to concentrate in a large settlement gained added force from the presence of armed bandits who infested the area in the 1950s and 1960s (ibid.: 116, 196). He was one of the first Buid to realise the necessity of large-scale settlement as a defence against land grabbing and banditry.

The chairman of the CNI in Mindoro in the early 1960s was one Sumbad, himself a member of a mountain group in northern Luzon (de la Paz, 1968: 39; Stickley, 1975: 176). He began a programme to register Mangyan land claims with the BFD. Yaum cooperated with this project and in the mid-1960s 1,156 hectares of land were surveyed as a Buid reservation (Lopez, 1981: 197). These plans fell through, and Sumbad absconded with the registration fees he had collected from Mangyan all over the island (Stickley, 1975: 194). But because of Yaum's prior contacts with the BFD, the surveys already completed received informal recognition from the local government (Lopez, 1981: 196). Yaum's biggest coup was to acquire for the Buid the right to pay taxes on these land claims, providing them with documentary evidence of prior occupation of their land (ibid.: 199). Tax receipts have proved instrumental on a number of occasions in blocking Christian claims to Buid land.

Not only does the municipal government profit from these semilegal taxes, but Yaum is also able to guarantee about three quarters of the Buid vote in local elections. He has enjoyed a close working relationship with the office of the mayor for many years. In 1976, Batangan was officially declared a *barangay*, the smallest unit of government after the municipality under the Martial Law regime. Yaum duly took over as *barangay* captain. It was at this time that PANAMIN took over from the CNI, and Yaum had been as assiduous in cultivating ties with it as he has been with all other government agencies in the past.

Because of his skilful manipulation of outside agencies, and of his ability to unite the Buid behind his leadership, Yaum has been able to use the mayor, the BFD, the police, the CNI, and now perhaps PANAMIN, to fend off land grabbers and ensure that some justice is done when a Buid is harmed by a Christian. He deals with most internal disputes himself and is said to have pocketed 1,000 pesos in fines from the Buid in 1979 (Lopez, 1981: 149).

Yaum's political activities have not led to a neglect of his economic interests. When he was working under the 'Mangyan gobernador' in the early 1960s, the latter lent him thirty head of cattle. Ten years later he had accumulated ten head of his own. He also struck up a business partnership with a local Tagalog swidden farmer living near Batangan in the early 1960s, one Sison. Sison began to hire Buid labourers to cultivate his land and to buy up their surplus crops. Eventually, Sison became wealthy enough to move into marketing full time and now owns a warehouse in Roxas with a storage capacity of six million kilogrammes of grain, giving him a near monopoly over grain purchases in southern Oriental Mindoro. Yaum continues to operate as his agent among the Buid, distributing the advance capital he gets from Sison among agents of his own who do the actual purchasing (ibid.: 237–40). Yaum also owns a piece of land on the National Highway worth 11,000 pesos, which he rents to a Christian tenant; a maize shucking machine; a cement house; and a jeep. This places him in the upper income bracket of provincial society. He is shown marked respect by all the local Christians, who address him as *meyor*.

From his base in Batangan, Yaum has been attempting to extend his influence over all the Buid. In return for invervening with lowland agencies in defence of their rights, for helping to solve local disputes, and for the respect he inspires among Christians, many outlying Buid settlements have granted him their allegiance. He actively encourages these outlying groups to form compact settlements of their own, headed by local leaders called 'consejal'. Yaum often uses these *consejal* as agents in his maize marketing enterprises. Aside from Batangan, he has two other *barangay*, Siangi and Tawga, in his *sakup* 'clientele' (ibid.: 142).

All the *consejal* in Yaum's sphere of influence meet regularly in Batangan to hammer out a consensus on policy toward the lowlands. The *consejal* act as conduits for transmitting decisions taken at the centre and information about the outside world to their local communities, and for keeping Yaum abreast of opinion in the outlying areas. If a Buid gets into a dispute with another Buid or with a Christian, it is very rare for him to go to a Christian official before consulting his *consejal* or Yaum first. To go outside with a problem is to risk ostracism by the other Buid. The Buid have maintained a remarkable degree of solidarity in relation to all outside agencies and this is one of the key reasons why they have been able to hold on to their land and to get a relatively good price for their cash crops. Yaum has been able to manoeuvre them as a bloc in his dealings with capitalists and government officials. In later chapters, the traditional institutions which Yaum has adapted for this purpose will be described in detail. The evolution of Buid society contrasts markedly with that of the Hanunoo in this respect, for the latter have collapsed under the impact of outside pressures and have often attached themselves individually to Christian patrons. They are ready to act as pawns for their patrons in court in disputes over land claims. They have, in short, become assimilated to the lowland type of social organisation which is characterised by vertical patron-client relationships and by feuding at the local level (Postma, personal communication).

The Buid of Ayufay since the war
As with the history of Batangan, it will be convenient to take the biography of the political leader of Ayufay, Agaw, as a reference guide

in the history of the Ayufay Buid. Agaw was born around 1940 in Ugun Liguma. When the Japanese invaded Mindoro, the Buid began moving around to evade them. Agaw's family fled to the headwaters of the Siangi (see Map IV). In 1948, the smallpox epidemic carried off much of the older generation and the survivors were dispersed even further. By 1950, there were almost no Buid left in Ayufay.

The first Christian pasture leases were granted in the area in the early 1950s. Ugun Liguma is a bowl-shaped valley containing some prime flat land on the right bank of the Bongabon river. In 1953 the Hernandez family from the town of Bongabon established two tenants on it, Ablo and Kolas. Two years later, Hernandez had his lease officially surveyed. In 1959, he applied to have his lease modified to allow the planting of tree crops. This proved uneconomic and two years later he moved to Manila, leaving his tenants in place.

In the early 1960s the Enriquez family acquired a lease for all the flat land on the left bank of the Bongabon river downstream from the Hernandez lease. They now have at least six Christian families as tenants on this land. In 1963 Luna acquired a pasture lease on the left bank of the Siangi river across from Fanuban (Luna, 1975: xvii). Luna also began bringing Christian tenants into the area to look after his cattle (see Maps V and VIII). Finally, in 1969, the Liwanag family acquired a lease for the entire Ayufay valley, despite the presence of a large number of Buid families there. Thus by 1970 most of the land, and nearly all of the flat land suitable for ploughing between the Siangi and Ambuan rivers, was legally in the hands of lowland capitalists.

Logging operations had removed most of the primary forest cover in this area. The Bongabon river valley proper was logged out in the 1950s and one of the small local outfits logged over the Ayufay valley in the mid-1960s. This logging involved the construction of roads into the interior, which facilitated the movement of Christian squatters into the area.

The squatters entered the area in three different ways. In the first place, the local Christian Bisayans operate an informal sort of bride-service. Thus in 1968 one of the original tenants of Hernandez, Ablo, married his daughter to another Christian, Totok. Totok came to work for his father-in-law and subsequently brought in his own father and brother and their families. Two years later, Ablo married another of his daughters to Doming. In the second place, the original tenants made a practice of 'selling' land rights to other Christians. In one case, a piece of land has changed hands three times in the past twenty years in this manner and is now being farmed by a tenant of the last purchaser. The third method of recruitment is tenancy. Many of the purchasers are in fact wealthy landowners resident elsewhere who bring in tenants to work the land. One of the biggest problems of the poor migrants in the mountains is the shortage of patrons, which are needed both as a source of credit and for protection from other Christians and from government agencies.

The biggest patron in the area is Nati Enriquez, sister of the mayor of Bongabon who originally acquired the land on the left bank of the river. She purchases virtually the entire maize crop grown by the Christian squatters and by the Buid in the whole of the Bongabon watershed. Several of the Christian families living around Ugun Liguma have got her to sponsor the baptisms and weddings of their children, thus making her their *comadre*. Map IX shows the current distribution of Christian land claims, with dates of occupation when known. The accompanying diagrams show the kinship and affinal relations among the Christian squatters, and the order in which the land was acquired by successive occupants.

Agaw's family, which had fled to upper Siangi in the early 1950s, gradually worked its way back toward Ayufay. Agaw married in Sigaw, but divorced his first wife and then married his second and current wife, Way-in, in about 1960. Around 1964 he moved with Way-in and her father to Ayufay. By 1968 Yaum was already trying to assert his influence in the area, get the local Buid to form a compact settlement, and reclaim the land from the Christians. But when the Ayufay Buid were left out of the CNI land survey in 1968, they became alienated from Yaum and refused to have anything to do with him for the next two years. Then the Liwanags, who had acquired the lease to Ayufay in 1969, cut down all the fruit trees which had been planted by Agaw and three other Buid in Ayufay. This act finally compelled the Ayufay Buid to form a settlement and seek Yaum's protection. The first settlement was built on Agaw's swidden half way up the Ayufay river and contained about ten households. Shortly thereafter Agaw met a member of the Liwanag family on his land. The latter threatened him with a gun, but Agaw faced him down, an unprecedented act on the part of an Ayufay Buid. Later that day, Agaw went to get Yaum and the two of them proceeded to the provincial capital and spoke to one of the CNI officials. The CNI brought the case before the land court, and the Liwanag family was forced to back down.

With this, the Buid had effectively reasserted their claim to the

Ayufay valley, but Agaw had further ambitions to reclaim Ugun Liguma as well, which was by now almost entirely populated by Christians. In 1977 Agaw made the first attempt to build a house in the valley. Not only was it the only land in the area suitable for ploughing, but its proximity to the logging road made it attractive for the sale of cash crops to the lowlands. He met with violent opposition from one Christian, but this man was killed by another Christian in an unrelated feud. The killer was also opposed to the Buid moving into the valley. With the help of Yaum, Nati Enriquez, PANAMIN, and a third Christian family which was feuding with the first two, Agaw finally managed to get four hectares of land set aside as a 'Mangyan reservation'. In 1978 the Ayufay Buid began constructing houses in this reservation, and by the time I arrived in August 1979 there were twenty houses under construction. The Buid continued to spend most of the year in their swidden houses, however, until January 1981 when they finally took up full-time residence in Ugun Liguma. I was on hand to witness this final move, and Agaw's continuing attempts to recruit even more Buid to live in the settlement.

There are several points worth emphasising in this history. The present Buid occupation of Ayufay and Ugun Liguma is the result of a protracted struggle against Christian landlords, tenants and squatters. They have succeeded by playing on the internal factionalism of the Christians, while maintaining a remarkable degree of internal unity. Leaders such as Yaum and Agaw have been able to use this internal solidarity in their negotiations with Christian patrons. Nati Enriquez, for example, makes a much greater profit from her trade with the Buid than she does with the more market-conscious Christians, and this makes it advantageous for her to protect the land rights of the Buid. It is the independent power base of Yaum among the Buid, his control of Buid votes, taxes and the marketing of their cash crops which has made it possible for him to wrest concessions from lowland government agencies, politicians and capitalists when other Mangyan groups have been fooled into parting with their land, labour and money in return for nothing. Yaum has naturally profited along the way, but his own interests coincide to a significant degree with that of the Buid as a whole. The process of concentrating the dispersed Buid population of Ayufay into a compact settlement parallels the process which occurred in Batangan twenty years ago, and, indeed, recalls the Spanish policy of *reducciones*. One of the first aims of the Spanish when establishing their authority over a new territory was to 'reduce' a scattered population to a single settlement 'within hearing of the church bells' (Phelan, 1959). What missionaries and government agencies had failed to do among the Buid for decades, if not centuries, was finally accomplished as a result of the Buid's own initiative.

3 Environment and Economy

In this chapter, the natural and social environments in which the Buid find themselves are sketched in. The nature of their mountainous terrain dominates Buid life and thought, and has important consequences for the way they interact with the non-Buid social world. In the second section, the traditional form of shifting cultivation is described and compared with similar systems in other parts of the Philippines and certain contrasts are noted between these systems and those of Borneo. Finally, the ways in which the penetration of the cash economy has affected the traditional economy are treated.

The Buid Environment

Mindoro lies between 12 and 13 degrees north of the equator in the humid tropics. Annual precipitation on the southern coast of the island is over 2,500 mm and can reach 3,750 mm or more in the interior mountains (Conklin, 1957: 21; Wernstedt and Spencer, 1967: 431). Southeastern Mindoro receives both the southwestern monsoon (*abagat*) from the middle of May until September, as well as the rains brought by the northeast winds (*amian*) in January and February. The period from October to December, when the prevailing winds are reversing, is characterised by a high risk of typhoons (*bagyu*). Mindoro is hit by 19 per cent of all Philippine typhoons (Wernstedt and Spencer, 1967: 431; Conklin, 1957: 20). Minimum rainfall occurs during March and April, the 'dry season' (*fangaraw*), but this is also the season for thunderstorms which can bring a great deal of rain. The temperature seldom varies beyond a range of between 23 and 26 degrees centigrade in the shade, although it can get much hotter than this in exposed grasslands during the dry season, and much colder when a typhoon is blowing. Humidity hovers around 80 per cent throughout the year (Conklin, 1957: 21).

The highland areas of Mindoro are composed of basement-complex rock materials which are slow to weather. They have developed into a topography of steep, serrated ridges and deep, steep-sided stream valleys (Wernstedt and Spencer, 1967: 430). This fact, taken with the abundant rainfall evenly distributed throughout the year, means that communications between Buid settlements are normally difficult and often impossible. Streams which may dry up completely when there has been no rain for two weeks can become raging torrents in a matter of hours. The upper Bongabon river can only be crossed for much of the year on precarious rattan bridges. This poses less of a problem for the Buid, who are excellent mountaineers, than it does for the Christians, who prefer to travel along the river valleys. The Buid maintain level trails running along the ridge tops into the interior, allowing them to maintain communications even when the rivers are in flood. These trails, called *baklayan*, are kept hidden from the Christians. One who arrives by means of them is a *famaklay*, 'visitor' from far away. Most other trails (*dalan*), however, run perpendicularly up and down the mountain slopes, and are difficult to follow during the rains. Most long-distance travel occurs after the grain harvest in September when generally dry conditions obtain, and when agricultural activity is at an ebb.

The mountains and forest provide the Buid with their best defence against Christian intruders, who are reluctant to brave the steep slippery trails, leeches, poisonous snakes and impenetrable undergrowth of the highlands. These are small obstacles for the Buid, who are habituated to them from youth. The Buid say that they find walking in the mountains less tiring than walking on the plains. The Christians, on the other hand, remain confined to the Bongabon river valley, having penetrated up it for 35 kilometres from the coast, stopping only where the mountains close in on either side to form a gorge above Alid (see Map IV).

In the area of my research, Buid swiddens range in elevation from 300 to 800 metres above sea level. The highest point in the area is over 1,100 metres above sea level, rising some 800 metres from the flood plain in just two kilometres. The Buid traditionally built their houses near the tops of ridges, in proximity to their swiddens, and hidden from the view of lowlanders by overhanging trees and folds in the topography. The views from their doorways are impressive, looking up and down the Bongabon river valley. The towering peaks to the north and west, home of the *bangun arungan*, or Taubuid, are often wreathed in cloud. The dense greenery of the primary rain forest which covers these mountains presents a stark contrast to the bare expanses lying downhill to the east, where the mountain chain quickly gives way to rolling hills and the flat littoral. The signs of Christian occupation in the lowlands are all too evident. Most of the land there has been denuded of forest cover by over-logging, and subsequent over-cultivation. Christian territory is a patchwork of light green grassland, brown ploughed fields, and scattered homesteads. Along the coast, one can make out extensive wet rice terraces and coconut plantations. On a clear day, one can even see the neighbouring islands of Tablas and Maestre de Campo 70 and 50 kilometres away respectively. The Buid have no names for these islands, knowing only that they are the original home of the Christians.

From their vantage points high on the mountain slopes, the Buid thus have constantly in view two opposed worlds. This must have been true for most of their history, for there have long been Christian settlements on the coast. Buid cultural autonomy is the product of an historical choice to eschew contact with the lowland world. By camouflaging their houses and trails, and by occupying positions where they can see without being seen, they have been able to vanish silently whenever an alien approached. Other, more specific injunctions have kept them from mingling with lowlanders, and these will be discussed below.

The Buid classify themselves and their neighbours in terms of their relative position on the slopes of the island. The concepts of *buid*, 'uphill', and *lod*, 'downhill', dominate their classification of spatial position and direction. Right and left have little practical or symbolic significance in their culture, nor are there any terms equivalent to the four cardinal points to indicate direction. It is concepts such as uphill/downhill, across, beyond, and near/far, together with the names of specific geographical features such as mountain peaks, streams and cliffs that are employed to identify localities and directions of travel. The standard greeting used throughout the Philippines (and in other parts of Austronesia) is 'Where are you going/coming from?' The standard Buid responses are *Uglaw am/gim buid* – 'I'm going/coming from uphill', or *Uglaw as/gis lod* – 'I'm going/coming from downhill'. No two points are thought of as lying at the same elevation. Transversal movement always involves ascent, descent, or a combination of the two. The uphill/downhill opposition has economic, social, and symbolic significance for the Buid, and it will make frequent appearances in the course of this book.

The traditional economy

The Buid practise what Conklin terms an integral system of shifting cultivation. By this he means that it does not form an adjunct to permanent field agriculture and that it is the only form of agriculture they are ever known to have practised. Further, the Buid have achieved a more or less stable equilibrium with their natural environment, and do not regularly pioneer new areas of virgin forest, unlike the Iban, for example (Conklin, 1957: 3; Freeman, 1970: 286). This system imposes quite specific constraints on Buid social organisation. The soils of the humid tropics, especially in mountainous areas, are subject to continuous leaching due to the constant percolation of warm rainwater through them. Leaching can be prevented only by maintaining a thick cover of vegetation over the soil, which locks the nutrients into living matter. The shifting cultivator of the humid tropics must concentrate these nutrients into a carpet of ash by slashing and burning the forest vegetation, at the same time ensuring that the forest cover is quickly replaced by a cover of cultivated plants which come to maturity at well-spaced intervals. In effect, he produces a controlled jungle ecology in his swidden (Geertz, 1963: 20 ff.). For this reason, intercropping is of the utmost importance for maintaining the fertility of the soil. Most of the shifting cultivators in Southeast Asia operate a complex system involving a succession of grain, root and tree crops on the same swidden before it is returned to fallow (Conklin, 1957: 77; Schlegel, 1979: 39; M. Rosaldo, 1980: 110; Karim, 1981: 105, 119; Freeman, 1970: 191–2; Leach, 1954: 72). The most careful of these studies has shown that over 400 specific plant types may be planted at one time or another in the swiddens of the group concerned. Among the Hanunoo, who are the Buid's neighbours, up to 125 plant types may be present in a single swidden during the first and most active year of a swidden cycle (Conklin, 1957: 77, 85; Schlegel, 1979: 38). To continue with the example of the Hanunoo, Conklin has carefully documented the extent of their preoccupation with the plant world. They are able to identify 1,625 specific plant types, of which over 1,000 have some specific use. Plants are the subject of 65 per cent of all after-dinner conversations, and appear in 74 per cent of the poems collected by Conklin, as opposed to only 5 per cent and 56 per cent, respectively, for animals (Conklin, 1955a: 72–3, 181–5).

Shifting cultivation, then, implies a deep familiarity with the natural environment and a recognition of subtle variations between micro-ecologies in a given area. The length of the fallow period required for a given plot to recover its fertility depends on the quality of the soil, the state of the surrounding vegetation and numerous other factors. De Schlippe has noted the failure of government programmes in Africa to impose fixed land boundaries and crop rotation cycles on shifting cultivators because they failed to give sufficient weight to local knowledge (de Schlippe, 1956: 150–2). The Buid exhibit a fascination with the plant world which takes on a religious significance to be treated later in this book. The roots of this significance lie in the fragile equilibrium between cultivated swidden and wild forest implied by their system of agriculture. The one is continually being transformed into the other.

The swidden cycle

Shifting cultivators in the Philippines generally classify land in terms of actual, potential and abandoned swidden sites. The Hanunoo recognise ten basic stages in the swidden cycle, the Tiruray recognise five (Conklin, 1957: 31; Schlegel, 1979: 22). The classification used by the Ayufay Buid is as follows (cf. Lopez, 1981: 162):

Normal stages

1	*gamasun*	swidden from selection to final clearing,
2	*sunugan*	burned swidden,
3	*namay*	grain swidden,
4	*tubas.*	harvested grain swidden,
5	*lamay*	root crop swidden,
6	*ginaru*	swidden reverting to forest, but still bearing tree crops,
7	*talun*	mature secondary forest, ready for recultivation.

There are, in addition, two types of land not normally involved in the swidden cycle. These are:

8	*furu ayu*	primary forest,
9	*ugunan*	grassland.

Slashing of new swiddens generally begins in late January and carries on until the beginning of April, so that the debris may be dried out as completely as possible during the height of the dry season. Burning occurs between mid-March and the end of April: those who wait until May may be overtaken by the monsoons and experience a poor burn. Planting is done a few days after burning and by May most grain crops are in the ground. Root crops may be planted at any time during the year, although unless its owner intends to plant a second grain crop on a swidden in the second year, it will be planted in root crops soon after the grain harvest in August. Old grain swiddens normally become root swiddens in the second or third year. The roots may be cropped for two or three years in succession, by which time some of the tree crops should begin bearing fruit. The most important of these are bananas, which form a substantial part of the Buid diet, especially when the more desirable root and grain crops are in short supply.

Although most of the integral shifting cultivators in Southeast Asia plant root and tree crops, in many of them, rice receives a disproportionate amount of attention.[1]

> In general, Southeast Asian shifting cultivation is further charac-
> terized by a strong emphasis on grain crops, the most important of
> which – qualitatively, from the standpoint of the cultivators, if not
> always quantitatively – is rice. (Conklin, 1957: 2)

This is true even where, as among the Hanunoo, the contribution of rice to the total diet is relatively small (ibid.: 30). In this respect, the Taubuid and the northern Buid are exceptional. The Taubuid, due in part to the high altitude of their fields, did not traditionally plant rice, and only now are some of those at lower elevations beginning to experiment with it as a cash crop (Pennoyer, 1978: 52). Only one man planted rice in Ayufay while I was in the field, and he was not born in the area. According to Lopez, rice was the major seed crop among the southern Buid, but it has now been largely abandoned in favour of maize (Lopez, 1981: 168). The Ayufay Buid probably planted more rice in the past than they do now, but it has always been regarded more as a ritual and seasonal feast food than as a staple. It is still seen as a necessary component of certain rituals, but, unlike most other Southeast Asian groups, is not itself the focus of much ritual activity. This attitude toward rice has had important consequences for the relative economic success of the Buid in recent years, for they have easily abandoned the cultivation of rice in favour of maize, which finds a ready market in the lowlands. Among the Hanunoo, by contrast,

> It is universally felt that the welfare of every individual, as well as
> that of the entire region, depends on the nature of the intimate
> relationship between the swidden farmers and [the] hypersensitive
> rice 'people'. (Conklin, 1957: 88)

For this reason, the Hanunoo have been unwilling to abandon rice cultivation, so central is it to their cultural identity. Upland rice is more difficult to grow, and more vulnerable to pests and bad weather than is maize. As a result of their cultural conservatism, the Hanunoo have suffered real economic hardship (Postma, personal communication). Much of the maize now grown by the Buid is used to purchase rice from the lowlands, so that they have in fact been able to maintain their rice consumption at or even above traditional levels.

Rice is eaten largely during the planting season in April, when it forms an obligatory part of the meal served to agricultural helpers, and in September, after the maize harvest, when money with which to buy it is abundant. During the rest of the year, the Buid rely on the produce of their *lamay*, non-grain swiddens, eating sweet potatos, yams, taro, manioc and bananas in roughly equal proportions. Maize is only eaten in its soft, immature form, either roasted or steamed as a snack, and is not dried and stored as grain except for seed. The Buid regard the Bisayan staple of cracked maize with contempt. There is no question that the Buid are better nourished than the Christians due to the wider range of dependable food sources at their disposal.

Once a swidden has reverted to *talun*, it must be left fallow for a period ranging from seven to twenty-five years (Conklin, 1957: 138). Because grain crops can be planted in a swidden for only one, or, at most, two years, new swiddens must be cleared continually to replace the old ones. In general, Philippine integral shifting cultivators prefer to build their houses near their fields, producing a pattern of dispersed settlement (Conklin, 1957: 13–15; Schlegel, 1979: 6; Frake, 1980: 86; Jocano, 1968: 37). The Ayufay Buid still maintain houses in their swiddens, in addition to the ones they have built in Ugun Liguma. During the periods of the annual agricultural cycle which require the most intensive labour, the central settlement becomes almost deserted (cf. Freeman, 1970: 164). While two households may farm adjacent swiddens, most swiddens lie about half a kilometre apart, or just within calling distance. The population is thus evenly dispersed across the landscape.

There seems to be a general agreement that the maximum population density which can be supported by Southeast Asian methods of shifting cultivation without damage to the environment is about fifty people per square kilometre (Conklin, 1957: 146; Schlegel, 1979: 69; Pelzer, 1945: 23). The actual population density of the Hanunoo varies between twenty five and thirty five people per square kilometre. This is in line with my own findings for the Buid inhabiting the area shown in the centre of Map V. This area is about thirty-five square kilometres and has a population of 700 Buid. Not all of this is arable land, some of it being unavailable for ritual or ecological reasons, making the effective population density some twenty-five or thirty people per square kilometre. Under traditional conditions, this would be well under the 'carrying capacity' of the locality, but due to the logging operations described in the last chapter, and to the destructive methods of the Christian settlers, the forest cover is rapidly receding. The land immediately adjacent to the settlement of Ugun Liguma is already suffering from severe erosion.

The Christian migrants who have taken up shifting cultivation in Buid territory tend to plant only a single cash crop, maize. Because of this, the lands they farm are subject to erosion which is exacerbated by the insufficient fallow period they allow before recultivating the same slope. The Christians are well aware of declining returns after two or three years, but because of their fragile tenure on the land, they hold the view that they ought to get as much out of it as they can, and be prepared to move on when the land is exhausted. Their survival depends almost completely on the success of their maize crop, which is highly vulnerable to typhoons. When a series of typhoons struck the area is 1978/79, the Christians were forced to rely on government relief and emergency aid, while the Buid simply continued eating their root crops (Lopez, 1981: 170).

Land tenure
The Buid subscribe to what may be called a labour theory of property. As Buid agriculture involves no permanent investment in the land, land in itself was not thought of in the past as being subject to private ownership. It 'belonged' to the spirits of the earth, and so long as these spirits were not offended, land was freely available to whoever wanted to farm it. A person owned only what he or she planted, and when the last productive cultigen in a swidden was harvested, all further claim to the plot lapsed. The same is true among the Hanunoo and Subanun: no rights whatsoever can be asserted over land which has once been cultivated but no longer contains any productive cultigens (Conklin, 1957: 35; Frake, 1980: 91. For a similar rule in Africa see de Schlippe, 1956: 13). Evidence for the Gaddang and Tiruray in the Philippines is less clear-cut. They do seem to retain some rights in abandoned swiddens, but whether these rights apply even to swiddens without any

surviving cultigens and, if so, how strong they are, is not clear from the literature (Schlegel, 1979: 23; Wallace, 1970: 60). None of these five societies possesses any corporate, property-holding group larger than a household. While current swiddens are considered to be the property of the whole household in the other four of these societies, among the Buid swiddens are owned by individuals, every adult man and woman asserting an independent claim to the cultigens in clearly differentiated plots.

In respect both to residual rights in abandoned land and to the existence of large property-owning corporate groups, the situation elsewhere in South and Southeast Asia appears to be quite different. Among the Kachin of Highland Burma, rights of usufruct are held by individual households; rights of access to uncleared land are held by the principal lineage in a village, which has the power to alienate those rights to other lineages; and chiefs assert political authority over the inhabitants of a defined territory (Leach, 1954: 115, 155). The Ma'Betisek of Malaysia have cognatic descent groups which hold corporate rights in land (Karim, 1981: 26). In Sarawak, Iban longhouses hold rights of access to uncleared land as against other longhouses, and individual households retain permanent rights over all the land they are responsible for once having cleared (Freeman, 1970: 143). In general, however, the evidence from Philippine shifting cultivators tends to support Frake's contention that

> Prior to the Oceanic migrations and to the innovation of permanent field agriculture in Malaysia, land must have been a free good. It is probable, therefore, that similarities in systems of land tenure between Malaysian permanent-field cultivators and the peoples of Polynesia and Micronesia are the product of a convergence under conditions of land scarcity and not of common cultural inheritance from the original Malayo-Polynesian speech community. (Frake and Goodenough, 1956: 172; cf. Goodenough, 1955)

The organisation of agricultural labour

Sahlins, citing Geddes and Izikowitz, views the hinterland communities of Southeast Asia as departing from the normal tendency of 'tribal' societies to incline toward 'generalised reciprocity', or the absence of precise calculation of returns. He attributes the emphasis on 'balanced reciprocity' in the area to the necessity for each household to accumulate a surplus of the basic staple, rice, for external trade. 'The principal relation between households is a closely calculated balanced exchange of labour service' (Sahlins, 1972: 224–5). This characterisation certainly applies to the Iban, whose labour-exchange system is governed by strict reciprocity:

> Thus if *bilek-family* A sends two women to weed on the farms of families B, C, and D, these three are each required, in return, to send two women to the farm of family A when its turn falls due on the rota [. . .] This principle of exact reciprocity is rigorously followed, so that if family A sends only one woman to work on the farm of family B, family B will send only one woman in exchange – employing its additional woman, on that day, in working on its own farm. (Freeman, 1970: 236)

The same notion of exact reciprocity seems to be operative among both the Kachin and the Ma'Betisék (Leach, 1954: 135; Karim, 1981: 104). Sahlins is cautious about extending his analysis to the Philippines, and it is just as well, for labour exchange in the groups that have been studied seems, for the most part, to be non-reciprocal in character.

Among the Buid, by far the largest amount of economic cooperation occurs between husband and wife, who, while belonging to the same household, maintain separate swiddens. There is a 'statistical' sexual division of labour, but it is not enforced by social or mystical sanctions. People can and do perform tasks normally assigned to members of the opposite sex. The work normally assigned to women is of the continuous, repetitive sort such as weeding, harvesting root crops and carrying moderate loads. Men tend to perform heavy, discontinuous work such as clearing thick underbrush, felling trees and building houses. Fetching water and firewood, cooking, feeding the animals and caring for children are all tasks shared equally by men and women. I have never known a Buid woman to hunt, but hunting is carried out more for the protection of crops than for its contribution to the diet, and no great prestige attaches to the successful hunter. There is no question of men being held responsible for the production of highly valued foods, and consequently receiving an exaggerated recognition of their economic contribution as among most hunter-gatherer groups, or even such hunter-cultivators as the Ilongot and Ndembu.[2] Among the Buid it is domesticated animals which are of social and ritual importance. Their production and ownership are not sex linked.

The Buid economy does not normally require the organisation and control of large groups. Most economic activities can be and are carried out by individual households, even if they contain only a single member. At certain times of the year, however, cooperation with other households in customary. That this cooperation is not imposed by economic necessity is demonstrated by the Ilongot, who practise virtually the same type of agriculture without having systematic recourse to cooperative labour except at harvest time (M. Rosaldo, 1980: 132–3; R. Rosaldo, 1979).[3] Among the Buid, the burning, planting and harvesting of swiddens is usually carried out by large groups. As each of these activities must be carried out by every household at roughly the same time, there is a potential competition for labour. Some means must be found to reconcile competing claims. Instead of relying on close kinsmen or contractual partners, the Buid resort to a more roundabout procedure.

Information about one's plans and intentions is communicated to others in a characteristically impersonal way. Every day at dawn and dusk, the adult members of a neighbourhood will gather on a cleared patch of ground and squat, all facing in the same direction with their gaze fixed on the mountain opposite. One by one they relate their experiences of the past day, gossip they have heard and their future plans. In a series of monologues like this, wills never come into conflict because no one is expected to make a direct reply to anyone else. Each individual can alter his or her plans without having to acknowledge that it is being done in deference to the contrary will of another. An individual may remain uncertain until the last moment just who will turn up to help on a given day. No one, kin or neighbour, has an obligation to help any other specific individual. No account is kept of the labour given to or received from other households. There is a general moral obligation to help when one is able, but it is an obligation owed the community as a whole. Each cooperative labour task – *tarugbungan*: 'mutual help' – is viewed as an end in itself. Not only is there enjoyment to be gained from the socialising which goes on during the task, but the owner of the swidden on which the work is done has an obligation to provide the helpers with a midday meal containing rice and a special side dish, ideally meat, but a vegetable cooked in coconut milk may be substituted. The owner of the field does not participate in the work, but stays discreetly out of sight preparing food for the others.

The situation among the Hanunoo appears to be very similar:

Nonritual feast labour (*pasapnung*) is the most common type of nonreciprocal group assistance in swidden work and may be recruited at any time, provided enough food (preferably rice) is available.

There is no exchange or reciprocal obligation attached to such participation, and since there is no binding contract involved, one can never be sure how many workers there will be until the morning of the feast. (Conklin, 1957: 53, 55)

As among the Hanunoo, Buid share the product of their grain swiddens with those who come to help harvest them. In the Buid case, a helper receives one third of what he or she harvests. While labour for the burning and planting of swiddens is usually recruited from within a local community, Buid travel widely during the harvest season, and the opportunity to help in distant harvests provides one of the chief incentives for initiating and maintaining social contacts with distant local communities (cf. Conklin, 1957: 54). Among the Tiruray, there appears to be a general expectation that cooperative labour will be reciprocated, but 'All in the neighbourhood who are able to help do so; those genuinely unable for any reason do not forfeit the reciprocating labour of the caller' (Schlegel, 1979: 19).

Other forms of sharing in the Buid economy

For convenience, I shall refer to all social and material transactions which do not indebt specific individuals or groups in Buid society as 'sharing'. Relations between members of a single household should epitomise the values of sharing and mutual help. The Buid divide cooked food into two categories: *fafa* 'cooked starch staple', and *ufi* 'side dish'. Only *fafa* is considered necessary for a meal. *Ufi* is prepared somewhat sporadically, as vegetables come into season. Normally, two meals are prepared each day, *yabas* in the morning and *yafun* in the late afternoon. Any member of the household may prepare and serve the meal, whether man, woman or child. Attendance at meals is informal. Household members need not eat together, but may wander in whenever they like. A friend or neighbour who happens to be present when the *fafa* is dumped out of the cooking pot on to a woven tray will be asked to share some. This is done by placing some food on an eating tray, turning away from the guest, and shoving it towards them. After an interval, the guest will begin to eat without otherwise acknowledging the offer. On the whole, however, *fafa* is not shared between households and is subject to little symbolic elaboration. It is not thought of as a scarce resource. This attitude contrasts markedly with that displayed toward meat, which is scarce, is always shared between households, and is the focus of a great deal of ritual concern.

I remarked earlier that for shifting cultivators like the Buid, the boundary between cultivated and uncultivated land, or between the human and non-human world, is continually shifting. In Mindoro, this shifting boundary exists not only in relation to plant associations, but also in relation to wild and domesticated animals. The pigs and chickens which live in the forest are exactly the same as those which live in human settlements. Domesticated pigs can always go wild, and wild pigs, if caught young, can always be domesticated. Humans must deliberately make each generation of pigs and chickens dependent on them for food and protection.

The life cycle of domesticated pigs and chickens is characterised by an outward movement. They begin life inside the house, often being fed by hand to develop a sense of dependency on their owner. When they mature, they are excluded from the house, but remain closely associated with it. Adult pigs are fenced beneath the house, which is raised about a metre off the ground. Adult chickens are left to roost in the branches of trees which overhang the roof of the house and to lay their eggs in baskets hung on its external walls. The two types of animals thus move from the inside of the house to the outside and end their lives by being shared with the members of neighbouring households.

Whenever a pig or chicken is killed, its meat must be distributed in exactly equal shares among all the inhabitants of a local community, regardless of their age, sex, or genealogical connection to the giver. With the exception of the meals provided to agricultural helpers mentioned above, domesticated animals are only killed on ritual occasions. These rituals are only performed by a household on its own behalf. Every household must maintain a stock of animals for such occasions, which may arise at any time, but which usually recur about once a month. An individual may expect to receive a share of meat from another household in the community about once a week. There is thus a continuous flow of meat through the community, which constitutes the most frequent form of transaction between households. The continual sharing of meat serves an important function in quickly integrating a new member into the community, for entitlement to a share is determined solely by current residence, not by pre-existing ties of reciprocity, kinship, or affinity.

Because a household performs a ritual on its own behalf, it does not indebt the undifferentiated recipients of meat shares, nor does it acquire any prestige by providing a feast. A household which is forced to perform frequent sacrifices is more an object of pity than of admiration, since the underlying cause of most rituals is an illness or death within the household.

The Buid obtain a large part of their animal protein from wild resources. When a large pig or monkey has been destroying swidden crops, spear or noose traps will be set, and groups of three or four men may gather to track it with spears and dogs. The product of pig and monkey hunts is shared in the same way as the product of sacrifices involving domesticated animals. A more important source of wild animal meat is the gathering of small animals, such as civets and bats. When caught in large numbers, these are also shared throughout the community.

Dam fishing in the Bongabon river is important not only for its contribution to the diet, but also for the opportunity it provides for large numbers of Buid to gather together from their isolated swidden homes. It is the only non-ritual occasion on which this happens and constitutes a social event in its purest form. Up to fifty individuals gather to construct a dam across part of the river bed, diverting the water and draining a portion of the stream, thus trapping fish among the exposed rocks. As it only takes a week of rainless weather to make this feasible, dam fishing exhibits only a moderate seasonality, occurring most frequently in the dry season from March to May. Men are responsible for shifting large rocks and cutting stakes. Women carry banana leaves and earth in baskets to pile against them. Finally, the children often prove to be the most nimble and are able to catch fish which have been trapped beneath the rocks. At the end of the day, all the fish are pooled and shared out equally among all the participants.

Sharing in general

The role of sharing in Buid society has already been discussed in many particular instances. As a value, it has a very general application in daily life. No Buid likes to be in debt to another for even a temporary period. (Most debts are incurred and paid off as a result of divorce settlements, see Chapter 4.) This caused certain difficulties for me at the beginning of my fieldwork. I was never able to initiate exchanges which would place Buid in debt to me or me in debt to Buid. On the few occasions when I was asked for a loan, it was always someone I did not know very well and my compliance with the request was enough to ensure that I did not see the individual again for a very long time. There was never any question of my giving direct compensation for help rendered or information given to me by Buid I knew well. This was a serious drawback in relation to the more tedious aspects of my work, such as language learning, for there was no way to compensate informants for the inevitable boredom. I was never able to pay people for carrying supplies or for any other work. In the end I managed to reach an arrangement with Agaw's family whereby I provided rice for all of us to eat, while the family provided the wood, water and labour needed to cook it. In my relations with the rest of the community, the large amount of assistance I was in fact given was always rendered in as anonymous a way as possible. Individuals would never come on their own to help me carry supplies across the Bongabon river, but the whole settlement would, on occasion, turn up *en masse* to do so. I would often wake in the morning to find fresh fruit or vegetables on my doorstep with no indication as to their origin. I was only able to collect samples of the material culture by displaying large numbers of glass beads to a gathering of the entire settlement, leaving individuals to decide how much the objects they brought in return were worth. The embarrassment caused by a barter situation in which a calculation of exact equivalences has to be made was in this way avoided by sub-merging the transaction in the relative anonymity of a group exchange. In the end, I was allowed to make general contributions to the welfare of the community as a whole, but I was not allowed to single out one individual from among the others.

The behaviour of the Christian peasants toward me provides an illuminating contrast. They were constantly trying to put me in their debt, or themselves in my debt, it did not really matter which. When relations between myself and a Christian family became strained for any reason, they immediately asked me for a further favour. To have refused the favour would have meant, in their eyes, that I had decided to terminate the social relationship entirely. Moral ties among the Christians are conceived in terms of *utang na loob*, 'debts of gratitude', which are left forever ambiguous (Hollnsteiner, 1973).

I give these examples of my attempts to create ties of reciprocity with the Buid because of my unique situation of dependency on others. I came only slowly to apprehend that attempts to build up relations of direct reciprocity with others were counter-productive. The principle of indirect sharing is so fundamental that it extends even to the characteristic mode of conversation among the Buid. I described above the way in which large groups will gather to discuss the organisation of collective work groups during the planting and harvesting seasons. Conflict is then avoided through each of the participants 'sharing' his or her thoughts with the group as a whole, without ever addressing anyone in particular. This is true of conversations more generally. Whenever Buid gather to chat, one will find that the majority are facing in the same direction, or sitting with their backs to one another. Eye contact is seldom made, and never when the topic of conversation may be in any way controversial. When a disagreeable statement is made, it may simply be ignored by the auditors, and the conversation may shift to an entirely unrelated topic, or else the auditors may simply sidle off and discontinue the exchange. This is easier to do when a large number of people are involved and one can slip away unnoticed. As an outsider whose business it was to ask a number of frequently tactless questions, this was often my experience. Just as I had to learn that the only acceptable way for me to participate in Buid social life was to share material goods with the group as a whole, so I had to learn that conversations were subject to the same rule and had to be shared with a group. Indeed, certain specific prohibitions make dyadic communication impossible in some contexts.

Not only are Buid prohibited from uttering the personal names of their parents and parents-in-law, but they are prohibited from uttering their own personal names. A namesake must be referred as *angku sangay*. For this reason, an effort is made to avoid the duplication of names within the local community. Much confusion was caused when a family moved to Ayufay from the other side of the island, as most of them had names in common with other Ayufay residents. Two Buid who meet for the first time must go through a lengthy procedure of indirect questioning in order to establish their mutual identities when there is no third party to supply the necessary information. I once accompanied a middle-aged man from Sigaw to visit the old man in Ambuan who has the best knowledge of regional genealogies. It took the old man over an hour to establish which members of his own generation were the parents of the younger man, and so identify his visitor. In collecting genealogies, I soon discovered that I received more complete and accurate information from third parties than from the individual with whom I was directly concerned.

Direct reciprocity and the calculation of equivalence in exchange is incompatible with the egalitarian values of Buid society. It places the parties involved in a potentially competitive situation in which one or the other must come out the loser. The Buid often become indebted to lowland Christian merchants, but they refuse to regard themselves as being under a moral obligation to them. The Christians are seen as attempting to exercise an illegitimate domination over the Buid, based on the threat of violence. From the Christian point of view, matters appear quite differently. Many of the Christians depend for their livelihood on 'buying cheap' from the Buid and 'selling dear' in the market towns on the coast. They attempt to build up stable, long-term relationships with particular Buid trading partners in order to guarantee their source of supply. They deliberately extend credit to the Buid, at an exorbitant rate of interest, to place the latter in a state of permanent indebtedness. Such relationships are an integral part of lowland culture and society. Rich landlords or merchants attach a number of clients to themselves by means of extending loans in times of crisis. This fundamentally asymmetrical relationship is expressed linguistically as one of reciprocity: a landlord and his tenant are both called *kasama* – 'companions' or 'partners', the former supplying the land and sometimes the capital for farming, the latter supplying the labour. After the harvest, they both receive their 'share' (*bahagi*) of the product. This relationship has a moral aspect. Because the tenant or client is in a state of long-term indebtedness, he owes his landlord a 'debt of gratitude' and should be ready to 'help' the latter on a diffuse, non-contractual basis. A patron may be said to 'hold' (*hawak*) a certain number of people in his 'sphere of influence' (*sakop*). Patron-client ties often receive ritual sanction through the institution of godparenthood, the patron being asked to sponsor the baptisms and marriages of his clients. The parents of the sponsored child then become the *compadre* or *comadre* of the patron, concepts which in other contexts have strongly egalitarian implications. Again, a fundamentally hierarchical relationship is represented as being one of mutual reciprocity.

Compadrinazgo ties cannot be created between Christian and Buid, because the Buid reject the rituals on which they are based. Instead, Christian traders try to resort to a more ancient institution, that of the *sandugo* – 'blood brother', literally, 'one blood'. *Sandugo* has now become a universal term of address for a Buid by the Christians. Like *compadre* it has the same moral implications of diffuse, enduring obligation; the same reciprocal character; and the same quality of masking a hierarchical relationship. To the Buid, the term is entirely without moral force. They regard its use by the Christians as an insulting imposition by people with whom they feel no moral connection of any kind. The Christian settlers among the Buid view the latter as standing in the same relation towards themselves as they stand in relation to their own patrons. They view the Buid's notorious unreliability in meeting their debts as an indication of their moral inferiority. The Buid view the attempt by the Christians to indebt them as an indication of the Christians' moral inferiority. Between the two groups there is a fundamental cultural divide.

Patterns of resistance to incorporation by the lowlands
The traditional Buid economy, as I have described it, has long been maintained against a background of permanent field agriculture in the lowlands. The Buid have only been able to maintain their social and cultural autonomy by systematically rejecting lowland agricultural methods. This rejection is expressed in Buid culture by a series of prohibitions. The most important of these is an injunction not to *agsagmak daga* – 'flatten the earth', a necessary step in the construction of wet rice terraces. To do so would be to anger *afu daga* – 'owners of the earth', spirits who are responsible for all fertility. These spirits are also angered by the use of ploughs and of water buffalo, the only available draught animal. Secondly, the construction of large settlements is believed to attract the attention of a variety of evil spirits. The Buid traditionally moved their house sites frequently in order to avoid localities which had become haunted by these spirits. This is much more difficult to do in a densely populated settlement. Thirdly, there was a prohibition against planting trees whose life expectancy was longer than that of a human. It was believed that since the tree would outlive the planter, it would somehow shorten the life of the latter.[4] One of the consequences of these three prohibitions is that they limit the period in which an individual or group can remain attached to a particular locality. Another is that they prevent the investment of labour in land, forcing each generation to start from scratch. Finally, despite a long-standing familiarity with Christian mythology, the Buid have always been extremely careful not to let Christianity interfere with ritual activity in any way. The significance of this fact will emerge only after the material on Buid religion has been presented. The point I want to make here is that these prohibitions have played an essential role in the perpetuation of the traditional

economy, and that they have had to be reformulated or abandoned in order for the Buid to participate in the market economy of the lowlands.

Trade and the impact of the market economy

External trade has always played an essential role in the Buid economy. As Freeman points out, shifting cultivation of the type practised by the Buid is almost unthinkable without iron tools, which must have been obtained from traders for many centuries prior to European contact (Freeman, 1970: 174–5; cf. also Leach, 1954: 229–30). The northern Buid do not construct the Malay piston-bellow forge in use among the Hanunoo, nor do they weave cloth on back-strap looms. The southern Buid are familiar with both techniques, and must have been one of the main suppliers of wrought-iron blades and cloth to the northern Buid in the past. In addition to iron, the Buid historically obtained salt, pottery and textiles from other highland groups. Salt was obtained from coastal groups such as the Hanunoo in the form of cakes, or simply of bamboo tubes filled with concentrated sea water (Conklin, 1958: 11, 55, 122). Pottery was produced by the southern Buid, who traded it with both the Hanunoo and the northern Buid (Conklin, 1953a). In return, the northern Buid traded, and still trade, their basketry, famous throughout the region; and resin, which is found only at higher elevations, and is used for torches.

Equally important for the Buid were certain prestige items such as beads and plates from China, and brass gongs and bells from Mindanao. These were brought in by Muslim traders from the south, who were stopping at the coastal market towns as late as 1940. All these items play an important role in Buid ritual life, and glass beads had an additional function as a medium of exchange (cf. Conklin, 1955a: 53, 82, for a similar situation among the Hanunoo). Beads are now obtained from Christian storekeepers in the coastal towns for 2.50 pesos a packet, a mark-up of about 75 per cent on the wholesale price in Manila. Most are now imported from Taiwan. They still play an important role in divorce settlements (see Chapter 4), but they have now been largely replaced by cash as a medium of exchange.

The increasing importance of maize as a cash crop
Maize has now almost entirely replaced rice as the grain crop planted in the first year of the swidden cycle. In Ayufay, the Buid sell about 90

per cent of their maize to Christian merchants, disdaining to grind and eat the dried grains as do the Bisayans. This means that roughly one quarter of the annual agricultural cycle is devoted to the production of a cash crop. In other words, the initial phase of the swidden cycle, the construction of *namay*, has been turned over to cash crop production, while the succeeding stages of *lamay* and *ginaru* have been preserved intact to ensure subsistence requirements. It is this 'mixed economy' which allows the Buid, for the time being, to have the best of two worlds. On the one hand, they remain relatively immune to most environmental disasters such as typhoons, which have less impact on root crops than on grain crops. On the other hand, they are now able to purchase a wide variety of lowland goods in addition to maintaining their consumption of rice by purchasing it from the lowlands.

The Buid spend a large part of their cash income on a range of cheap 'luxury' items such as transistor radios, electric torches, blankets and lowland clothing, and on more practical items such as aluminium pots, salt, matches, iron tools, nails and even ploughshares. Many of these items have been substituted for traditional Buid manufactures such as cotton loincloths and skirts, and clay pottery, thus weakening the system of internal trade. Only a few of the more remote Buid settlements continue to prefer the traditional goods. In the settlement of Batangan, which is the most heavily involved in the cash economy, there are still a few individuals who continue to produce clay pottery for trade with the Taubuid, who will not use aluminium.

It is difficult to determine the precise extent of Buid dependency on the lowland market. In settlements like Batangan, dependency is almost complete, while in settlements like Ayufay, most of the goods obtained in the lowlands are regarded as frivolous 'extras' unnecessary to economic production. In Ayufay, most individuals make no attempt to budget their cash income, but squander it as soon as they receive it on items such as cakes, biscuits and even brassières. But there is one context in which participation in the cash economy has become vital to production. Paradoxically, this is due to the persistence of the traditional system of labour sharing.

The sponsor of a collective labour team during the maize planting season in April is obliged to provide a rice meal for the helpers. Because planting is done some seven months after the last harvest, most Buid are forced to borrow rice from Christian merchants at a staggering rate of interest. The normal arrangement is that rice worth 25 pesos is loaned by the merchant in return for one *kaban* (about 60 kilos) of maize at harvest time. Now, a *kaban* of maize sells for 50 or 60 pesos at that time, netting the merchant a profit in excess of 100 per cent after only five months. Admittedly, the merchants face a high risk of their debtors defaulting. The Buid often evade payment, sometimes moving right across the island to avoid their creditors, and there is little the latter can do about it. Nevertheless, if a Buid does want to maintain a stable trading relationship with a merchant, he or she must pay through the nose.

The sister of the mayor of Bongabon controls most of the Buid maize trade in the area. It pays her to deal with the Buid rather than with the Christian squatters since the Buid are more easily intimidated and less sophisticated about market mechanisms than the Christians. For the same reason, it is in her interests to protect Buid land claims against the squatters and to encourage them to adopt a more settled way of life, as this makes debt collection easier. She tries to bring pressure to bear against recalcitrant Buid through the agency of Agaw and other local leaders. Agaw has a great deal at stake in maintaining a good working relationship with this patron. Her support is vital in protecting Buid land against the poor Christians (most of whom regard themselves as her clients as well), in maintaining good relations with the Bureau of Forest Development, in which one of her nephews is employed, and as a counter-weight to the influence of Yaum.

Approximately half the maize harvest each year goes toward the liquidation of debts incurred over the previous year. The other half is sold either directly or through agents to large dealers in town. At the end of the 1980 harvest, after all loans had been paid off, eleven Buid from Ugun Liguma decided to hire a logging lorry to take their surplus straight to the warehouse of Sison in Roxas (see Chapter 2), where they thought they would get a better price than from the local traders. One third of the load belonged to Yaum, representing repayments of loans he had made to local Buid during the preceding year; one third belonged to Agaw, representing the product of his ploughed fields; and the other third belonged to the rest. The total load came to 6,327 kilos and sold for 7,281 pesos. Of this, Yaum received 2,132 pesos, Agaw received 2,221, and the remaining nine participants divided the remainder of 2,928 pesos among themselves, yielding an average income of under 300 pesos on the year's crop. I would estimate that this figure represents about half the total average cash income for a Buid in the Ayufay area, which is equivalent to about 40 pounds sterling.

Agaw was the first Buid in the area to break the prohibition against ploughing the land. He now owns two water buffaloes, and has taught himself and his son how to use them in ploughing. Because of his political prestige, and his willingness to innovate, he has been able to appropriate the unused flat land around the settlement of Ugun Liguma for ploughing. He planted a second maize crop on this land after the September harvest, which yielded a substantially smaller harvest in January. Along with many of the more 'progressive' Buid, he is succumbing to the temptation of indefinitely intensifying maize production. Swidden size used to be limited to the area needed to produce a subsistence crop. Among conservative Buid it is still limited to the area required to produce a cash crop which will just meet traditionally defined needs. But for those Buid more familiar with the unlimited range of goods available on the market, and with the desirability of providing their children with a lowland education and officially recognised land titles, the need for additional cash induces them to expand the size of their swiddens and to recrop them at more frequent intervals, leading to a loss of soil fertility.

Other sources of cash income
In addition to maize, some of the up-river Buid in Alid and Fawa grow substantial crops of squash (*labasa*) for sale to the lowlands. The 'progressive' elements in Ayufay have broken another prohibition by planting commercial tree crops such as coffee, cacao and mango which are just beginning to bear fruit. As often as not, the primary motivation for planting tree crops is the need to establish occupancy of an area in the eyes of the government. The collection of forest products such as orchids, honey, bamboo and rattan also provides a certain income, but the sale of timber is of greater significance than all these other sources of income combined. Strictly speaking, all logging in the area is illegal, and cut timber is subject to appropriation by the Bureau of Forest Development.

Both the Buid and the Christian squatters laboriously fell and square logs with hand tools, and then hide them by the side of the logging road to be picked up by lorries during the dry season. Some of these lorries operate only under cover of darkness, but others are owned by organisations which have contacts within the law enforcement agencies. I heard of a variety of arrangements, the most common of which was to allow the BFD to confiscate a certain proportion of logs which its members could then sell on their own account, in return for turning a blind eye to other shipments. Hard wood was fetching

1.30 pesos per board foot (144 cubic inches) in town, and soft wood was fetching 0.60 pesos. Semi-finished timber of good quality was selling for 1.80 pesos, and finished boards for 2.50 pesos. But the Buid were getting no more than about 0.25 pesos per board foot, after their local Christian contacts, the contacts of those contacts, and the law enforcement officers had taken their cut. Lorries can carry up to 3,000 board feet. On one such load, the Buid contributed 1,300 board feet and received just 330 pesos in return, or about 20 pounds sterling for several weeks of labour by four different men. On another occasion, a Buid had 1,500 board feet of wood confiscated by the BFD. A sympathetic Christian said he would do what he could to try to get the BFD to share 50 per cent of the profits with the unfortunate Buid, but by the time I left, it seemed he would be lucky to get half that amount. This same lowlander acquired a power saw, capable of cutting 600 board feet a day, ingratiated himself with the local Buid and persuaded them to cut and haul logs to the roadside for him. He had arranged to sell these logs to a timber dealer from northern Mindoro, who had acquired the right to 300 cubic metres of wood from the owner of the local logging concession to supply a major soft drink company in Manila with wood for crates. The BFD agreed to this operation on condition that the logs used were 'abandoned' and not freshly cut. The Buid who participated in this scheme were never paid the 400 pesos they were owed.

Logging is, in short, a very risky business, which can yield a much higher rate of return on invested labour than can maize, but which requires an extensive familiarity with the political system and business practices of the lowlands. The Christians are much more adept at circumventing government regulations than are the Buid, and generally receive twice as much for their wood as a result.

Changes in the system of land tenure

Under Philippine law, no land with a slope exceeding 18 per cent can be released for settlement. In 1975 a Presidential Decree ordered a Forest Occupancy Survey to be carried out to determine the presence of 'primitive tribes', *kaingineros* (shifting cultivators), and squatters within government forest reserves, and the 'extent of their respective occupation and resulting damage or impairment of forest resources'. The Decree made it mandatory for 'any person who shall cut, gather, collect, or remove timber or other forest products from any forest land' to have a permit to do so (P.D. 705, 1975: sec. 68). In order to legalise their position, the Buid had three alternatives. First, they could appeal to the PANAMIN to have their land declared a tribal reservation. From what they knew to be the consequences of such an action for the Hanunoo in the south of Mindoro, the Buid were unanimously opposed to this option. By the time the land within the 'Mangyan reservation' in Buyayaw was divided up, there were only two hectares of land per family to go round. What is more, the Hanunoo on the reservation had been developed as a tourist attraction.[5] Second, they could try to have their land released for private ownership. Although there was some enthusiasm for this idea, the Buid were in the end dissuaded, again by the experience of the Hanunoo. The Christians had been able to acquire Hanunoo lands in 'released' areas by buying the titles from unsuspecting Hanunoo, or simply by using Hanunoo as fronts to advance their own claims. Whole river valleys, which belong to the Hanunoo on paper, turn out, on closer inspection, to belong to Christian landlords, who use the Hanunoo as pawns in suits brought before the Presidential Advisory Commission on Land Problems (PACLAP). No Hanunoo or Buid has sufficient influence or capital to pay for a formal survey, and so they must rely on lowland backers. In any case, most Buid land has a slope in excess of the maximum allowed for private ownership.

The third option was to apply to the BFD for *kaingin* permits, which allow a household to claim up to seven hectares of previously farmed land. In consultation with Yaum and the Enriquez family, this is what the Ayufay Buid decided to do. In anticipation of the Forest Occupancy Survey (FOS) carried out by the BFD in October, 1980, the Buid asked me to prepare a map of the lands they would be claiming. The result is shown on Map X. One of the interesting things about this map is that the Buid parcelled out the entire Ayufay watershed into equal allotments to be claimed by each adult man and woman as their exclusive property. This constituted a fundamental transformation in Buid notions of land tenure and is indicative of both the persuasive power of Yaum and Agaw, and of the seriousness with which the Buid take the threat from the squatters. At a deeper level, however, the principle of equal shares for all was rigorously adhered to. There was absolutely no quarrelling within the settlement of Ugun Liguma about how much land each should get (but see Case 2 in Chapter 8). Provision was made for families with a greater number of children and those such as Agaw who started out with the largest claims gave much of it away in succeeding months.

As it turned out, one of the chief difficulties the Buid had with the surveyors lay in convincing them that the land was being claimed by individuals, and not by male heads of households. The surveyors refused to believe that women had an equal right to have land registered in their names and this fact is likely to have important repercussions on Buid practices of marriage and divorce, not to mention on the general status of women. Divorce, which is frequent among the Buid, is virtually impossible under Philippine law, so that the question of dividing conjugal property seldom arises in the lowlands.

Although government legislation is designed to protect forest lands for commercial exploitation, and to protect watersheds, it often has the opposite effect of increasing the threat of soil erosion and the spread of grasslands. This is true of the provision that 'squatters' are allowed to farm the lands they already have in cultivation, but are prohibited from making any new clearings. Shifting cultivation requires the regular return of swiddens to forest fallow, and a fallow to swidden ratio of at least 8:1. During their survey, the Forestry officials had to be convinced of definite 'improvements' to the land before they would register it as occupied. As a result, the Buid now feel that they are obliged to keep as much land as possible under continuous cultivation to prove their occupancy. One solution is to plant commercial tree crops, an option which the government actively encourages. But this removes land from the swidden cycle and places an additional burden on the land retained for subsistence crops.

The planting of tree crops appeals to the Buid since they do not regard land as such as being subject to private possession. The ownership of tree crops establishes their right to a certain area in their own eyes as well as in those of the government. They have had to break the prohibition against planting long-lived trees, but the Buid seemed to regard the empirical validity of the consequences of breaking this prohibition as a matter for speculation, and as being, in any case, less fundamental than the rules relating to property.

A further consequence of the changes in land tenure is that the possibility of accumulating productive property has been opened up. This is especially true of those who have taken up ploughing. They must make a long-term investment in clearing the land of all obstructions. One of the effects of the prohibitions against planting trees and ploughing was to ensure that land was regularly returned to the common pool of fallow forest, and that a relative equality of access to productive resources was maintained. Only a few of the Ayufay Buid realise the potentialities of the new economic system and are actively exploiting them. Foremost among them is Agaw, who has taken to investing the profits from his ploughed fields in buying land back from the Christians and in the planting of coconut trees. It is interesting to note, however, that he does not display the same proprietary attitude towards his swidden land, in which he has made no long-term investment of labour.

The final agricultural prohibition against flattening the land was broken while I was in the field, partially as a result of my presence. This was a more serious matter than the planting of trees, the owning of water buffalo and ploughing, for it directly angers the spirits of the earth. Towards the end of my stay, I asked the Buid what they would like from me in return for all their help. After much deliberation, they hit upon an idea which would allow me to share my gift equally with the entire community, in conformity with the principle of sharing. They wanted a cement terrace on which they could dry their maize prior to selling it. Such terraces function as drying platforms, basketball courts, and symbols of wealth in surrounding Christian barrios. For the Buid, it would constitute a 'concrete' proof of their occupation of the settlement site of Ugun Liguma. Work on levelling the ground and collecting sand and gravel from the river bed 500 metres away proceeded smoothly until we were ready to pour the cement. The Buid then became extremely nervous about what we were doing, as not only were they *agsagmak daga* – 'flattening the earth', but they were *agsagmak unay binagaw* – 'flattening the sand of the Bongabon river', which has its own powerful spirits, as well. The crisis was only resolved when a ritual was peformed to appease these spirits.

As noted in the last chapter, Yaum obtained the right for the Buid to pay land taxes to the municipal authorities about ten years ago. While the legality of this tax is somewhat dubious, the Buid do receive receipts in return for paying it, and these receipts have proven useful in countering Christian claims to their land. They have even been produced as evidence in court. Nothing makes the Buid more anxious than the idea, often advanced by well-intentioned bureaucrats from the provincial administration, that they should not be paying it. The annual payment of the land tax has developed into a festive occasion when hundreds of Buid from all over the municipality of Bongabon converge on the central Buid barrio of Batangan. The town officials come up and address the assembled Buid with patriotic speeches, and are feasted with rice and pork (cf. Lopez, 1981: 223). For many of the interior Buid, this is the time when most of their purchases of lowland consumer goods take place. Although the average tax payment per individual land holding is only 25 pesos, most Buid have parted with at least 100 pesos by the time the event is over. This necessitates a further round of borrowing from the Christian traders, since the tax payment is made in January, after the proceeds of the September harvest have already been spent. Many lowland traders are attracted to the barrio by the large numbers of Buid and set out displays of aluminium pots, bush knives, cloth, sweets, toys and cosmetics. The payment of the land tax may be seen as a sort of ritual acceptance of the new order, and as a nominal submission to lowland authority. It confirms and makes explicit the changes which have occurred in the Buid system of land tenure over the last twenty years.

Continuity and transformation in the Buid economy

The Buid have jettisoned many of their traditional beliefs and practices which kept their subsistence economy separate from the lowland market economy in the past. But it should also be noted that most of the changes have taken place at a technical level, and have not affected social relations. The planting of trees, the acquisition of water buffalo and ploughs, the abandonment of rice in favour of maize, and even incipient terracing all represent a break with tradition. At the level of social relations, however, the Buid have made every attempt to preserve the spirit of the traditional system of social organisation. They are prepared to borrow rice at exorbitant rates of interest during the maize planting season in order to provide the traditional midday meal, and so as not to have to recruit labour by means of wages or dyadic contracts. They have maintained the principle of equal access to the land in a new form by amicably allotting every adult an equivalent plot. They have resisted the lowland notion that the household constitutes a life-long corporation under the authority of its senior male. This last point is of fundamental importance, for as I shall argue in the next chapter, the Buid view the strength and solidarity of the community as varying in inverse proportion to the internal strength and solidarity of its component households. Finally, the Buid continue to adhere to a labour theory of property, adapting it to the lowland notion of land as private property by making permanent improvements to it, such as the planting of trees and clearing it for ploughing.

On the other hand, certain very important changes have occurred at the level of social organisation. The most dramatic of these has been the construction of large-scale, permanent settlements, which has given rise to social tensions of a type previously unknown. I shall be dealing with these later in the book. Other changes have affected the Buid population unevenly. The majority of the Buid view cash crops as merely new means to achieve the old ends of sustaining their rice consumption at traditional levels and of purchasing a small number of exotic goods once a year. These Buid are not terribly disconcerted by the fact that they are being systematically cheated by the Christians in their commercial transactions. If by investing an equivalent or slightly reduced amount of labour in the cultivation of maize than they used to invest in the cultivation of rice and the manufacture of trade goods, they are able to meet their perceived material needs, they do not view themselves as being intolerably exploited. Many of them accept the fact that systematic underpayment by their lowland patrons is a necessary price they must pay for the protection of their land against the poor Christians. The less sophisticated continue to view the latter as their real enemies. In effect, these Buid are merely buying time for their traditional social organisation.

There is, however, a less obvious but potentially more dangerous threat to Buid society which comes from within. Those leaders, such as Yaum and Agaw, who have been able to take advantage of the market to increase their productive capital and to use their authority among the Buid as a bargaining counter in their dealings with lowland patrons, are gradually transforming the nature of Buid society. For the time being, the Ayufay Buid can afford to treat Agaw as merely their agent in dealing with the lowlands, but as time goes on and the role of the market and lowland society acquires an increasing dominance in their social life, leaders such as Agaw will become indispensable. This has already happened in Batangan, where the question of who shall succeed Yaum is a matter of real concern to all Buid. As the taste for lowland commodities takes hold of ever increasing numbers of Buid, and as their sophistication about lowland affairs reaches the level already achieved by Yaum, his followers will be less ready to pay the usurious price demanded by their lowland patrons for the preservation of their traditional society. But before the analysis is carried any further, the nature of that society must first be described.

II
Social Organisation

4   Idioms of Social Organisation

This chapter is divided into three parts. In the first part, I wish to situate my analysis of Buid kinship within the broad framework of theories which have been developed to deal with so-called cognatic or bilateral kinship systems. In the second part I describe the levels of Buid social grouping, beginning with the most inclusive level, the in-marrying region, and ending with the minimal group, the married couple. I then give an account of Buid marriage practices which attempts to demonstrate the fundamental importance of what I term 'spouse-sharing' for the cohesion of Buid society, and for the maintenance of the equality and autonomy of all adults. I show that the relationship between spouses is based on the sharing of the same sorts of activities as is the relationship between members of the same region and local community, differing only in intensity. In the third part, I describe the cultural constructs relating to shared kinship substance and their role in social life.

Social structure in Southeast Asia

In a classic paper written in 1935, Radcliffe-Brown set out what he took to be the 'necessary conditions for the existence of a society'. These were:

> 1. The need for a formulation of rights over persons and things sufficiently precise in their general recognition as to avoid as far as possible unresolved conflicts.
> 2. The need for continuity of the social structure *as a system of relations between persons, such relations being definable in terms of rights and duties* (Radcliffe-Brown, 1952: 47, my emphasis).
> To provide continuity of social structure is essentially a function of corporations (ibid.: 45).
> . . . unilineal institutions in some form are almost, if not entirely, a necessity in any ordered social system (ibid.: 48).

He modifies the last assertion elsewhere in his essay by admitting the possibility of 'an incorporated local community which was completely

61

endogamous and which would therefore not have to face the issue of choosing between matrilineal and patrilineal succession'.[1] If, however, inter-marriage were to occur between two such communities, the result would be 'to produce a loose and indefinite structure' (ibid.: 46).

When British anthropologists trained in the Radcliffe-Brownian tradition came to look analytically at social structure in Southeast Asia and Oceania, they found it very difficult to apply this definition of social structure. Radcliffe-Brown cites approvingly the work of one of his students, Embree, in Japan, but when that same student came to compare Japan with Thailand, he was constrained to characterise the latter as having a 'loose structure', i.e. reciprocal rights and duties between individuals were not clearly marked and carried out, and there were few corporations to provide continuity (Radcliffe-Brown, 1952: 193; Embree, 1950). In a similar vein, other writers talked of 'strongly' versus 'weakly' structured kin units (Firth, 1957: 5), or of 'definitive' versus 'optative' descent group systems (Firth, 1957: 5; Barnes, 1962: 7). What all of these authors were trying to account for were societies in which there was little continuity in corporate groupings, and/or a lack of rules for the allocation of rights over persons at birth 'sufficiently precise' to 'avoid unresolved conflict'.

In particular, a whole debate arose over the functional analogues of the unilineal descent groups of Africa and Australia in societies which lacked a clear and consistent rule of descent. Certain writers preferred to reserve the concept of descent group for groups recruited solely on the basis of descent, in effect reserving the term for unilineal systems (Fortes, 1959; Goody, 1961; Leach, 1962), while those who had conducted fieldwork in non-unilineal systems preferred to adopt a more flexible approach, and used it to describe groups in which descent was a crucial, although not a definitive criterion for group membership (Goodenough, 1955; Firth, 1957, 1963; Davenport, 1959; Scheffler, 1965, 1966). Finally, Sahlins pointed out that one cannot infer the non-unilineal character of a system from the composition of local groups alone, as the latter is affected in any society by extraneous demographic, economic and political factors (Sahlins, 1965). One had to identify clearly the functions or operations controlled by an ideological principle, and not confuse dogma with practice. He noted that there seems to be a sort of continuum between agnatic and cognatic descent groups and ideologies, some societies insisting more than others on doctrinal purity in the recruitment of local-group membership (Sahlins, 1963). Scheffler refined the distinction between descent categories, which may be fully cognatic in character, and descent groups which may have a strong patrilineal bias (Scheffler, 1965: 44).

It had long been apparent, however, that there were other simple societies in the area which lacked descent groups of any kind. One of the earliest and clearest accounts of such a society was that by Freeman on the Iban (1958). He argued that the fundamental corporate group in Iban society was the *bilek*, or longhouse apartment domestic group, which achieved continuity through the generations much like a lineage by incorporating in-marrying spouses and cutting off out-marrying spouses. Recruitment to the *bilek* was fully bilateral in character, with no significant difference in the rates of virilocality and uxorilocality. In many ways, the Iban appeared to conform much more closely to the received view of an 'ordered social system' than did the ambilineages of Polynesia in which an individual retained potential rights to membership of numerous descent groups, whichever one he happened to be affiliated to at a given time. There were clear and precise rules allocating individuals to groups, and the groups were corporate and enduring.

In the first collection of essays devoted to the kinship systems of the area, Murdock identified a 'social type' which he termed 'bilateral' in opposition to 'ambilineal' and 'unilineal' systems. At a higher level of contrast, he grouped bilateral, or Eskimo type, quasi-unilineal, or Carib type, and ambilineal, or Polynesian type under the general heading of 'cognatic systems' (1960: 8–9). The use of these terms varies widely between different authors, but here I shall follow Murdock's usage (cf. Appell, 1976: 9–11 for a discussion of different terminologies). Murdock defined bilateral systems according to eight criteria, two of which concerned kinship terminology, i.e. the lack of extension of sibling terms to cousins, and of parental terms to uncles and aunts. Three criteria were negative in character, involving the absence of distinctions in marriageability of different kinds of first cousin, the absence of functionally important descent groups, and the absence of a unilocal residence rule. Only three of the criteria were fully positive in character. These were the prominence of small domestic units, prevailing monogamy, and the presence of bilateral kindreds (Murdock, 1960: 6). It is these three positive features which have given rise to most controversy. It has been noted that the existence of small domestic units is characteristic of many types of society, and that it is only the absence of larger kinship groupings which gives them a prominence (in the eyes of the ethnographer) in bilateral societies (King, 1978: 13). Secondly, a high incidence of extended family domestic groups has been reported in a number of otherwise 'bilateral' societies (Whittier, 1978; and Sather, 1978). The same can be said for 'prevailing monogamy': there are very few societies in which polygamy can be said to 'prevail'. Finally, if the personal kindred is defined as a category of consanguineal kinsmen as it is by Murdock and Freeman (1961), it may either be too broad a concept to identify bilateral systems, as such categories may well exist in unilineal systems; or too narrow if native categories include affines as well. We are on even shakier ground if we wish to assert that kindreds play an important role in the recruitment of social action groups. In many otherwise 'bilateral' societies, this is simply not the case.(cf. King, 1978: 11).

The suggestion has been made that the category of bilateral societies is in fact defined by what its members lack, and that it therefore cannot provide the basis for proper internal comparison (Needham, 1966). Murdock made the confident assertion that

> The degree of identity in diagnostic characteristics among the peoples mentioned [as having a bilateral social system] is extraordinary. . . . However great or slight its social and cultural complexity . . . if a society for any reason maximizes the small domestic unit and minimizes lineal descent groups it tends automatically to arrive at a single uniform configuration of marriage rules, kin alignments, and kinship nomenclature. (Murdock, 1960: 6)

As we have seen, this claim does not, in fact, amount to much. Having constructed a category, Murdock notes the fact that the societies included in it meet its criteria, which is hardly surprising. The so-called uniform configuration of marriage rules (i.e. their absence), kin alignments (i.e. the presence of 'kindreds' which are not unique to the type), and kinship nomenclature (bilateral: again not unique to the type) breaks down when examined closely. Indeed, it could be argued that since the presence of other marriage rules, kin alignments or terminologies would exclude a society from the category, the statement that all these features are common to the members of the category is meaningless.

It would, perhaps, be better to recognise the fact that in many so-called bilateral systems kinship does not provide the underlying idiom for the organisation of social life, and that comparative analysis should concentrate instead on some other organisational feature such as residence or ranking (King, 1978: 10). While most of the societies studied in Borneo and the Philippines do have prominent small domestic units, and these are often the only fully corporate groups in them, many of them lack the continuity through the generations characteristic of lineal descent groups and the Iban *bilek*.[2] Such societies seem to lack all the criteria for an ordered social system demanded by Radcliffe-Brown. Nevertheless, they do persist, and they do not seem to be subject to a greater degree of social disruption than the 'tightly structured' societies of Africa. Much of the difficulty can, I think, be traced back to Radcliffe-Brown's insistence on social structure as being based on inter-personal relations, and the clear definition of rights and duties obtaining between persons.[3] The suggestion has been made by Kirsch that the real difference between Thailand and Japan may lie in the articulation between person and society, the person being allowed a greater degree of autonomy in the former case (Kirsch, 1969: 57). More generally, it seems to be the case that in many parts of Southeast Asia social action is thought of as being continuously constructed on the basis of certain shared rules, and not as being defined in advance by a rigid code of conduct prescribing correct behaviour between an individual and structurally defined others. There seems to be a further emphasis on achieving an exact equality between actors within a group, an equality which is much more fragile than an instituted hierarchy of roles. Geertz asserts that in Bali 'rights and duties are apportioned with strict equality, deliberately blind to differences of general condition' in the context of any given group, whatever the ends to which that group may be devoted (1975: 165). There is a hierarchy between groups based on descent which is in continual conflict with the principle of equality between coresidents in a defined territory (ibid.: 167). In the Philippines, Renato Rosaldo asserts of the Ilongot that 'only equals, as they saw it, could work together in improvised and coordinated equality' (R. Rosaldo, 1980: 146). Michelle Rosaldo states that the overall tendency in Ilongot life is to 'deal flexibly with such distinctions as could promote a sense of strict dependency and obligation, provide grounds for hierarchy, or undermine the autonomous posture of adults who must cooperate in day-to-day affairs' (M. Rosaldo, 1980: 13). The goal of an Ilongot youth is precisely to achieve the status of an autonomous and equal adult through the taking of a head and/or through marriage (ibid.:

173). Establishing social ties with other local groups is a long and complex process of exchanging first formal speeches, then gifts, and ultimately women, so converting a balanced dyadic opposition into a solidary unity based on sharing between equals (ibid.: 207). Unlike the Balinese, the Ilongot do not appear to see an opposition between kinship and locality, for the largest social group, the *bertan*, is defined by shared putative origins and a knowledge of shared movement in the past. Genealogies are not remembered and there is a preference for local group endogamy (R. Rosaldo, 1980: 225, 1975).

These two examples are highly relevant to the Buid case. While descent groups are built up out of a selection of dyadic links of filiation, so individuating group members and placing them in a potential hierarchy, groups based on common locality can define all members as a community of equals differentiated only by relative age and sex (cf. Needham, 1966). The importance of residence and locality in ambilineal systems for defining discrete corporate groupings has often been noted, but their significance in bilateral systems is even greater. The largest discrete social group among the Hanunoo, Subanun, Tiruray and Sulod in the Philippines is a settlement of a handful of households whose members are not necessarily related to one another by ties of kinship (Conklin, 1957: 12; Frake, 1960: 53; Schlegel, 1970: 10). Among the Mandaya, the largest discrete social group is the household (Yengoyan, 1973: 166). All of these authors emphasise the importance of non-discrete neighbourhoods or communities. It is also important to note that all of these groups shift their residence regularly and that co-residence is to be defined not in terms of common occupation of a fixed locality, but in terms of coordinated movements through space and time (R. Rosaldo, 1980: 224). Settlements, while they may be discrete at any one time, can dissolve and reform with a different composition on an almost annual basis. Among the shifting cultivators who have been studied in the Philippines, the Ilongot appear to be unique in their concern to maintain the continuity of local group composition through successive moves, although even they do not often achieve this goal.

I would argue that given the economic advantages of frequent movement in a regime of shifting cultivation, the high cultural value placed on the autonomy and equality of adults in social interaction, and the weakness of these societies in relation to those which surround them, an emphasis on moral rights and obligations which tie the individual to the group in which he happens to be living and not to other specific individuals, represents a highly coherent form of social organisation, which may also be highly adaptive (cf. Yengoyan, 1973: 164).[4] The problem is that most ethnographers have been content to describe the lack of permanence in social group composition, and the weakness of ties between specific categories of kin, without going on to describe the mechanisms by which new and temporary group solidarity is continuously being constructed. Among the Buid, these mechanisms involve the sharing of certain key activities.

The sharing of space and activity as the basis of social groups

The Buid as a whole may be defined by their use of a mutually intelligible language and by the sharing of a common set of values which mark them off from the Hanunoo to the south and the Taubuid to the north. As I noted in Chapter 1, the line between the Buid and the Hanunoo is much sharper than the one between the Buid and the Taubuid. The Hanunoo practise secondary burial, while the Buid have a great fear of corpses and would never dream of disinterring one. The Taubuid, on the other hand, possess powerful shamans who are ranked in a hierarchy, while Buid spirit mediums have little influence outside their ritual speciality and are organised more as a college of equals.

The Buid are internally divided into two large groups defined by the way in which they have borrowed culture traits from their neighbours. The southern Buid weave cloth and write the ancient syllabic script like the Hanunoo, while the northern Buid smoke pipes like the Taubuid. Each of these groups is again subdivided into two, producing the four groups mentioned by Tweddell (see above, Chapter 1). At this level, distinctions in dialect play an important differentiating role, which are correlated with the low frequency of interaction between the groups. The 'script-writing Buid' of the extreme east have been cut off from the 'cloth-making Buid' of the south by Christian settlers. The Beribi of the west are cut off from the 'pipe smokers' of the northeast by the difficulty of the terrain.

For the Buid of Ayufay, the most important division at this level of contrast is between the 'basket weavers' to the north of the Siangi river, and the 'potters' to the south of it (see Map V). They say that it is dangerous to marry a potter because it offends the spirits of the earth, and that one must be careful to make a substantial offering to the latter if a potter is married. There was no one living in Ayufay while I was in the field who had been born south of the Siangi river, although there was one old man in Ambuan who had left Batangan many years before because he disapproved of Yaum's modernising tendencies.

The region

The next less inclusive social grouping among the Buid, which I shall call the region, is more difficult to characterise. We may begin by comparing it to similar units elsewhere in the Austronesian culture area. A Buid region is essentially an in-marrying local group of between 500 and 1,000 individuals. Bloch has given a detailed description of the ideology of the Merina of Madagascar, among whom 'intermarriage is the sign both of pre-existing kinship and of the strengthening of such pre-existing kinship.' (Bloch, 1971: 202). Ideally, the in-marrying group, the local group, and the kinship group should all coincide for the Merina, although due to their history of expansion, this is rarely the case now. This ideology led Bloch to adopt the term 'deme' from Murdock: 'we shall regularly employ "deme" for an endogamous local group in the absence of unilinear descent, especially when we are regarding it as a kin group rather than as a community' (Murdock, 1949: 63). Less far away, Dozier has also employed the concept of deme to characterise the members of Kalinga regions, who 'were bound to one another by common residence and consanguinity' and who 'married among themselves, observing only the prohibition on marrying close cousins' (Dozier, 1966: 56). Ilongot *bertan* have also been referred to as demes (R. Rosaldo, 1975). The endogamous regions described by Macdonald are again very similar (1977: 117–18). Finally, among the Hanunoo, Conklin has noted 'a marked tendency toward regional endogamy' (1959: 634). Now, an essential feature of all these societies is that they place a high value on the consanguineal tie: so much so that among both the Merina and the Hanunoo there is felt to be a certain contradiction between the incest taboo and local endogamy. Among the Merina, this contradiction appears as a balancing between the idea that all marriages with kinsmen are incestuous, and the idea that one should marry as close as possible in order to retain rice land within the local group (Bloch, 1971: 58). Among the Hanunoo, the difficulty is resolved through the payment of a ritual 'fine', graduated according to the closeness of the consanguineal link between the prospective spouses (Conklin, 1959: 634).

Buid regions resemble those of the Kalinga, Hanunoo and Merina in that they exhibit a strong tendency toward local endogamy. They differ in that they are not thought of as being kinship groups. Among the Buid, the ideal social relationship is that which exists between spouses: marriage is a social relationship between equals, freely terminable by either partner. By contrast, kinship is viewed as a biologically given relationship with hierarchical implications, and is played down. Rather than stressing the desirability of marrying within a set of kinsmen, the Buid stress the disadvantages of marrying outside their region. These disadvantages mainly relate to the difficulties involved in obtaining a divorce from an outsider. Buid living up-river were said to be extremely violent and possessive of their spouses, while those living in down-river regions were said to be too greedy in their demands for compensation when divorced. The full significance of these statements will become clear later on. Although no marriages occurred between the Ayufay Buid and those south of the Siangi, marriages are sometimes contracted with other basket weavers from up-river. There was one such marriage between an Ayufay woman and a Fawa man while I was in the field, but the two of them were continually quarrelling and having to make sacrifices to the spirits of the earth as a result. They were pointed out to me as an example of the dangers of marrying outside one's region. It was not really their fault that they quarrelled: they were simply *bukud fag taw* 'different kinds of people'.

Members of a Buid region do not think of themselves as constituting a body of kinsmen. Most Buid are ignorant of ties of filiation which relate individuals they have not known personally. There are some old men who make it their business to memorise and recite genealogies which link the oldest living generation with the original culture heroes. These genealogies are linear in form, paying no attention to the sex of the individuals constituting the connecting links, or to branching. Their purpose is more cosmological than social in character: they are not used as 'charters' for membership in social groups, nor are they used as a means of establishing rights to property. Most Buid are entirely ignorant of the names of their own great-grandparents, since there is a general reluctance to utter the names of the dead. What matters in terms of group affiliation is social commitment in the present, not the biological relationships which have resulted from the social and biological activities of one's ancestors.[5]

This lack of emphasis on shared descent accounts for the relative openness of Buid regions. As I noted in Chapter 2, much of the Ayufay population fled to upper Siangi during the Second World War and the subsequent smallpox epidemic, and they still retain links with that area. It is entirely possible for a Buid individual or family to move to a new region. So long as they conform to the local expectations of proper social behaviour, they are accepted as equal members of the new community. It is because kinship is not a necessary criterion for regional membership that I hesitate to use the term 'deme' for these regions. In my view, a more satisfactory approach is to define a Buid region in terms of shared values and expectations regarding the settlement of disputes. Among feuding peoples such as the Kalinga or the Nuer, the largest jural entity is often described as that unit within which there are formal procedures for mediating a dispute and arranging for the payment of compensation.

> We speak of 'law' here in a sense which seems most appropriate when writing of the Nuer, a moral obligation to settle disputes by conventional methods. (Evans-Pritchard, 1940: 169)
> We may say therefore, that there is law . . . between tribesmen, but no law between tribes. (ibid.: 121)

Among the Kalinga, Barton defines the region as the area within which formal mediators act to resolve disputes and within which a cessation of hostilities is obligatory while mediation is going on. Such mediations are nearly always successful (Barton, 1949: 164–7). Among the Buid, however, homicide is so rare, and so opposed to the basic pacific values of the society that there are no conventional means of dealing with it. The typical dispute in Buid society centres on a divorce. In this sense, then, one can define a Buid region as the largest jural entity within which marriage, divorce and remarriage can be arranged with a minimum of trouble according to accepted rules of compensation. The region is a group based, not on an ideology of kinship, but on an ideology of marriage, such that a Buid thinks of his or her region as containing a set of past, present and potential affines, and not as a kindred or a bilateral descent group. What this means in practice will become clear below when I discuss Buid marriage practices. For the time being a more positive definition of a Buid region would be that it is a spouse-sharing community whose members regard one another as equals who must submit their marital disputes to the collective mediation of the other members of the region.

The in-marrying region, so defined, constitutes the largest social unit among the Buid which is conscious of itself as a group, comes together for collective ritual activity and shares a minimal dialect. Dialect is extremely important in the maintenance of group identity, a fact which may help to account for the extreme fragmentation of Buid dialects.[6] The region asserts its collective identity in a series of rituals following the death of one of its members. Post- mortem rituals are described in Chapter 7.

Map IV shows the Buid regions I have been able to tentatively identify. Of those which are indicated, I only know the Ayufay region in detail, although I have visited five others, i.e. Fawa, Alid, Mungus, Lower Siangi and Batangan. I have been told that Upper Siangi, Tawga, and Habang Safa constitute similar regions. The Ayufay region is shown in greater detail on Map V. It should be noted that it has been cut in half by the influx of Christians close to the Bongabon river valley, and a number of Ayufay Buid have relatives living across the Bongabon river. Because of the barrier provided by the Christians living along the logging roads running along the valley, social inter-action between the two parts of the region is declining in frequency. The major rival to Agaw's leadership is now living across the Bongabon river, a factor which further contributes to a reduction in social contacts.

The local community

The Ayufay region is subdivided into six local communities, formed by the populations living along the Ayufay, Ambuan Ugbut, Sigaw, Fayagnun, Akliang and Hagan rivers. The members of a local com-munity are bound together by the regular sharing of meat, labour and speech, described in the last chapter, and by regular participation in rituals designed to fend off the attacks of predatory spirits. Again, they are not thought of as kinship groups: any person who resides in the area is entitled to an equal share in any distribution of meat and is obliged to share his or her own meat by virtue of their residence alone. Of course, most of the people in the local community could trace some sort of kinship tie with one another, but the point is that they do not. They speak of themselves as companions of a more regular sort than is implied by membership of the region.

If there is one core symbol which constitutes the ideal image of social behaviour among the Buid, it is that of a group of companions engaged in some cooperative enterprise. The prototypical enterprise is that of a shared movement through space. Those who live in a *garakbangan balay*, 'house cluster', travel together in a group when venturing into the lowlands to acquire goods they cannot produce themselves, and are described as a *gufudan*, 'companion set'. The smallest moral unit, the *talsawa*, 'spouse set', may also be referred to as being composed of a pair of *kuyugan*, or 'habitual companions'. The terms *guyan*, 'to follow a leader on a trail', *gain*, 'to join someone on a trip', and *taban*, 'to take someone along on a trip', are used in a more general sense to describe the initiation of a social relationship. Finally, the term *sama*, cognate with the Tagalog word for companion, functions as a universal term of address among the Buid. So common is the usage of the term *sama* among the pipe-smoking Buid that they use it to denote their particular dialect: to speak Buid like a pipe-smoker is to *agsama*.

Similarly, words such as *gubun*, 'to abandon someone', *galin*, 'to leave on one's own', *aglius*, 'to desert a companion', *agsaman* 'to separate', *agbaya*, 'to deliberately avoid', and so on are used in a more general sense to describe the abrogation of social relationships, usually marital ones. This idiom of companionship implies that social actors come together as autonomous agents to pursue a common goal. They are not obliged to cooperate because of some ascribed relationship based on shared kinship substance or shared locality, nor are they obliged to cooperate with specific individuals because of debts incurred in the past. It is shared activity itself, and the amicable sentiments generated by habitual cooperation which constitute the basis for the relationship. The activities which provide the rationale for a relationship in the first instance become after a time only a means of expressing a deeper sentiment of amity and fellowship.

Yengoyan's illuminating discussion of the concept of *kaban* in Malaysia is relevant here. He points out that Freeman's definition of its meaning among the Iban is at variance with its meaning elsewhere in the area. It generally has a broader connotation than Freeman's 'kith and kin'.

> The concept of *kaban* or togetherness embraces kinship relationships and interpersonal behaviour stemming from kinship obligations, but other cultural and non-cultural variables also help to promote and maintain 'belongingness'. Economic relationships based on reciprocal and non-reciprocal ties, spatial factors, ritual cooperation, nonkin social groups and interactions are critical

forces in the development of the concept of *kaban*. . . . In general, most insular Southeast Asian societies appear to have mechanisms such as *kaban* which demarcate spheres of social discourse at the widest level of inclusion and at the highest level of abstraction. (Yengoyan, 1973: 168)

This discussion accords very well with my own understanding of the Buid concept of *abari* and with Bloch's discussion of the concept of *havana* among the Merina (1971: 58–60).

Traditionally, the component households of a community were evenly dispersed throughout its territory either singly or in *garakbangan*, 'clusters', of two or three. One of the members of each household in a cluster would normally be related as parent, child or sibling to one of the members of another of the households. Such clusters did not constitute discrete groups, however, as a family normally maintained more than one house at a time and alternated its residence between them. The rule of post-marital residence requires, for example, that a couple regularly alternate between the cluster of the husband's parents and that of the wife's parents. The community of Ayufay included about forty households while I was in the field, grouped into eleven clusters of close kin (see Figure 1).[7] Of these forty households, thirty had built houses in Ugun Liguma and ten were still resisting settlement. The average household size in Ugun Liguma was 2.9, giving a total population for the community of Ayufay of about 115. The pre-settlement distribution of the clusters can be seen from Map X. Clusters F, G and H lived, and for the most part clusters G and H continue to live, along the upper Ayufay and one of its tributaries. Clusters A, B, E and J occupied the middle Ayufay and formed the core of the original settlement on Agaw's land (number 6 on the genealogy). Cluster C occupied the slope to the south of the Ayufay. Finally, clusters D, I and K were too small and fragmented to form residential agglomerations of their own, but lived interspersed among the others.

Every ten years or so, a local community hosts a *fanaludan*. Unfortunately, Ayufay had held one just a month before I arrived in the field and none were being held in the vicinity for the rest of my stay, so I have only fragmentary statements from informants about them. Essentially, they seem to consist of a large feast given by one community for the members of other communities, and attendance does not seem to be based on kinship ties. Conklin gives a brief description of a similar ceremony among the Hanunoo. During the first dry season after the

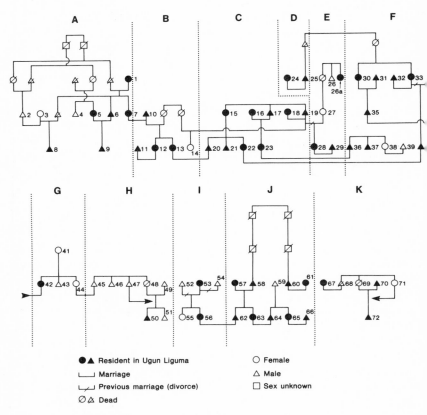

Figure 1 Principal kinship and affinal links among Ayufay Buid.

burial of a corpse, its bones are exhumed. They are then 'Cleaned, clothed, housed, fed, talked with, danced with, and consulted (by weight divination) on serious matters such as crop harvests, encroaching Christians . . . at a two or three day socio-religious feast, a *panludan* (Conklin, 1955a: 54). They may be attended by hundreds of kinsfolk and require months of preparation, including the construction of dance pavilions, houses for the bones and structures in which to make offerings. It is the most important event of the year, expressing many of the strongest values of Hanunoo culture. Everyone behaves as if he or she were an eligible bachelor or maiden, dressing in their finest clothes and ornaments, and engaging in courtship, singing, gossiping, gift-exchange, dancing, telling of stories and the consumption of rice and meat. It constitutes a celebration of life in the face of death (ibid.: 54–6). Much of Conklin's account is similar to what I was told about the Buid *fanaludan*. They dwelt on the social aspects, as the subject of death and ghosts is avoided whenever possible. The Buid admitted to making a small offering to the collective dead during the feast, but played down its importance in favour of the festive aspect of the ritual. I shall discuss Buid funerary customs in Chapter 7. I raise the question of the *fanaludan* at this point to indicate its function of providing an occasion for the assertion of the solidarity of a local community in opposition to its neighbours. In any event, it would seem that the ritual aspect of the event is of concern only to the host community, while its social aspect is what interests the guests.

Most Buid households possess a hoard of exotic goods, such as brass gongs and bells from Mindanao, and ceramic plates from China. These are brought out for display only during the *fanaludan* and are kept carefully hidden at all other times. I referred in the last chapter to the fact that it was impossible to gain prestige within a community by sponsoring feasts of meat, as these were a sign of household misfortune. In the inter-communal context of the *fanaludan* however, rivalry comes to the fore and everyone is concerned to show off his heirlooms to maximum effect. *Fanaludan* should not be contaminated by any Christian influences and everyone wears the traditional loincloth or tubular skirt. The Ayufay Buid were convinced that it would soon die out in their area, as the younger generation forgot the *ugali magurang*, 'customs of the elders'. What stuck in their memories of past *fanaludan* were the number of pigs and sacks of rice consumed, of poems recited and flirtations negotiated, and the purity of expression of Buid culture in general.

Given my lack of direct observation of this ceremony, I feel entitled to advance only the most tentative interpretation of its significance. It is definitely connected with death and the regeneration of life, reproducing on an expanded scale the post-mortem rituals described in Chapter 7. It also provides the only opportunity for competitive display in Buid society. When the households of a community bring out their heirlooms and kill all their adult pigs, they are achieving prestige at the expense of other communities, not at the expense of other households within their own community. Finally, it provides an opportunity for reinforcing contacts with distant communities and maintaining a larger sense of the cultural unity of the Buid as a whole.

There is no sharp conceptual distinction between the Buid region and community as I have defined them. Both are social groups based on shared social and ritual activity. Activities which unite the members of a region are relatively rare, occurring in the event of a death or divorce, while those uniting the members of a community occur daily in the context of agricultural labour, the routine repulsion of predatory spirits and the sharing of meat. The distinction between the two levels of grouping is being made sharper at present due to the fact that each community in the Ayufay region is in the process of forming a compact settlement. Were the whole of Ugun Liguma to be set aside for the exclusive use of the Buid, it is conceivable that the whole region would concentrate there, as happened in Batangan. At the moment, however, the intensity of intra-communal collective activity is increasing at a faster rate than intra-regional activity due to the periodic 'mitings' held in each settlement. I shall deal with this phenomenon in the next chapter. Here it should be noted that, under the traditional dispersed pattern of residence, social contacts with the members of other households were a matter of deliberate choice. When conflicts arose between the members of different households, they could usually be dealt with through simple avoidance. In the case of severe conflict, one could always move one's house and swidden further away, or even move to another community. By contrast, members of a single household cannot avoid one another for extended periods, and must find a way to either resolve their differences or formally liquidate the household.

The household

The mean household size in Ugun Liguma was 2.9, the median 2.5 and the mode 2. These are extraordinarily small values and reflect the fact that no more than two adults are ever resident in the same household. Households ranged in size from 1 to 6 members, representing different stages in the developmental cycle. For the Buid, the ideal household contains a married couple plus at least one child, not necessarily their own, and no one else. Only thirteen of the thirty households in fact conformed to this model, but it can easily be shown why the others deviated from it.

The first thing a boy does when he reaches maturity, at about the age of fifteen, is to build a house of his own and clear his own swidden. He may not reach full economic independence from his parents for a number of years, continuing to eat with them or with the members of other households, but he will sleep away from his parents' house with increasing frequency. Six of the households in Ugun Liguma were of this type, containing a single bachelor youth. Once he has found his feet economically, he will marry and acquire the help of a wife on his swidden and in the house, as he will in turn help on his wife's swidden. There were two households of this type in Ugun Liguma. With the birth of a child, or by marrying someone who already has a child, an individual will become a member of a co-resident nuclear family, the ideal type, of which there are thirteen in Ugun Liguma. Due to Buid practices of birth spacing, resulting in an average three-year gap between births, and a high rate of infant mortality, a household will seldom grow beyond six members before its elder sons begin to set up households of their own, or its elder daughters move out to live with widows (see below). Eventually, the household will be reduced to the original married couple, once all their children have left. There were three households of this type in Ugun Liguma. Often they will take charge of a grandchild for at least part of the time. The Buid say that an elderly couple like to have a child around 'to have someone to talk to'. A child is especially likely to be left with its grandparents if its own parents feel they are still too young to cope with the responsibility. Finally, one or the other of the elderly couple will die. The survivor remarries if at all possible, but due to the fact that husbands are usually older than their wives, and because Buid men tend to die younger than women, there are always a certain number of elderly widows in the community. These widows are not left to live alone, but are provided with an adolescent girl to 'help fetch wood and water', as the Buid say. There were five solitary widows in Ugun Liguma. One of them was living with her dead son's adolescent daughter, one with an unrelated adolescent girl, two had a remaining unmarried daughter with them, and the fifth had two small children. There were two elderly single men in the vicinity, and there was every indication that they would soon marry two of these widows: one marriage was being delayed for supernatural reasons and will be discussed in Chapter 8. The other three widows had no immediate prospects.

The ideal composition of a Buid household derives from the fundamental value Buid place on the autonomy and equality of all adults. To have more than two adults in a single house would place an intolerable strain on domestic harmony. Even if the house of an ageing parent is only a few metres away, it would be inconceivable for them to actually move in with their adult children, given the former dependency of the children on them.[8] The relationship between husband and wife, on the other hand, is egalitarian, but it is also extremely fragile, often ending in divorce.

The married couple

The only adults who cannot avoid one another on a day-to-day basis are spouses. There is no formal ceremony to mark the initiation of a marriage.[9] Two individuals begin to share a single house and to engage in the regular sharing of agricultural and domestic labour, of food and of sexual intercourse. The fact that the relationship is based on the sharing of the same sort of activities as is the relationship between members of the same region and local community places it in the same series. They continue to maintain separate swiddens and separate ownership of their valuables. The unity of a married couple is symbolised by their joint ownership only of the house in which they live and of the domesticated animals they raise together. These animals are fed, like all the other members of the household, with the crops produced by the respective swiddens of the husband and the wife. The symbolic role of houses and domesticated animals in ritual is examined in Chapter 7.

The sharing of food, labour and sexual services within a domestic unit is so fundamental to Buid social life that ideally no adult ever remains single for more than a few weeks at a time. The marital relationship constitutes the most intense bond of companionship and sharing in Buid society, in that it requires the daily cooperation of two individuals who cannot avoid one another for long without threatening the relationship itself. Now, there is no expectation among the Buid that any particular marriage will endure indefinitely. As soon as one of the parties decides to leave the other, the relationship is finished. Spouses do not acquire long-term claims to the labour or sexual services of their partner when they marry. In Ayufay, I estimated that an individual will contract, on average, five serial unions in the course of his or her marital career. A total of ten serial unions is by no means uncommon. While accusations of laziness in helping with agricultural and domestic chores, and of stinginess in providing food, are sometimes given as the reasons for marital breakdown, by far the most common grounds for divorce arise from one spouse taking an outside lover.

Social conflicts among the Buid are settled by means of a *tultulan*, 'collective discussion', when they cannot be simply ignored. This is the case when a conflict arises between spouses, who are, by definition, co-resident. Any member of the community is entitled to come and participate in a *tultulan*. Whether or not a marital dispute was occasioned by one of the spouses becoming involved with a third party, in the context of a *tultulan* the dispute is defined as being between the two spouses alone. The primary object of a *tultulan* is to bring about an end to quarrelling, either through the reconciliation of the couple, or through their definitive separation. As often as not, a *tultulan* functions as a public arena in which the couple can ventilate their accumulated grievances against one another, and ends in a renewed commitment by the couple to live together in harmony. This result will then be ritually validated by a *fanurukan* ceremony, as described in Chapter 7.

A divorce is achieved by one spouse paying the other a mutually agreed sum of compensation. In a divorce case, one spouse is always defined as the one being abandoned (*gubun*). The abandoned spouse is entitled to demand however much compensation he or she feels necessary to assuage the emotional distress caused by separation. In the early phase of a separation, this demand is likely to be impossibly high. During the course of the *tultulan*, communal pressure will be directed toward the reduction of the demand to a 'reasonable' level, a level which is in fact more or less standardised throughout the in-marrying region. Moral opprobrium attaches to a spouse who is felt to be exhibiting a possessive (*kongit*), jealous (*kaingli*), or aggressive (*kaisug*) disposition during the proceedings. The amount of compensation demanded normally decreases as the passions of the abandoned spouse cool down, so that after an interim period which may last for days or months, a settlement is reached.

The rules for division of property following divorce are quite simple. Household utensils and domesticated animals are divided equally. If there is an odd number of the latter, one is killed and eaten. The house goes to the spouse who was 'abandoned'. As far as children are concerned, I was given a variety of conflicting 'rules'. One informant said that, if there were a male and a female child, the boy would stay with the mother and the girl with the father. Another said that a younger child would stay with the mother, and an elder child with the father. In practice, children seem to alternate between the households of their biological parents until they reach the age of about ten, and then they are free to stay with whoever will have them, whether they are their parents or not.

The institutions of the *tultulan* and of compensation serve as a means of channelling potentially violent quarrels into socially acceptable processes of negotiation and compromise, in which the primacy of reason over emotion can be re-established. All adult Buid are in possession of a stock of valuables with which to lubricate the often uneasy transition from one marital partner to another. Indeed, one of the primary functions of these valuables is to serve as a circulating societal fund for the *dissolution* of marital relationships. They thus constitute a sort of inverted bridewealth, in that they are used not to create alliances, but to sever them. The unilateral transfer of valuables from one individual to the other cancels the bonds of sharing and companionship which formerly united them. Social recognition of these bonds is formally granted only when they are dissolved. There may be no marriage ceremony among the Buid, but there is a highly elaborate divorce procedure.

While compensation was formerly calculated and paid in terms of fathoms of glass beads, it is now calculated and largely paid in terms of cash. As cash income has gone up, so has the rate of compensation, until divorce settlements reaching 3,000 pesos have been demanded and paid in the wealthiest community of Batangan. In the northern Buid area, settlements seldom exceed 500 pesos. This difference is the result of two factors. The first concerns the interference of Christian missionaries, who discourage divorce as much as possible, giving their backing to the party who is being 'abandoned'. The second is simply the greater amount of disposable income in the southern areas. I could find no evidence that the southern Buid divorce less often than the relatively poor northern Buid. If anything, they do so more often.

Case histories of divorce

Nearly all divorces result in the immediate remarriage of one of the spouses, and in the eventual remarriage of the other. Since most of the adults in the community are already married, one divorce is likely to spark off a whole chain of other divorces as abandoned spouses search for new partners. The practical implications of divorce may perhaps be made clearer by looking at a few case histories. In Figure 2, the marital relationships between the principals in two separate divorce cases are shown. The diagrammatic conventions are the same as in Figure 1. In Case 1, C is initiating a divorce from D and hoping to remarry her former husband B. B is trying to divorce his present wife A. Individuals 11, 12 and 51 also appear on Figure 1.

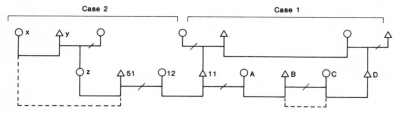

Figure 2 Links among those involved in divorce cases 1 and 2.

Case 1

Individual 11 was included in these negotiations as step-brother to D. When D had married C, he had had to pay compensation to B. Not having sufficient funds at the time, he borrowed 200 pesos from 11. As D was now in the position of receiving compensation in his turn, since his wife was initiating a divorce, 11 was hoping to collect the debt. Now C was divorcing D because she wanted to return to her former husband who had in the meantime married A (a former wife of D's step-brother, 11). A did not consent to a polygynous marriage, as she could have done, and was demanding compensation from B.

In practice, when a woman initiates a divorce, it is her prospective husband who pays the compensation directly to her current husband. This is in part due to the fact that settlements are no longer paid in beads, to which both men and women have equal access, but primarily in cash, to which men have greater access. B was thus in the situation of having to pay compensation to both D and A. His wife A was asking only 200 pesos, but D lodged an initial demand for 1,500 pesos, or about three times the annual income of a Buid. All the individuals involved were under the age of twenty-five.

This was the situation when a *tultulan* was convened in the house of D's uncle. More than fifty people attended, some from miles away. The negotiations went on from early morning until midnight. Most of the talking was done by neutral mediators, many of whom were in no way related to the principals. The first step was to get D to moderate his demand, which was eventually reduced to 600 pesos. The meeting then moved on to the determination of the value of the goods B was offering in kind. Some of his relatives helped out by placing notes of two and five pesos on a tray in the centre of the floor, along with five armlengths of beads, valued at fifty pesos. A small pig was trussed and placed beside the tray, valued at 100 pesos, then an old aluminium pot, valued at thirty pesos, and so on into the night. C, who was the cause of the whole business in the first place, became increasingly agitated as negotiations dragged on. At sundown, she became hysterical and feverish, and went into convulsions. The meeting continued regardless, but B was unable, in the end, to meet the demands and it ended inconclusively. The marriage between C and D remained in force, the couple were seemingly reconciled, but I was told that after the next maize harvest, when B was able to pay off D, the divorce would take place. And so it happened.

Case 2

Individual 12 was interested in these negotiations, as she shared a child with 51, who alternated between their respective households. After divorcing 12, 51 had married a girl ten years younger than himself and gone to live near her father Y and step-mother X. Now X was also about ten years younger than her husband, which made her about the same age as her son-in-law 51. They took a fancy to one another and began to flirt. Noticing this, Y became extremely angry and threatened 51 with a bush knife, forcing the latter to flee and hide in the forest. This was clearly an unusual case because of the normal restraint which marks relations between parent-in-law and child-in-law. It was overridden in this case by the fact that X was only the step-mother of Z and was close to 51 in age. The heaviest moral censure fell on Y for his threatended violence. After a long series of *tultulan*, 51 promised to desist in future from flirting with his mother-in-law and was reconciled with Y and with his own wife. They all continued to live together in a *garakbangan balay*, 'house cluster'.

Discussion

What is remarkable about these and other cases I witnessed (see Chapter 7) is the apparent ease with which disputants may be reconciled as a result of *tultulan*, however violent their initial reactions to a proposed divorce. In many cases, all that is needed is an opportunity to vent one's grievances against a spouse in a public forum. In Case 1, C clearly achieved some sort of temporary catharsis, as she was able to go on living with her current spouse for some months. In Case 2, a man bent on homicide was brought round to accepting a situation in which he came into daily contact with his adversary. Of course, not all quarrels end so amicably. One of the reasons advanced for the violent behaviour of Y was that he was a 'Bangun'. I shall discuss a case in Chapter 5 in which a divorce dispute ended in homicide, and an exceptionally protracted series of *tultulan* took place to arrive at an appropriate sum of compensation for this unusual crime. This case also involved 'Bangun'. Moral opprobrium attaches to possessiveness and aggression, not to infidelity.

The negative value attached to jealousy and possessiveness receives at times a semi-ritual expression. The entire adult population of Ugun Liguma often gathered on moonlit nights to engage in a sort of mock orgy. Men would try and reach up women's skirts with their hands or with symbolic phalluses such as aubergines or realistically carved pieces of wood. The meaning might be made even more explicit by spitting on the tip of the object. The women would retaliate by ganging up on one man, wrestling him to the ground and trying to squeeze his genitals. During these free-for-alls, distinctions of age and marital status break down. Among the women, it is the older ones of the grandparental generation who are the most aggressive. Among the men, it is the young bachelors. I never observed any breach of the incest taboo which obtains between parents, children and siblings, however. No one is in the least restrained by the presence of their spouse. It is as if everyone reverts to the free and easy joking relationships of youth, before they became attached to their particular spouses. These events may be seen as an informal assault on the exclusivity of marriage, which divides the adult community into distinct couples.

Summary

The typical Buid marriage may be said to involve the transfer of an individual from the household of one spouse to that of another, mediated by the payment of compensation to the abandoned spouse. Robert Fox, in discussing the marriage system of the Tagbanuwa of Palawan, a system almost identical to that of the Buid, wrote:

> Possessiveness, if it leads to jealousy on the part of either spouse, is condemned and a cause for divorce . . . the exchange of a fine or fee is a deeply moral act which either creates − or absolves the individual of − social as well as psychological responsibility . . . all instances of *pang-agaw* (spouse stealing) automatically initiate a remarriage as well as a divorce. (Fox, 1954: 112–3).

This account can be applied in full to Buid society, whose members also speak of *fangagaw* or *garagawan babay*, 'reciprocal wife-stealing', without the slightest hint of moral condemnation. The Tagbanuwa, as it happens, go much further than the Buid in extolling the virtues of a high marital turnover. 'A requirement for entering the underworld is to have had exactly *seven* spouses or lovers' (ibid.: 101, cf. also 224).

All the adults in an in-marrying region are expected to be willing to submit their marital disputes to the assembled community and to abandon their claims on their current spouse according to an established procedure. Although the marital relationship as such constitutes an ideal model of companionship and sharing, it is not intended to involve a long-term, exclusive attachment to a particular marital partner. There is a constant circulation of adults between the component households of the region which operates to minimise the development of loyalties to any one individual or household. By Buid cultural definition, all adults 'need' a spouse, but they are not dependent on any particular spouse. Every adult Buid is entitled to regard every other adult of the opposite sex, excluding those covered by the incest taboo, as a potential marital companion. Potential spouses become actual spouses through the mediation of the *tultulan*. In effect, one is dependent on the community as a whole for access to marital partners. The fragility of the marital bond and the right of the community to intervene in internal marital affairs ensures the primacy of the community as an object of allegiance over the household.

Put in a slightly different way, it may be said that it is the community as a whole which possesses the ultimate right to regulate the sexuality of its members, just as the prior claim of the community to the food and labour of its members is asserted on the occasions of animal sacrifices and seasonal collective labour parties. Moral obligation exists primarily in relation to the encompassing community: one is obliged to share one's labour, meat and spouse with the rest of the community, but one is not obliged to share any of these things with any particular individual.

The 'statistical consequences' of Buid marriage practices

Let me begin with two concrete examples of the complex network of ex-marital ties which exist within a Buid region. Figure 3 represents the relationships between five women who gathered one morning to discuss an imminent divorce:

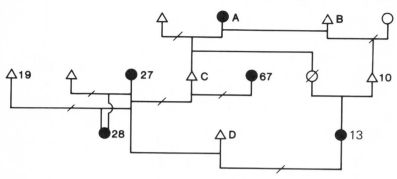

Figure 3 Links among five women by former husbands.

Case 3

Individual 27 was proposing to leave her current husband C and return to her former husband D. Actually, she had been alternating between the two of them for quite some time, and they had jointly fathered one of her children (see below). The woman 28 had been the product of a similar polyandrous marriage in the past between 27 and two other men. The group which gathered to discuss the case was composed almost entirely of women who were entirely unrelated to one another with the exception of 27 and 28. They were, however, connected to one another through past marriages to the same men. 27 and 67 had both been married to the son of A. A was now married to the grandfather of 13. 13 had been married to the former and future husband of 27 and so on. It would doubtless be possible to trace some distant kinship tie between them, but such links would not be as relevant for understanding their current relationships as the fact that they had shared the same men, albeit not at the same time, as husbands in the past. Each of these women was connected with yet another women through different past marriages.

A more extensive example of these ex-marital networks is given in Figure 4, which shows some of the sequences of marriages converging on individual 19, who also appears in Figure 3. To my knowledge, 19 has been married six times, and has had children by at least three women. 27 has been married to at least four different men, and has had children by all of them. These are the only two individuals shown in the diagram for whom I feel I have complete information regarding the number of their productive marriages, and even for them I am not sure that I have a complete list of the unproductive marriages.

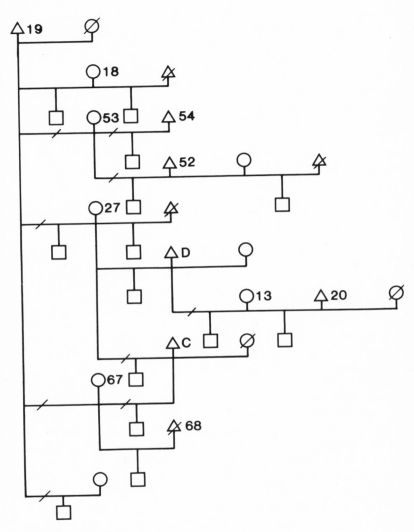

Figure 4 Example of ex-marital network.

On the whole, I feel justified in assuming that a Buid will share a house with about five different spouses during his or her lifetime. If one marries five times, and if each of those spouses marries an additional four times, then, by the time one has reached old age, one will have 'shared' a spouse with twenty members of one's sex and age group. A man or woman who marries ten times, as is not uncommon, will have 'shared' a spouse with virtually every other man or woman in their age group in the in-marrying region. Earlier in this chapter, I stated that a Buid thinks of his or her region as containing a set of past, present and potential affines, not as a kindred or descent group. This is true not only of one's own generation. With each new marriage, one acquires a new set of stepchildren and parents-in-law. With each new marriage contracted by an individual's parents, a new stepparent and set of stepsiblings are acquired. And with each new marriage contracted by one's children, a new child-in-law is acquired.

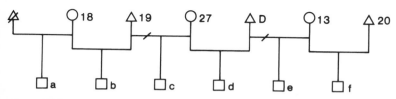

Figure 5 The creation of half-sibling chains by 'spouse-sharing'.

In Figure 5 a chain of productive marriages has been extracted from Figure 4 in order to show the practical consequences of widespread spouse-sharing on the subsequent generation. If a particular marriage is unproductive, it is possible for the couple to have nothing more to do with one another once they have divorced. On the other hand, ex-spouses who share a child will remain linked through that child. Viewed from the perspective of the junior generation, a series of productive marriages results in a chain of half-siblings. In Figure 5, a shares a mother with b, b a father with c, c a mother with d, and so on. a is a step-sibling of c, and c is a stepsibling of e. b is not a stepsibling of d, because 19 and 27 are divorced, and the step relationship does not survive divorce. They may, however, have once been stepsiblings sharing a single household, and continue to regard one another as quasi-siblings. Whether or not their parents remain married, the incest prohibition does not apply to them, and stepsiblings may marry.

One of the consequences of having a large number of half-siblings is to increase the number of close kin possessed by an individual. By sharing only a single parent with most of his or her siblings, an individual is likely to have nearly twice as many siblings as would be the case if both parents were shared. In the second generation, an individual will have twice as many first cousins, descending from the half-siblings of the parents; in the third generation, twice as many second cousins; and so on. Within an in-marrying region of 500 members, the probability that one will be able to trace a relationship within the range of third cousin is extremely high. In practice, most Buid do not bother to remember genealogical connections past the level of their grandparents, and so only first cousins are of much significance to them. They are the nearest relatives with whom one may engage in sexual intercourse, although they are too close for uncomplicated reproduction. It is not the sharing of a common ancestry which binds the Buid together; it is the regular redistribution of personnel between households over time, the potentiality of shared living space which gives the society its sense of cohesion.

The sharing of substance

In the last section, I gave an account of the series of social units which are based on shared space and activity. In this section, I shall deal with the cultural constructs which relate to shared physical and spiritual substance, and which primarily govern the relationship between the mature and the immature members of the community. Maturity is defined among the Buid in terms of the ability of an individual to engage in sexual intercourse, to cultivate a swidden, and to produce enough food for subsistence needs. It is only when an individual is capable of these activities that he or she is in a position to engage in social interaction as an equal, autonomous social agent, and so to participate to the full in social life. An individual begins his or her life in a state of absolute dependency on specific members of the senior generation, and only gradually begins to generalise his or her dependency on a wider section of the community. The process of socialisation among the Buid may be said to consist in the progressive elimination of dependency on specific others, and in the progressive integration of maturing individuals into the communal circuits of sharing and companionship. This process of maturation is reflected in the Buid theory of the personality, which is held to begin its development in the infant in a state where it is completely dominated by purely physiological needs and desires, and to progress ideally to a state in which it is dominated by reason and the imperatives of moral conduct.

The Buid hold that a man must have repeated sexual intercourse with a woman over several months in order for conception to occur. This belief implies that a woman must remain in constant association with a man in order to conceive his child, so that conception normally occurs in the context of a marriage. On the other hand, if a woman engages in regular sexual intercourse with more than one man during the period immediately preceding a pregnancy, then each man is held to have contributed equally to the substance of the child, and will be socially recognised as one of its genitors.[10] Polyandrous unions which result in live births are thus fixed in the social memory by the appearance of multiple genitors in the genealogies of the children produced by them.

The initial substance of the child is held to derive solely from the father and the mother is said to act merely as the vessel for the father's semen. The mother contributes her substance to the child by nourishing it in the womb in the same way as she nourishes it with her milk after it is born. Children are not for this reason held to be more closely 'affiliated' to their fathers than to their mothers. Each contributes to the substance of the child in a different, but equal, manner.

Conception and childbirth are recognised consequences of sexual intercourse, at least some of the time, but they are not seen as the primary purpose of sexual intercourse, or, *a fortiori*, of marriage. As discussed in the preceding section, marriage consists in the sharing of food, residence, labour and sexual intercourse by an adult man and an adult woman. Sexual intercourse is, in one of its aspects, a social transaction clearly differentiated from the mating of animals. This may be seen from the fact that the Buid make a rigorous linguistic distinction between the mating of humans (*sinud*), the mating of pigs (*lufis*), the mating of chickens (*tuktug*) and the mating of dogs (*ugwan*). Further, it is taboo (*fayawan*) to laugh at animals observed in the act of mating, as this draws attention to a disturbing similarity between animal and human activity. It is a matter of Buid dogma that human and animal intercourse have nothing in common: the former is a social activity, the latter an instinctive one.

The fact that this distinction is asserted dogmatically and must be enforced by an explicit rule indicates that there is another aspect to human sexual intercourse which is non-social, but that this aspect is suppressed by convention. In addition to being a mutual social transaction between companions of the opposite sex, intercourse is also the gratification of a selfish desire, in which the partner may be viewed as a mere instrument for the fulfilment of one's own needs. A spouse who is possessive or jealous of his or her partner, who tries to control the sexuality of the partner by insisting on the continuation of the relationship against the latter's wishes, is thought to have allowed selfish desire to overcome reason. The weight of public opinion is brought to bear against such an individual in the *tultulan*, as we have seen.

There is a third aspect to sexual intercourse, which consists in its causal link to procreation. This aspect is not considered to have a great deal of social significance, or to be the occasion for much public concern. There are no social groups which have an interest in the birth of a child as a new recruit because of its specific parentage, nor do adults feel the overwhelming need to produce descendants common in many other traditional societies. Parents have no claim to the labour of their children, nor are children obliged to provide for their parents' physical or mystical welfare either before or after the latter's death. Childbirth is an entirely private affair at which the husband normally acts as midwife. It is entirely up to the couple to decide for themselves whether to abandon the child to die in the forest, to foster it with the adults of another household, or to raise it themselves.[11]

The abandonment of a newly-born child in the forest is not considered to be an act of aggression against an autonomous human being. An infant is born with a 'soul' (*falad*), but it does not yet possess a 'mind' (*fangayufan*). It is accompanied by a 'companion' (*ufud*), the afterbirth, which is also said to have a *falad*. The afterbirth is always abandoned in the forest. At this stage, then, there is little to differentiate the infant from its 'companion', and both may be abandoned without further ado. Infants are so closely identified with their parents that the latter have complete control over their fate. Individuals become fully human only after they have developed the capacity for autonomous social action. This capacity depends in turn on the ability to speak (*gawang*), and to reason (*gayufan*). These abilities develop in a child only after birth, as a consequence of social interaction. The first recognition of the developing individuality of a child comes when it receives a personal name after one or two years. Even then, its name may be changed from time to time as a result of chronic illness, and its individual identity remain in a state of flux until the age of five or six. The *falad* is intimately linked to the physical aspect of the person: physical illness is the result of mystical attack on the *falad*, and the *falad* is the source of all individual needs, emotions and desires. Like the body itself, it is given to an individual at birth by its parents, and retains a close connection with them.

The Buid recognise that a series of procreative acts in successive generations (*sukfunan*) links every individual to a large number of ancestors and the descendants of those ancestors, creating what is known in anthropology as a genealogy for every individual. The Buid also possess a terminological system which categorises individuals according to their position on ego's genealogy. The terms themselves are polysemous, but one of the senses of each term is a specifically genealogical one, in the sense proposed by Keesing in his discussion of Oceanic kinship terminologies in general:

> Kinship terms denote genealogical positions in that the classification of close kin is not contingent on their assuming the social identities connoted by them, or enacting their roles. When a kin term is used to label a pattern of role behaviour by someone not meeting those genealogical criteria, it *is* contingent on that social identity being relevant in the context of the moment. (Keesing, quoted in Eggan, 1972: 12)

The internal logic of the Buid kinship terminology is relatively simple and quite similar to that of the Hanunoo, whose terminology has been elegantly analysed by Conklin (1964). It is not my purpose here to give an exhaustive account of Buid kinship terminology, but to examine its articulation with the social role system in general and with the age and sex role systems in particular. As it is only close genealogical kinsmen whose identities as kinsmen are relevant to ego, I shall concentrate on them. It should be understood that when I write of 'close genealogical kinsmen', I am referring to those individuals recognised as such by the Buid.

Buid kinship terminology

Terms for kinsmen who are normally co-resident are all non-reciprocal in character, while all other kin terms are reciprocal. The non-reciprocal terms are as follows:

1 *ama* Father. Addressed as *mama*.
2 *ina* Mother. Addressed as *didi*.
3 *kaka* Elder sibling. Addressed as *kaka*.
4 *fuyu* Younger sibling. Addressed by personal name.
5 *anak* Child. Addressed by personal name.
6 *faduasay* Sibling. This term may be used as a cover term for 3 and

4, and is reciprocal in character. It is rarely used by siblings who are co-resident, however.

7   *ulung* 'Step'. This term may be appended to any of the foregoing to indicate that the relationship is based not on consanguinity, but on a marriage in the senior generation.

The reciprocal terms are as follows:

8   *fufu* Parent's parent, or child's child. If the former, it may be qualified as either *fufu ama*, 'grandfather' or *fufu ina*, 'grandmother'. If the latter, no gender distinction is made. This term may also be applied to the parent's parent's sibling and to the sibling's child's child, with the same optional qualification of gender in the senior generation. The senior generation is addressed as *fufu*, the junior by personal name.

9   *bapa* Parent's brother, parent's sister's husband, sibling's child (male speaking), or wife's sibling's child. The senior generation is addressed as *bapa*, the junior by personal name.

10   *bayi* Parent's sister, parent's brother's wife, sibling's child (female speaking), or husband's sibling's child. The senior generation is addressed as *bayi*, the junior by personal name.

11   *folibapa* Parent's parent's sibling's son, or parent's sibling's child's child (male speaking). The senior generation is addressed as *bapa*, the junior by personal name.

12   *folibayi* Parent's parent's sibling's daughter, or parent's sibling's child's child (female speaking). The senior generation is addressed as *bayi*, the junior by personal name.

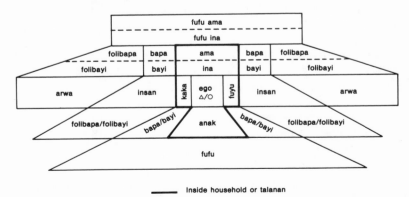

Figure 6 Buid kinship terminology

13 *insan* Parent's sibling's child. Addressed by personal name.
14 *arwa* Parent's parent's sibling's child's child. Addressed by personal name.
15 *atlu* Parent's parent's parent's sibling's child's child's child. Seldom recognised. Addressed by personal name.

Analysis

The words *ama* and *ina* mean simply 'male' and 'female', so that an individual's closest kin are identified in terms of the most basic social opposition in Buid society. *Ama* and *ina* may be used to specify the sex of any human or animal category: sexual dimorphism, and its role in procreation, is recognised by the Buid as being common to both the human and animal worlds. The relationship between parents and children is, in the first instance, an entirely 'natural' relationship based on the facts of procreation. The term for child, *anak*, may be glossed as 'immature individual (of either sex)'. Again, it may be used to qualify both human and animal categories. The sexual identity of children, as opposed to that of parents, is seen as irrelevant to the genealogical relationship which links them. The distinctions of age and sex, by which the terms *ama, ina* and *anak* are differentiated, derive from the given, biological nature of the individuals to whom they are applied. Together, they make up the *talanan* 'parent/child set', or nuclear family, which is a 'natural', pre-social group.

The terms for the other close genealogical kinsmen follow the same pattern of differentiating only the members of senior generations according to sex. These latter terms are all reciprocal in reference, however, unlike the terms within the *talanan*. Lack of reciprocity within the *talanan* extends even to members of the same generation, in that elder siblings are differentiated from junior siblings. The only relationship in which the age and sex of both parties is irrelevant is that between cousins.

Only kinsmen in senior generations and elder siblings are addressed with the appropriate kinship term. All other individuals are addressed either with their personal names, or with the all-purpose term of companionship, *sama*. The avoidance of the personal names of senior kinsmen in address emphasises the given, hierarchical nature of the relationship. In the case of the most extreme form of dependency, that of children on their parents, this avoidance is extended to include a prohibition on uttering a parent's personal name even in reference. To break this prohibition is said to result in a painful swelling of the offender's head. Parents are instead addressed with specialised terms: *mama*, 'daddy', and *didi*, 'mummy'. The existence of a kinship relationship between two individuals is relevant only when they stand in a relationship of dependency and authority to one another. More generally, it may be said that all relationships of legitimate hierarchy and dependency in Buid society are associated with the genealogical constructs which govern behaviour between children and adults, while all relationships of equality and autonomy are associated with the constructs of companionship which govern behaviour between adults. This principle may be illustrated by the fact that the spouses of senior kinsmen are treated terminologically and behaviourally as if they were kinsmen, while the spouses of kinsmen in ego's own and in descending generations are not.

Children among the Buid are by definition incapable of conducting an autonomous existence. They are dependent on members of the senior generation for physical, emotional and mystical care and protection until they reach maturity. Normally it is one of their senior kinsmen and the current spouse of that kinsman who play the role of provider. If their own parents are divorced, children will regularly alternate their residence between the household of their mother and stepfather, on the one hand, and that of their father and stepmother, on the other. During the day, small children are likely to be left in the care of a grandparent, aunt or uncle (and their respective spouses). At a later age, they may decide to live permanently with one of these close kinsmen. The social role of provider, then, is nearly always played by one of a number of sexually differentiated couples in the senior generation, only one of whom is a genealogical kinsman.

Now, it is through one's 'real' parents that one is related to a wider genealogical network of kinsmen, so that it is important for an individual to be able to distinguish between them and his or her step-parents. This is done by means of the modifiers *arungan*, 'real', 'authentic', and *ulungan* 'false', 'steprelative'. It is not necessary to make this distinction between more remote 'real' relatives, such as aunts and uncles, and their spouses. The latter are simply treated as if they were senior kinsmen. By contrast, genealogical terms are not extended to ego's own spouse, to the spouses of kinsmen in ego's own or descending generations, or to the senior kinsmen of any of these spouses. These individuals are instead referred to by a distinct set of 'affinal' terms.

Buid affinal terminology

16   *indugan* Husband. Addressed by personal name.
17   *babay* Wife. Addressed by personal name.
18   *nugang* Spouse's parent or child's spouse. Addressed as *sama*.
19   *tagyaw* Husband's sibling or woman's sibling's spouse. Also wife's sister or man's brother's wife. Addressed by personal name.
20   *ai* Wife's brother or man's sister's husband. Addressed by personal name.
21   *balayi* Child's spouse's parent. Addressed by personal name.
22   *bilas* Spouse's sibling's spouse. Addressed by personal name.

Analysis

The contrast between intra-household non-reciprocity and inter-household reciprocity in reference is maintained in the affinal terminology. But the implied hierarchy in the non-reciprocal terms used to refer to spouses is overridden in address. This is the inverse of what happens between consanguines of different *talanan* and generation, where the implied equality of reciprocal terms of reference is overridden by non-reciprocal forms of address. Another distinctive feature of the affinal terminology is the existence of a special term, *ai*, for a man's brother-in-law. The relationship between *ai* is often very close, lacking the hierarchical implications of junior and senior siblingship. Why there should not be a parallel term for a woman's sister-in-law, I am unable to say.[12]

The term *nugang* is of special interest as it describes a relationship of marked hierarchy which nevertheless occurs between individuals who are non-kinsmen and who have never occupied the same household. In this instance, the reciprocal term of reference is contradicted by the fact that the junior partner in the relationship is prohibited from uttering the personal name of the senior even in reference. A further peculiarity is that instead of employing the affinal term in address, the junior resorts to a term of companionship, which emphasises precisely equality, *sama*. *Nugang* is also the only category in which no gender distinction is made in an ascending generation.

Since these affinal terms apply to individuals who are likely to have achieved adulthood, ego is unlikely to be involved in a relationship of dependency of authority with them. They need not associate with one another unless they choose to do so. While 'affines' of this type often form warm, cooperative ties with one another, such ties are the product of a voluntary, freely terminable agreement. The relationship is thus more 'companion-like' than 'kin-like' in Buid terms. The relationship between parent- and child-in-law is more ambiguous, given the past authority and continuing influence of the former over one's spouse.

The Buid life cycle

The ultimate goal of Buid child-rearing is to bring children to a point at which they can take their place in the community as mature, autonomous adults capable of engaging in the sharing of food, labour and sex on an equal basis. The initial absolute dependence of an infant on its parents is gradually diluted and diffused among a growing number of adults, until it is on the community as a whole that an individual depends, and toward the community that an individual feels a sense of obligation. Particularistic ties with specific members of the community are discouraged as a threat to communal solidarity. In the following discussion, I shall focus on three principal mechanisms which contribute to the detachment of children from specific adults, and to the gradual lessening of dependency on them.

In the first place, children experience frequent shifts of residence from an early age. They come into contact with a large number of step- and half-siblings on both their mother's and their father's side. Their loyalties will not be to any particular domestic group, but to all the domestic groups in which their immediate genealogical kinsmen happen to be living at any given time. The child will learn to regard all relationships based on the marital tie as temporary, and that all adult members of the community may be regarded as potential steprelatives.

In the second place, children are encouraged to spend most of their time in peer groups, away from adult supervision. These groups include all of the children of both sexes in a local community from the age of five until puberty. Relationships with the peer group are governed by the same norms of companionship and sharing that govern relationships among adults. Older children often return home only to take their meals and to sleep, and not always then. Children are accorded the privilege of being able to eat in any household in the community, and are prone to rapid materialisation on the doorstep of whichever household is preparing a particularly desirable side dish. Older children frequently sleep at a friend's house, even when its adult occupants are absent. By the age of ten, they are quite capable of cooking their own meals. A great deal of learning takes place within the peer group. Older children teach the younger ones how to catch fish and small animals, and how to prepare them; how to play games which develop physical dexterity and endurance; and how to behave in general in a socially acceptable way. The sexes begin to separate only with the onset of puberty. It is at this point that boys build their first house and clear their own swidden. They begin to spend most of their time in the company of other young bachelors, exchanging the romantic poems used in courtship, indulging in joking behaviour with the adolescent girls, and travelling further and further afield. It may be two or three years before they are married and fully independent, but they move out of their parents' house as soon as they are able. Adolescent girls, as I have noted, tend to move out of their parents' house and into that of an elderly single woman. In summary, then, contact between adults and children is held to a minimum, thereby encouraging a feeling of self-sufficiency from an early age.

In the third place, there is a general minimisation of the authoritarian aspect of the parental role. Buid never command their children.[13] Faced with an explicit request, a child is most likely to respond by saying *U dayu*, 'I don't want to'. They are always concerned to assert their autonomy in such situations, and will carry out a request only after a significant period has elapsed. Such behaviour on the part of a child is not regarded as reprehensible, but as a natural consequence of the child's relative lack of sensitivity to the needs of others. I never heard an adult raise his or her voice to a child, much less did I ever see a child physically punished. Particularly anti-social children, who are subject to frequent bouts of quarrelling, sulkiness or tantrums, are deemed to have been 'bitten' by one of a number of evil spirits named after the emotional disorders they cause. A suitable ritual of exorcism may then be performed which effects, on the mystical level, a separation of the soul of the child from the intrusive spirit and, on the psychological level, a distancing of the child from its anti-social behaviour. The child is brought to regard its anti-social behaviour as having an external and frightening origin. Repudiating such behaviour then involves the child in no loss of face. The child is not forced to submit to the moral will of its parents, but encouraged to reassert its self-control. Children are thus seldom put in a position of having to comply with the unintelligible moral judgement or command of an adult superior.

In summary, then, Buid kinship constructs are thought to have positive implications for proper social behaviour primarily in relation to the roles of immature dependant and mature provider. The ultimate goal of the provider is to eliminate the dependency of his or her charge. Childhood dependency is not extended into adulthood, for senior kinsmen have little ritual, political or economic authority over their mature junior kinsmen. Parents do retain a certain amount of control over their children in the early stages of the latter's marital careers. They have the right to demand a fine called *inuyu* if they disapprove of a particular marriage, which was traditionally fixed at the rate of two fathoms of beads, but one informant had heard of a case in Batangan in which 1,000 pesos, a pig and a sack of rice had been demanded and paid. Parents also have the right to demand a fine known as *inawid* if they disapprove of an offspring's divorce. It was also traditionally fixed at two fathoms of beads. Beyond these limited rights to intervene in a child's marital affairs, however, parents have little control over their children once they have left home.

There is one apparent exception to the rule that the existence of a kinship relationship ceases to govern social interaction once both parties to it are mature. There is a statistical tendency in each generation for some marriages to last longer than others. Long-lasting marriages are likely to produce groups of full siblings. In all the flux of Buid social life, the relationship between full siblings stands out for its stability. While half-siblings may go off to live with different stepparents, and one's own parents may remarry other individuals one does not like, a full sibling has exactly the same relatives as oneself and is likely to share the same residential history. Full-sibling sets tend to disperse when they first marry, but they tend to reconstitute themselves in middle age in a *garakbangan balay*, to which is attached each of their current spouses, children and children-in-law. Now, not everyone has a full sibling. The greater moral density of full-sibling sets within the general population exerts a 'gravitational effect' on the more atomised fraction of the population and full sibling sets end up forming the core of household clusters. If we refer back to Figure 1, it will be seen that there are five significant sets of full siblings in Ayufay: Clusters A, C, F, G, and H. Three of these have banded together to form the settlement of Ugun Liguma, while two of them, Clusters G and H, form a separate *garakbangan balay* in the interior.

I have already shown the marital history of the senior member of the full sibling set in Cluster C in Figure 4. His brother, 17, has also had children by three different wives, and his sister, 15, has had children by three different husbands. In most cases, these sibling sets do not constitute the core of a residential group which continues into the following generation. The chain of half-siblings produced by the members of the full-sibling set in Cluster C are scattered throughout the region, and show little sign of regrouping in future. They have grown up in different households from one another. In the traditional system, this would represent a typical process. Certain sets of full siblings would be produced in each generation, only to dissolve again in the next as those siblings entered into a number of marriages, while new full-sibling sets would emerge as a result of stable marriages in different sectors of the population.

The solidarity between full siblings is greater than that between each of these siblings and their children, if those children are shared with an ex-spouse. The children will be alternating between the households of their two parents when they are young and will move away entirely when they marry. Full siblings are more likely to share a common residential history than are parents and children. This lack of inter-generational solidarity means that there is little incentive to advance 'familial' interests from one generation to the next. It is only when the members of a full-sibling set begin themselves to make stable marriages that the elements of an inter-generational group capable of advancing its interests at the expense of others begin to emerge. Such a development would constitute a direct threat to the traditional system of social organisation and to the values of communal equality and solidarity on which it is based.

The point is that even full siblings tend to disperse at first, and only come back together *as companions* once they have established their mutual autonomy and equality. They do not form a 'kinship group' in the sense usually implied by that term. It is because they are long-term companions that they are bound to one another, not because they share a common substance. The fact that such groups do not perpetuate themselves down the generations also indicates that we are not here dealing with a social grouping based on shared descent.

This is not to say, however, that the existence of a kinship relationship ceases to have any other significance once both parties to it are mature. On the contrary, as we shall see in Chapter 7, a kinship tie survives even death. But it comes to have mostly negative associations. The norms associated with kinship between adults are mostly concerned with ensuring that the dependency of children on their parents and their initial identification with them is not extended into adult life. The role of the incest taboo in ensuring the separation of close kinsmen is also relevant here, but will be dealt with in Chapter 7 because of its mystical implications.

Conclusion

The Buid system of marriage and residence nullifies two common tendencies toward hierarchy in social life. On the one hand, it prevents the emergence of descent groups in which senior members would have authority over junior members. What authority there is remains confined to that of the adult members of households over the immature children living with them. Even so, the authority of the parental generation is diffused among a large number of real and stepparents, aunts, uncles and grandparents. On the other hand, it avoids the hierarchical relations between wife-givers and wife-takers which arise when women are regarded as a good under the control of senior men, who must be compensated for their loss when they are given in marriage. The exchange of women by men involves not only the subordination of women to men, but also of unmarried junior men to the senior men who control the women. In the Buid system, no one is in a position to control the marital choices of anyone else. The principle of 'reasonable' compensation for abandonment by a spouse allows for the reconciliation of the offended spouse with the offender without giving the former the power to prevent the latter from re-marrying.

5 Transformations in Social Organisation

In this chapter, the transformations which have occurred in Buid social organisation as a result of the introduction of cash cropping, settlement in large-scale communities and the acquisition of lowland patrons will be described. Some of these transformations are relatively superficial, affecting only the details of social life, while leaving the basic system of values untouched. Others threaten to strike at the heart of that system. Among the most fundamental changes is a transformation in attitudes towards marriage and child-rearing, which is discussed in the first section of this chapter. The full implications of this transformation have yet to be realised on the ground. In the second section, I argue that from a relatively amorphous collection of households, the local community has increasingly acquired the characteristics of a corporate group with a recognised leadership, policy-making process, corporate property and identity. This has been accompanied by the emergence of a degree of hierarchy in Buid society which has not yet been legitimised in terms of the traditional system of values. The political leader of Ugun Liguma continues to defer to the will of the community as elaborated in political meetings, and to act as the servant of the community. His behaviour stands in marked contrast to that of the leader of Batangan, who has created ties of personal dependency between himself and other Buid, and who openly employs his influence with lowland politicians in order to impose his will. The traditional system of values is being rapidly eroded in Batangan due to the rise of economic stratification, daily exposure to Christian culture, the presence of Protestant missionaries and the existence of patron-client ties between Yaum and his followers. Even so, the Batangan Buid have managed to preserve a great deal of their internal solidarity. In the last section, I identify the basic problem of Buid society as the creation of a community based on the constructs of shared space and activity, as opposed to the constructs of shared origin and substance, characteristic of kinship-based society, and use these constructs to introduce my material on Buid religion.

101

The emergence of kinship groups

In the last chapter, I argued that while groups of full siblings may have provided the core of local residential clusters in the past, the chances were that not all of these siblings would make stable marriages and that their children would tend to disperse as a result of the latter's lack of a common residential history during childhood. The reproduction of a full-sibling set in the second generation has far-reaching political and economic consequences. In the first place, the second generation will be able to capitalise on the centrality of their parents in the local community. In the second place, due to the undivided loyalties of the children to one set of parents, and of parents to the children they share with a single spouse, the parental generation will be encouraged to think of advancing their children's interests and relative position in the longer term. Such attempted advancement of the interests of one's children would have little meaning in the traditional system which did not permit the accumulation of wealth or power. Because of the political and economic changes in the last ten years described in Chapter 3, however, accumulation is now a real possibility. The individual most aware of the possibilities in Ayufay is Consejal Agaw, and it is not surprising both that he is a member of a full-sibling set himself, and that his stable marriage to his current spouse has produced another generation of full siblings.

Agaw is an extremely astute man. He has been almost solely responsible for encouraging the members of the Ayufay community to form a single large-scale settlement and to have their lands surveyed and taxed. He also recognises the necessity of building up a large, stable domestic group in order to cope with lowland pressures. He admits that it was Buid practice in the past to expose unwanted children in the forest and that he did so himself with the child of his first marriage. Faced with the numerical superiority of the lowlanders, however, he now holds that it is necessary for all Buid to have large families. With the rise of a hierarchy in power and wealth, we can see here the emergence of an ideology of stable domestic groups and a concern for their perpetuation from one generation to another. As land becomes subject to the norms of exclusive private ownership, it becomes necessary to ensure the 'patrimony' of one's children. Agaw is busy doing just that. He was careful to see that his eldest son, not yet married, had a land claim registered in his name, and that his own holdings and those of his wife will be sufficient to provide for his four other surviving children (four others have died). Indeed, he devotes himself to the future welfare of his children with a quite un-Buid intensity, and this devotion is reciprocated by the children. The younger children have grown up with a sense of their father's pre-eminent position in the community, and are aware of the deference he receives from poor Christians, who address him as *consejal*. They show this awareness in their deportment. I have seen his three youngest sons, aged four, six and ten, face down Christian children twice their size, while most Buid children take to their heels at the slightest hint of aggression. The eldest son is about eighteen and was born before his father returned to Ayufay from Sigaw and became a political leader. He is much closer in behaviour to the young men of his age than he is to his younger brothers. Agaw is training his ten-year-old son as a potential leader. This son is being sent to school in Batangan, where he is doing very well. The younger brothers also exhibit a quite uncharacteristic degree of sibling rivalry. They are constantly quarrelling with one another and competing for their parents' attention. Unlike most other Buid children, they have never lived in another household with different sets of half- and stepsiblings.

Agaw's realisation of the potential of kinship relations for building up a power base has not been limited to his family of procreation. When the first large settlement was built in Ayufay, he started with a core group composed of his own household, and those of his mother, brother, sister and sister's husband's daughter. His brother has since died, but has been replaced as a supporter by the latter's son. His own son now has a house of his own, bringing to six the number of closely-related households in his cluster. He has, in addition, taken into his protection the households of two unrelated elderly widows and of the niece of one of the latter, who has no other close relative in the community (these households are indicated as being part of Clusters A, B, E and K in Figure 1). Together, these nine households now form one quarter of the settlement of Ugun Liguma (see Map XI). Agaw is now actively negotiating to bring over a large number of close kin from Sigaw, including his wife's brother (who is also his second cousin), his deceased brother's former wife, her current husband (who is also Agaw's first cousin), and her first cousin. Land has already been set aside for the members of these three households in Ayufay (plots 3, 3a, and 4 on Map X).

In addition to these close kin, Agaw has also managed to attach kinship Cluster J to his faction. They have built their houses in his half of Ugun Liguma and their land claims lie between those of his own cluster and those of his sister's husband's cluster. Cluster J is composed of five households focused on the couple 63, 64, and not on a full-sibling set. It is held together by the exceptionally strong bond of companionship between 64 and his wife's father and brother. The couple 60, 61 arrived from the other side of Mindoro just before my departure. Their case is discussed in more detail below. Because Cluster J is based on ties of companionship and not siblingship, it possesses little long-term cohesion and follows the lead of Agaw in most matters.

The fourteen households so far discussed constitute the core of Agaw's faction in Ugun Liguma. Cluster F, containing five households, is loosely united by two elderly sisters and is rather reluctant to get very involved in lowland affairs. Its members rarely contribute to settlement meetings. One or two of its younger members generally back Agaw's initiatives. Cluster D is composed of a single household and has deliberately marginalised itself, building its house outside the settlement fence. Its male member was once married to a Christian, the only case I know in which this has happened. Agaw has been unable so far to attract the members of Clusters G and H to live in the settlement. They are based on two groups of full siblings, and show no desire to put themselves under Agaw's leadership. Cluster I is now attached to Cluster J by marriage.

This leaves Cluster C and part of Cluster K unaccounted for. Individual 70 is planning to marry 15, which will bring the two groups together through an alliance in the senior generation. Already the two groups are acting in concert in political and economic disputes. Cluster C is the only group focused on a set of full siblings in the senior generation aside from Agaw's Cluster A, and it constitutes the core of resistance to Agaw's authority in settlement affairs. While some of the members of this group are better versed in lowland affairs than is Agaw (21 has even attended a year of high school), none of them possesses his political ability to find compromise solutions acceptable to the most conservative as well as to the most progressive. Further, as I indicated in my discussion of 19's marital history, they have not yet adopted a long-term perspective enabling them to act in unison to advance their children's interests. At least this is true of the older generations. 21 shows signs of personal ambition. Although he is twenty-five years old, he says that he will wait until he has had some further education and obtains a secure source of income before he marries.

It is interesting to note the total contrast between Agaw's manipulation of kinship and stable affinal ties in building up a settlement under his leadership, and the traditional political system which was based on a continual undermining of such ties. It is as if they were always there, waiting for someone with the enterprise to utilise them. Of course, it is not merely a question of one man's initiative, but of a change in the wider political environment brought about by land scarcity, cash cropping and the need for patrons. It is because of Agaw's willingness to deal with lowlanders and to negotiate with government agents that the other Buid consent to follow his lead in these matters. I shall discuss the transformation of the political system in more detail in the next section. Here, I wish merely to draw attention to the role that a breakdown in the sharing of spouses has played in this transformation. When confronting the Christians, Agaw must have a group of dependable supporters behind him. The traditional system was well adapted to a situation in which the Buid could respond to external aggression by fleeing into neighbouring regions, as they did during the war. Now that they must stand and fight for their land, they are forging links of dyadic dependency and authority among themselves. The transition from a defensive to an offensive strategy has necessitated a certain abandonment of egalitarian values and an acceptance of leadership, reinforced by the beginnings of an ideology of kin-group solidarity. Agaw's kinship cluster shows signs of becoming a sort of bilateral descent group. His children are not only more tightly knit that are other sibling groups, but they are on very close terms with their first cousins who live in adjacent houses. Those individuals who are now growing up with minimal ties with their half-siblings and no ties at all with their first cousins will be operating in future under a distinct disadvantage.

Put simply, what is happening in Ugun Liguma is that intra-household ties, and the ties between specific households which are their result in the second generation, are beginning to take precedence over the ties between the individual and the community as a whole. If close kinsmen begin to cooperate with each other more intensively than they do with non-kinsmen, then the principle of equal sharing between households breaks down. The generalised and diffuse subordination of the junior generation to the senior generation is replaced by the subordination of children to their own parents, and of junior siblings to senior siblings. The right of the community to intervene periodically in the composition of households disappears when marriages become more stable. In the past, a high rate of divorce meant that most marriages involved the transfer of an individual from the household of one spouse, who had minimal rights over him or her, to the household of a new spouse, under the supervision of the community as a whole. A low rate of divorce means that most marriages involve the transfer of a man and a woman out of the households of their respective parents and the formation of a new household. This in turn means that marriage will come to resemble more an alliance between kin groups than a sharing of spouses. Because of the authority exercised by parents over their children, and of the debt children owe their parents for their upbringing, the right of parents to control the actions of their children is qualitatively different from the rights one spouse exercises over the other. The fact that an individual is acquiring a spouse not from another spouse, but from the potential spouse's parents means that an individual is under great pressure to conform to the expectations of his or her parents-in-law.

In short, it seems that an attack on the single principle of frequent divorce has enormous consequences for the social system as a whole. The sort of situation described in the last paragraph has not yet been fully implemented in Ayufay. I give it only as a logical extrapolation of current trends toward the accumulation of heritable property and toward the political manipulation of kinship ties. It also serves to illustrate the centrality of spouse-sharing to the maintenance of communal equality by way of negative example. It was the sharing of spouses which allowed Buid society to preserve a remarkable degree of individual equality and autonomy. This practice is now being replaced by a new emphasis on kinship ties to focal political leaders and the emergence of long-term debt relationships.

The local community as emergent corporation

The first step in the subordination of the Buid to the lowlands was their settlement in large villages, a process which recalls the early Spanish policy of *reduccion*. Yaum's community of Batangan was the first to follow this path in the early 1960s. Yaum has since encouraged the settlement of Buid communities from Tawga in the south to Ayufay in the north. In each of these local communities he has his representative, the *consejal*, who acts simultaneously as the local community's spokesman. Yaum is himself addressed by the Christians as *meyor*. As the Buid themselves are well aware, Yaum was able to achieve a decisive break with the old political culture by *aksakbaw gubyirnu*, 'entering the government', i.e. by allying himself with the local politicians and wealthy Christian families, thus reinforcing his influence among the Buid with external political support. In this he constitutes an exceptional case among Buid leaders, most of whom continue to operate within the traditional framework. I shall deal first with the local leaders such as Agaw, and ignore for the time being their dependence on Yaum.

I have given numerous examples already of the ways in which a local community operated in the past as a more or less coherent ideological whole. Nevertheless, it lacked a recognised leadership, a formal policy-making process, corporate property and a clear definition of its membership and collective identity. All of these features are becoming increasingly evident in the communities of settled Buid.

Leadership

Local leaders such as Agaw are just beginning to establish their authority in their respective communities and are engaged in a constant struggle simply to hold their settlements together. The local *consejal* tend to be the same individuals who functioned in the past as mediators in divorce cases and their present position continues to depend on the skills which they employed in that role. They must be able to guide communal policy without engaging in what is defined as 'proud' (*buagun*) or 'aggressive' (*maisug*) behaviour. Violence and aggression may be said to constitute the most extreme expression of negative reciprocity. For the Buid, they are seen as a potential consequence of all dyadic reciprocity. The Buid concept of *isug*, 'aggression', connotes all that has a negative value in social life: aggression, the uncontrolled expression of egoistic emotions and the attempted exploitation of others. They regard *maisug* behaviour as being typical of the Christians. The word has a wide distribution in the Philippines. Among the Tausug Muslims of the Sulu archipelago, it connotes all that is positively valued in men: virility, courage and the ability to stand up for one's honour (Kiefer, 1972: 53).[1] The Tagalog equivalent of *isug, tapang*, has a more ambiguous meaning, referring, on the one hand, to the virtues of courage and bravery and, on the other, to men who are dangerously violent or fierce in the manner of wild animals. The Buid language has many words for fear, fleeing and leaving others behind, none of which carries a negative moral connotation. By contrast, it lacks words expressing a positive evaluation of courage or the reciprocation of violence. *Isug* is put into the reciprocal form of *garisugan* to describe quarrelling of a serious nature. Slightly less serious than *maisug* behaviour is *buagun*, 'boastfulness', 'pretension', 'deceit'. This is said of individuals who draw undue attention to their achievements, or tell stories without foundation. One is expected to be modest in comportment and to stick to what one knows from personal experience.

Now, Agaw is in many ways one of the most shy and retiring men in Ayufay. Several more aggressive individuals who have ambitions to replace him have been relegated to the periphery of communal affairs, despite their greater knowledge of lowland ways. Agaw's enhanced political and economic standing derives from his own industry, and not from an ability to appropriate the labour of others. The Ayufay Buid think of him as a sort of specialist in lowland affairs and defer to him in such matters. He is not for that reason thought of as a superior in other contexts. Buid attitudes toward him are similar to their attitudes toward more powerful spirit mediums whose particular competence in the superordinary domain gains them no special status in other fields of endeavour. Christians, on the other hand, are always anxious to recognise status distinctions. They make a point of addressing Buid leaders as *consejal* and, in the case of Yaum, as *meyor*. The Christians, in fact, treat Yaum with extreme deference due to his high relative income, possession of tenants, ties with local politicians, and to the fact that he is known to have had two interviews with the President of the Philippines. The Buid, on the other hand, treat him with no such deference, address him with his personal name, and constantly require him to demonstrate that the projects he is continually initiating are really in their own interests. When rumours began to circulate in 1981 that Yaum might be taking a job with a government agency which would take him away from Batangan for the greater part of the year, it was the local Christians who were most upset at the prospect of losing their *meyor*, or patron. The Buid, by contrast, seemed entirely unmoved at the prospect. While they admit that his influence has been advantageous for them in many particular instances, they are highly critical of what they see as his boastful behaviour, and certainly feel no sense of moral obligation or gratitude toward him as a result of his actions.

Agaw's duties as *consejal* include attending meetings with the other Buid leaders in Batangan to discuss matters of interest to all Buid, and attending meetings in the coastal towns to mediate in disputes involving Ayufay Buid and Christians. In return, the other members of the community 'help' on his swidden. Unlike Yaum, Agaw does not demand a fee from the particular individuals he helps, but remains embedded in the traditional system of sharing. He is thought of as working in the interests of the community as a whole, and as receiving their collective help in return. A subtle difference has, however, been introduced. The traditional system of sharing may be represented schematically as follows, with each household represented by a letter, and the community as a whole by a group of letters in brackets:

$$A <=> (B, C, D) <=> B <=> (A, C, D) =$$
$$C <=> (A, B, D) <=> D <=> (A, B, C)$$

What this scheme is intended to convey is that what each household gives to, and recieves from, the community is roughly equal. Agaw has built up his position by maintaining, on the one hand, an equivalence between what he gives to, and receives from, the community, while at the same time intensifying his exchange beyond what is normal for other households:

$$A <=> (B, C, D) > B <=> (A, C, D) =$$
$$C <=> (A, B, D) = D <=>(A, B, C)$$

How Agaw's leadership works in practice may be illustrated by the role he played in two collective labour projects designed to benefit the community as a whole. On one occasion, he mobilised the residents of Ugun Liguma to build a fence around the settlement in order to clearly demarcate Buid land from the land of the surrounding Christians. He took it upon himself to slaughter two of his pigs to provide food for all of the workers. On another occasion, when the cement for the terrace was being poured, he organised the collection of funds with which to purchase rice to feed the workers (I contributed a pig). In both instances, Agaw supervised the cooking and distribution of the food. He was clearly acting as a representative of the whole community, not in an individual capacity as sponsor of a collective labour feast. Such communal projects represent a more developed form of the traditional system in which the group helped one of its parts. The group is now conscious enough of its own identity to conceive of itself as an entity which can benefit as an entity from its collective activity. But it still requires an individual to act as sponsor for its collective activities, and to stand for, and speak in the interests of, the whole. Unlike the traditional swidden work-group, Agaw takes an active part in communal projects and sets an example to others through his superior industry. He does not play a supervisory role. He reconciles in this way the egalitarian values of the culture and the need for someone to provide a focus and direction to group activity. Money which is collected for communal purposes, such as the feeding of visiting government officials or of communal work groups, is always placed in the safe-keeping of a member of kinship cluster J who is a highly respected spirit medium, and who adopts a neutral position in most policy-making decisions. Agaw's power within the community ultimately rests on his skill in achieving group consensus. He cannot be seen to be profiting personally from the policies he advocates.

The political 'miting'

Community policy is formed through a series of community-wide assemblies, called after the English term 'meeting'. These meetings contrast with the traditional *tultulan* in a number of ways. In the first place, they are clearly focused on the *consejal*, who dominates the proceedings with long speeches concerning recent developments in other Buid communities and in the Christian lowlands. In the second place, all adult men and women in the settlement and, if possible, even those who have not yet joined it, are positively encouraged to attend. In the third place, they are held in a corporately built and owned structure, the 'barrio hall' (again, the term is derived from English). Finally, they are reserved for the discussion of corporate affairs, both internal and external.

A great deal of these meetings is taken up with the reports of Agaw on the intelligence he has received from his meetings with the other *consejal* in Batangan and from the lowlands concerning government initiatives as regards the Buid (usually transmitted via Yaum as their recognised leader); the course of disputes between Buid and Christians over land claims, debts, assaults and so on; and proposals originating in Batangan for the cooperative marketing of timber, maize and other cash crops. No one interrupts the opening speech of the *consejal*, which is usually phrased in broad and tentative terms. Auditors restrict themselves to voicing agreement from time to time, or remaining silent when they disagree. When the *consejal* has finished, other elder men begin monologues of their own. The course of the discussion may meander in many directions as everyone speaks in turn, until a 'sense of the meeting' emerges. Women tend to play a less active role than men, although they are present in equal numbers and sit interspersed among the men. They usually confine themselves to whispered asides, lowland affairs being generally regarded as the business of men. Real criticism goes on outside these formal meetings and becomes known to the individuals being criticised through third parties. Meetings may in fact be devoted to nothing more than the clearing up of back-biting and gossip which has been circulating behind people's backs.

Because these meetings are devoted to issues felt to concern every member of the community equally, it is expected that everyone will attend. Indeed, it is a bad sign if a significant group stays away, as it means that it is impossible to reach a consensus and that the group concerned may be harbouring a grievance. Agreement to participate in a meeting already implies a certain willingness to go along with the weight of communal opinion. Much of the real political bargaining, then, occurs outside the context of the formal meeting. A skilful leader like Agaw must always make it appear that a particular plan of action has originated with the meeting and not with himself. Authority does not rest with the leader, but with the assembled collectivity which gives its consent to a particular policy.

Meetings take place in a public arena which has no equivalent in traditional Buid society. All large-scale Buid settlements now have a barrio hall, and its existence is a symbol of their existence as a group. In Ayufay, it consists of a large roofed enclosure surrounded by benches but without walls. The participants sit on these benches, or on the ground in the middle of the floor tending fires which are kept for light and, on cold nights, for warmth. Meetings are always held at night to secure privacy from nearby Christians and perhaps also to provide speakers with a certain sense of anonymity. The use of the barrio hall for political meetings is restricted to matters touching on the interests of the group as a group. Traditional disputes such as divorce cases continue to be held in private houses. The holding of meetings in the barrio hall provides a clear contrast to the holding of a *tultulan* in a private house to discuss issues of direct relevance to only one of the component households of the community. In the first instance we are dealing with a self-referential process, in the second with the intervention of an encompassing group in the affairs of an encompassed group. In the traditional system, the community became aware of itself only in the context of events occurring in one of its parts, such as a death or divorce. To a certain extent, the interests of the whole were identified as being the sum of the interests of the parts. I say 'to a certain extent', because there was a notion of the mystical interdependence of the whole, but this notion received little practical expression except in ritual. At present, the community is made continually aware of its practical, corporate interests through political meetings in a determinate time and place.

Intracommunal disputes, formerly restricted to *garagawan indugan/babay*, 'mutual stealing of wives/husbands', have become more generalised in the past ten years. With the growth of large-scale settlements, land scarcity and the market economy, accumulations of wealth and power have become possible. This has led to the rise of political factionalism and to the growth of kinship solidarity as political forces. Such internal squabbles are, however, dwarfed by the threat presented by the Christians. There is a very strong feeling among the Buid that all internal disputes must be resolved without reference to external agencies, as the Buid can only maintain their economic and political position by functioning as a bloc. As I have said, leaders such as Agaw have not become patrons of individual families, but are engaged in a balanced exchange of services with their communities as a whole. Internal cleavages are subordinated to communal solidarity, which is based on the maintenance of horizontal bonding between households, and a continued resistance to the growth of vertical bonds between them. The Buid stand in marked contrast in this respect to the Christian peasants among whom kinship and not locality is paramount in the creation and maintenance of social bonds. A peasant's loyalty is to his kin and patron, not to his neighbours. As his kin tend to be widely dispersed, given the migratory character of his society, he is left heavily dependent on vertical ties to his patron, and prone to conflict with those of his own class. The pioneer Christians in the mountains are continually feuding with one another and trying to involve the Buid on their own sides. Murders are not uncommon, as every man stands ready to avenge an affront to his honour, even years after the original incident. Feuds may be temporarily patched up by patrons, to whom the peasants go to arrange compensation, only to break out again. This places the patrons in a very strong position, as clients are dependent on them, not only economically, but also for physical protection. As I shall show later, Buid settlements also have their lowland patrons, but such patronage tends to be extended to whole communities as indivisible units, and not to individual Buid or their families. Before an adequate explanation of the way in which Buid communities have been able to retain their internal solidarity can be attempted, material regarding religious beliefs and practices will have to be introduced. Here it may be said that, in general, beliefs concerning the predatory spirit world act as an effective incentive towards ritual cooperation and the sharing of sacrificial meat between disputing factions. Buid egalitarianism is a social construct. In the past, the system of residential dispersion and ritual aggregation prevented the accumulation of wealth and power, so that equality could be constructed in reality. In the present, equality is increasingly becoming a fiction, carefully maintained in the form of political meetings, to bolster the bargaining power of emergent *gurangun*, 'big men', in their dealings with the Christians.

The Buid consciously strive, then, to maintain a united front against Christian attempts to steal their land, government plans to make them abandon shifting cultivation, and general lowland harassment. Working through their patrons, they attempt to get better collective rates for the sale of their cash crops. More importantly, they never involve the lowland legal and political system in their disputes with other Buid. I noted in Chapter 3 the effects of internal divisiveness on the Hanunoo in relation to competing land claims, in which Hanunoo served as pawns in the land courts for their respective Christian patrons. There was one incident in which one of Agaw's rivals for leadership took a dispute with a Christian over land to the local Christian barrio captain (the barrio, now called *barangay*, is the next smaller unit of governmental administration under the municipality) without consulting a Buid community meeting first. He was roundly and universally condemned for this infringement of Buid solidarity, even though his dispute was with an outsider. Many Buid now say that ultimately they would like to possess a clear title to their land, as the only guarantee that they will be able to continue to hold it in the face of any Christian challenge. In view of the way in which they dealt with the Forest Occupancy Survey discussed in Chapter 3, it is not clear how well they understand the implications of full private ownership, with the right to alienate title to outsiders. This brings us to the third feature of the local community as an emergent corporation: the existence of communal property.

Corporate property

Before the survey was made, the issue of which lands each adult member of the community would claim was discussed in a series of meetings. Boundaries were modified and names were changed as the Buid examined my map until everyone was satisfied that an equitable distribution was being made. The fact that residence in the settlement of Ugun Liguma entitled one to a share of communal land was made explicit by the inclusion of claims for potential members of the settlement, i.e. for Agaw's relatives in Sigaw (plots 3, 3a and 4 on Map X), and for the refugee family from Occidental Mindoro (plot 60). I argued in Chapter 3 that this treatment of communal lands represented a transformation of the traditional system in that it recognised permanent rights to a determinate area, while preserving the more fundamental rule of equal shares for all. Inclusion in the survey was predicated on the willingness of individuals to function as full and active residents of Ugun Liguma. The two kinship clusters who continued to live along the Yaman were also included as long-standing members of the community and as potential members of the settlement. Up to now, the registration of land claims has been admitted as a necessity in relation to the government and lowlanders, but the notion that it should operate to prevent some Buid from having access to any land of their own, or that they should have to rent land from other Buid, is strongly rejected. When the Buid say that they would like to have full title to their land, they are thinking in terms of the ability of Christians to dispossess them, not in terms of expanding their acreage at the expense of other Buid. I would argue that the Buid have come to regard all the land in Ayufay as the corporate property of the members of the settlement of Ugun Liguma in the sense that the latter have the right to decide who is to farm what part of it.

The corporate nature of the settlement itself is even more strongly marked. The land on which it is built has received limited recognition from the government as a 'Mangyan reservation' set aside for the use of any Buid who wishes to build a house on it. As I noted in Chapter 2, this was accomplished with the help of Yaum, Nati Enriquez and the government. Most settled Buid communities impose certain rules on their members, such as the prohibition of gambling, drinking of alcohol, and free passage of Christians within the settlement. Ugun Liguma is no exception. The purpose of constructing the fence referred to above was to establish a moral barrier to Christians, who could then be asked to explain their purpose if found inside it. Aside from the land itself, the communal property of the settlement includes all that has been built on it by the community as a whole, such as the fence, the barrio hall and the cement terrace. The initiative for all of these projects came from the community, not from the government. Just as I was leaving the field, the Buid decided that they wanted to build a water pipe from the spring to the settlement, access to which would be denied to the Christians. All these projects have a material motive, but their symbolic value as a concrete representation of corporate activity is equally significant.

The emergence of a corporate identity

In the past, Buid communities had indefinite boundaries. It was possible for an individual to live on the margins of two different communities, or to alternate residence between several. So long as the functions of communities were mainly ritual, this was of little consequence. While there continues to be some overlap in community membership, some households alternating between Ayufay and Akliang (numbers 70 and 72 for example), they have, on the whole, become increasingly discrete. Communal identity now has a focus in a compact settlement and leader. One can refer to the members of the Ugun Liguma settlement either by its name, or as *anda Agaw* 'of Agaw's group'. I have already examined the hierarchical implications of the present politico-economic situation, including the rise of differential accumulations of wealth and power, the recognition of dyadic obligations between kinsmen and dependency on external patrons. To these may now be added an ideological factor. As the community begins to think of itself as a corporate whole, it must take one of its parts as standing for the whole in its relations with outside world. If power is defined as the probability that a command will be obeyed by a given group of persons, then Agaw is powerless. Even if we adopt Weber's wider definition of power as the ability to impose one's will against resistance, Agaw's power is still negligible (Weber, 1947: 152). In fact, power and authority continue to reside in the political meeting, which is made up of the entire membership of the corporation, and which jealously guards its prerogatives. Because of the notion that consensus must be reached on all policy, one cannot even say that power rests in the hands of the majority. Looked at from the standpoint of classical Weberian analysis, one would have to conclude that Buid communities are not corporate groups at all (ibid.: 146). This would be highly misleading, however, for the real basis of Agaw's power lies not in his ability to impose his will on other members of the community, but in his ability to mediate between the corporate group and outside powers. He has privileged access to the counsels of Yaum and lowland politicians. Within the group, he is merely an equal, but in relation to the outside world he is the first among equals. It is the relationship between Buid communities and lowland patrons, who are in possession of real power, that must now be examined.

Power and patronage in the lowlands
The qualitative difference between Yaum's leadership and that of Agaw may be illustrated by an examination of the one murder case I came across in Buid society. It originated in a divorce case between Miun and Gimnayan of the Fawa region, on the extreme northern edge of Buid territory (see Map IV). The earliest events in this incident were recorded by Lopez while she was in the field. Miun was well known throughout Buid territory as being extremely *maisug*, 'aggressive', and in possession of powerful *amurit*, 'black magic'. His wife accused him of frequently beating her and she demanded a divorce. Miun insisted on a compensation payment of 400 pesos which Gimnayan and her relatives were unable to pay. One of the latter had good friends in Batangan, whom they asked to get Yaum to intervene. The two factions from Fawa were eventually threatened and cajoled into bringing their dispute to Batangan, where Yaum gave them a long lecture on his ability to have people imprisoned in a lowland jail if they behaved violently. Together with four *consejal* from Batangan, Yaum eventually got Miun to accept 160 pesos and two iron pots as compensation. Fifty additional pesos were demanded from Miun by the Batangan officials as a *fangabaya*, 'restraining fee'. Gimnayan's group paid 100 pesos to Yaum, and 50 pesos to two of his aides in return for their services. As I have said, traditional mediators received no compensation of any kind. (This part of the account is taken from Lopez, 1981: 149–50).

This is how matters stood when Lopez left the field. A few months later, Miun went to the house of his ex-wife's father, killed Gimnayan, burnt down the house and slaughtered all the animals. A few days after that, Miun was found dead. It was generally assumed that he had killed himself, although some hinted that Gimnayan's father had been responsible. Gimnayan's kin held Miun's kin responsible for the death of the former and demanded compensation. In February 1980 Yaum called a meeting in Ugun Liguma, the last outpost of his influence, to arbitrate between the two sides. He set the compensation at 3,000 pesos, one thousand each for the death, for the house and for the animals. By October, nothing had been paid, and Gimnayan's father was becoming increasingly dangerous. A second meeting was set to take place in Ugun Liguma, but Miun's relatives were afraid to venture so far from home because of Gimnayan's father's violent mood and did not come. Finally a second meeting was arranged nearer to Fawa. Damages were reduced to 2,000 pesos. Miun's brother explained that he was busy trying to collect minor debts from relatives, but was having little success. He continued to live in fear of his life from Gimnayan's father. Clearly, 2,000 pesos is an enormous sum by Buid standards, representing between five and ten years' income for an inhabitant of Fawa.

This case is interesting in several ways. In the first place, it shows that non-violence is a moral value, not always lived up to in practice. Once a cycle of violence is started, it may well lead to an open sequence of retaliatory killings. Rare incidents of this type may be enough to enforce a general feeling that any expression of physical aggression may have terrible and uncontrollable consequences. Miun's violent tendencies were interpreted not as a praiseworthy defence of his honour, but as a symptom of his possession of black magic. Having committed a murder, he immediately killed himself, an outcome which may have been due in part to Yaum's threat to bring in the police. Most Buid would rather commit suicide than be taken for a long time into a lowland prison. Indeed, Yaum's clumsy intervention may well have exacerbated the whole situation. Instead of allowing a tense situation to resolve itself by degrees through a series of *tultulan*, he forced the issue and gave Miun a deeper sense of grievance by humiliating him in front of the whole Batangan population, who despise 'Bangun' in any case. Yaum's appeal to the external source of power at his disposal ran right against the Buid tradition of mediation and the working out of a consensus in which no one loses face. He overplayed his hand by attempting to impose a judicial settlement on a group which he has not as yet made politically and economically dependent. The Fawa Buid earn a fair amount of cash from the sale of *labasa*, a kind of squash much desired in the lowlands, but they sell it to Christian middlemen once a year and avoid contact with the lowlands at most other times. Their land is as yet under no direct threat from Christian loggers and settlers, they have not yet felt the need to form compact settlements, and they do not recognise *consejal* in their region.

I have given this example to illustrate the radical difference between the traditional Buid political culture as still practised in Ugun Liguma, and the lowland model which Yaum is increasingly adopting. Now, it would be going too far to assert that the traditional culture has been completely abandoned even in Batangan. Matters of public interest are still submitted to settlement-wide meetings and Yaum must tread a careful path between the manipulation of his lowland-derived power and conformity with the indigenous value system. Only a small number of Batangan households are dependent upon him personally. If he is to get broad public support for his projects, he must achieve consensus in the accepted way. But the traditional political culture in Batangan is in a state of decay, due to a number of factors. In the first place, Buid households there have achieved a differential success in their exploitation of the market. Apart from widows with large families and the physically disabled, all households are able to grow enough food for their subsistence needs. But the top 20 per cent of Batangan households receive 51 per cent of the settlement's total cash income, and have average landholdings of 34 hectares each, while the bottom 20 per cent receive only 4 per cent of the total cash income, and have average landholdings of 5.8 hectares each (Lopez, 1981: 257). This difference in income is eroding the old sense of equality. In the second place, the Batangan Buid have been unable to maintain a rigid physical segregation from the Christians. The amount of disposable income in the settlement has attracted a number of Christian shopkeepers who trade for Buid produce on a full-time basis. Batangan also has a government-run school, and most children attend it at least part of the time. As a result, many of the younger generation are beginning to imitate lowland behaviour. They are bringing up their own children in a state of emotional dependency, playing competitive games such as basketball among themselves and against Christian opponents for monetary wagers, and furtively consuming alcohol. In the third place, missionaries have long played a central role in the settlement. In Chapter 2 I noted that Yaum's first allies in the founding of the settlement were the missionaries of the O.M.F. While only a quarter of the settlement now adheres to Protestant Christianity, the rest identify themselves as nominal Catholics. Christianity is seen as a necessary component of Filipino identity. The nominal Catholics continue to practise elements of the traditional religion, but these elements are losing much of their former coherence and rationale, as they are practised in private. They no longer serve as they once did as a focus of communal solidarity. The situation among the Protestants is much more extreme. As I have said, the Protestant missionaries oblige their converts to give up all animal sacrifice, thus enforcing a clean break from their unconverted kinsmen and neighbours. The sharing of sacrificial meat within a group is the most powerful statement of social solidarity and equality in Buid society. The Protestant Buid may have gained a new social identity in their church, but it has nothing to do with the traditional value system. Finally, Yaum has begun to establish patron-client relationships with certain individuals. He grants loans to others on the *alili* system, where 25 pesos at planting time is repaid with a sack of maize worth 60–70 pesos at harvest time; he charges fees for mediating in disputes and his authority is backed up by force. The traditional values of communal equality and solidarity are thus being simultaneously undermined on the economic, cultural, religious and political levels. Against this background, however, one must not lose sight of the fact that the Batangan Buid continue to attend political meetings in large numbers, that they do not hesitate to express their opposition to policies with which they disagree, and that they maintain a remarkable degree of solidarity in the face of external threats. Unlike the atomised Christian peasant population which surrounds them, they constitute an organised political force to be reckoned with. Why this should be the case is easier to understand by making a comparison with a Buid community at an earlier stage of integration into the lowland political and economic system, such as Ayufay, where the sense of communal solidarity is still intense.

Community and Religion

In the first chapters of this book, I have attempted to explicate the nature of Buid society as being founded on the concepts of sharing and companionship. The Buid conceive of the community as being made up of a group of people speaking the same language and following the same traditions, who live close to one another and who habitually share food, labour and help in times of crisis. Given the strong positive value attached to equality and personal autonomy in Buid society, it must find ways of creating solidary groups without resorting to ties of interpersonal dependency and authority. The idiom of companionship provides the most powerful metaphor for expressing an egalitarian form of solidarity: it implies a voluntary relationship between equals, and not the ascribed relationship between juniors and seniors implied by the idiom of kinship. Companionship also implies the occupation of a common place in the present and continuous shared activity, as opposed to the emphasis on a common point of origin in the past and a shared physical substance which unites people however long they have experienced spatial separation in societies which take kinship as the basis of moral solidarity (cf. Bloch, 1973). The Buid do not recognise long-term moral obligations to other specific individuals. They have no one but their neighbours to fall back on when crisis threatens. It is doubly important, then, that an individual maintains good relations with the other members of the community and that this community be as large as possible.

At the symbolic level, the household stands as a paradigm of the community, in that it constitutes the most intense arena of companionship and sharing. The marital relationship is virtually defined in terms of the continuous co-residence of an adult man and woman. It is initiated when a couple take up residence together and it ceases when they separate. Co-residence involves the daily cooperation of spouses on their respective swiddens, the sharing of the produce of those swiddens, and the sharing of sexual services. Each spouse retains his or her own personal autonomy and identity throughout. Their mutual commitment is always in question and must be continually reasserted. Households are composed of individuals who reside together voluntarily, except in the case of small children, although even they begin to have a fairly wide choice of residence at an early age. The terms for the core members of the household, *ama*, *ina* and *anak*, are also the terms for man, woman and child, and can be taken as denoting the basic divisions of society, divisions which have nothing to do with kinship.

But if the household represents a paradigm of society as a whole, it also forms the minimal and most exclusive unit within the community. Given the fact that households are not bound to one another by ties of filiation and descent created in the past, they can only be bound together by a series of transactions in the present. Indeed, since companionship is the ideal type of social relationship in Buid society, the potential exclusiveness of households represents a threat to the integrity of the society as traditionally constituted. The solution adopted by the Buid consists in the practice of frequent divorce which results in a periodic redistribution of the population among the community's component household units. Individuals are brought to think of the members of other households as past, present or potential members of their households, and of the members of their own households as only temporarily co-resident. The sharing of a common place of residence with others at some point in the life cycle may be compared with the sharing of a common substance in kinship-based societies as a principle of social solidarity.

This account of companionship, co-residence and sharing begins to answer the question raised above (p. 67) concerning the way Buid society deals with the problem of creating new and temporary social groupings, given their lack of permanent descent groups and rules of conduct which establish in advance the rights and duties which obtain between specific individuals. Every individual in Buid society may be thought of as standing in the centre of a series of circles of social interaction, ranging from those with whom a house is shared, to those with whom a river valley, a minimal dialect, a language, or merely the highlands of Mindoro are shared. There are rules which specify how anyone is to behave toward the members of one's household, community, region and tribe, but these rules apply to types of encompassing group, not to specific individuals. One is always free to join a new household, community or region, so long as one agrees to follow the accepted norms of behaviour within the groups one joins. Moral obligations are established between the individual and the group, not between specific individuals. These recognised obligations dwindle until the limits of the social world are reached with the inhabitants of the lowlands. The Christians are the opposite of companions: they are not *sama* but *luktanun*, 'aliens', whose customs and values make no sense.

The central problem of Buid society is the creation of a community based on shared social space and activity in order to counter the threat of external exploitation. In the next part of this book, I intend to show that Buid religion is primarily concerned with just these issues and that the notion of 'community' is largely a religious construct. The integration of Buid society cannot be understood without reference to notions of collective vulnerability to mystical agression and the need to sustain a broad alliance among households in order to counter it. This is achieved through a series of rituals which take two basic forms: the seance and animal sacrifice.

III
Religion

6 *Spirit Mediumship*

In this chapter I describe an aspect of Buid religion which immediately imposes itself on an outside observer. Almost every night in a settlement the size of Ugun Liguma, one will hear a low but persistent chanting which goes on from dusk until dawn. A continuous and routine contact with the spirit world is taken for granted by all Buid. Although all Buid suffer from the effects of this contact at one time or another, it is only the practised mediums who are able to 'see' the spirits by means of their familiars. The spirit world is populated by a host of normally invisible beings, some of whom are men's allies, but most of whom are their predatory enemies. It is to prevent the predatory spirits from attacking members of the community that mediums chant. Through their collective power, the mediums of a community construct an invisible wall around each of its component households. No single medium is strong enough to do this on his own. All adult men possess a familiar, although not all are equally powerful. The younger, less experienced mediums support the efforts of their elders, and only gradually acquire the ability to 'see' for themselves.

In order to understand what the Buid mean by 'seeing' and combating spirits, we must begin by examining in more detail the Buid concept of the person. In the second section, I describe the seance in all its varieties. In the third section, I contrast Buid spirit mediumship with 'shamanism' as practised elsewhere in Southeast Asia. Finally, I offer a few observations on the specificity of the Buid phenomena, attempting to clarify the concept of an egalitarian legitimation of belief. Mystical truth in Buid society is verified not by reference to a hierarchy of religious specialists or to received tradition, but by the personal experience of individuals caught up in collective ritual action. Because of this, there are broad differences of opinion concerning the detail of religious belief and much metaphysical speculation among those who are so inclined. There is no one with the authority to reach a final decision on such matters, but they are not felt to be of great practical importance anyway. What is felt to be important is that spirit mediums reach a consensus on what it is that they are fighting, and that there should be general agreement on the essentials of ritual practice. Beyond that, everyone is free to think what they wish.

The Buid concept of the person

A person is made up of three components: a physical body (*abilugan*), a soul or vital principle (*falad*) and a mind (*fangayufan*). The physical body is doomed to decay after death. As the Buid say, it then becomes the meat of the ghouls which infest graveyards. The body may also be attacked through its animating principle, the soul. While an individual is alive, the predatory spirits may bite, gnaw, stab or slash at the soul, causing it, and the body it inhabits, to weaken and eventually die. It is only when the soul departs from the body at death that the latter begins to corrupt and can be directly consumed by the spirits. The soul forms a sort of invisible double of the body, the latter reflecting the state of the former in visible form. The soul is said to reside in the upper torso and shoulders, and is the seat of the emotions. Buid describe an intense emotional state such as anger or jealousy in terms of the soul rising up from the chest into the neck. If it is not controlled, it issues forth in bitter words or violence.

The Buid have no notion of temporary soul loss: mystical damage is done to the soul while it is in the body. The Buid also have no concept of spirit possession: no more than one soul can inhabit a body at one time. Predatory spirits which have 'bitten' the soul of a person can be chased away, but they are never thought to have taken over the physical body. These facts have obvious implications for my discussion of spirit mediumship, for mediums are neither 'possessed' by their familiars, nor do they experience the mental dissociation often associated with 'soul loss'.[1]

The third component of the individual is the *fangayufan*, literally 'that which thinks' or 'thought (noun)'. I shall refer to it as the mind, with all the metaphysical overtones of the word. The mind is less closely associated with the body than is the soul, and is capable of detaching itself from the latter, or, rather, it is not thought of in terms of spatial localisation. The mind is associated with perception, especially hearing and sight, and with speech and understanding. The very old and the very young are thought to have a weaker mind than those in their prime, and are for this reason thought to be more vulnerable to all types of danger. Ordinarily, humans only see with the aid of an external source of light, such as the sun. During the night, they must rely on torches or on spirit familiars. It is the control of the mind over the emotions, the senses and language which gives an adult the power to master the physical and metaphysical environment. But the mind gradually weakens, and disappears at death. Unlike the soul, it does not survive in a new form.

The concept of mind is similar to a number of other reified mental processes which are formed in the Buid language by a process of adding affixes to root verbs, such as *sungun*, 'depression', *kasaya*, 'desire', *isug*, 'aggression', and so on. The beings referred to in these terms attack a victim's soul and must sometimes be driven off with an elaborate ritual of 'exorcism'. Of all the harmful mystical entities recognised by the Buid, only these beings are without a describable form. Like the mind, they are abstract in character. It was hard for me to tell whether the Buid meant such statements as *fansungun nangagat Agan*, 'a *fansungun* has bitten Agan', to be taken literally. What was clear was that undesirable mental states were often thought of as coming from outside the individual and could be rectified by chasing away the agency which caused them. The same ambiguity attaches to the concept of *fangayufan*. When a medium says *Angku fangayufan aglayug sas tungud, u nuglai, uglag ka labang glaw sas baba daga*, 'My mind flies up above when I chant, and I see the spirits walking on the earth below', it is not clear whether some mystical substance is supposed to leave the medium's body for the duration of the seance, or whether a simple extension of the medium's normal powers of perception is involved. In English we say 'my thoughts were far away' without intending to imply clairvoyance or astral projection. As we shall see, there are reasons to accept both the literal and the metaphorical interpretations of the statement.

The connection between mind, speech and perception can perhaps be made a little clearer by reference to the spirit familiars, the *lai*. The mind of the medium comes into contact with his *lai* by means of a specialised form of speech, the *lai*, meaning, in this case, 'a chant'. Thereafter, the medium operates through a heightened form of perception which allows him to 'see' in the dark and at a remove from his physical location. He does this in order to repel attacks which have been made on the souls of community members. In relation to the invisible world, the soul plays a passive role as victim, and the *fangayufan* an active role as protector. An ageing medium who is going deaf or blind loses the ability to chant and transfers his familiars to his wife. This is the only set of circumstances under which women can acquire familiars of their own.

The nature of the soul may also be explicated by a consideration of its spirit counterpart, the *labang taw*, 'human spirit or ghost', into which it is transformed at death. A ghost remains near its former body, which in normal cases is buried on a mountain peak, for three months after the death. In the case of a typical suicide, accomplished by hanging oneself from a tree in the forest, the body is not buried but left to rot where it hangs. Its soul is transformed into a *fanagbung*, 'that which has been hanged'. This spirit is characterised by an elongated neck, and must wander the earth for ever. Individuals who die by drowning are buried under a heap of stones by the river bank and are also thought not to make a successful transition to the underworld. These spirits are condemned to walk the earth, cold and damp, in a perpetual search for a fire to warm them. The ghosts of those who have received a proper burial eventually go to the underworld, where they lead a life similar to that of humans, but with a few inversions. Night and day are reversed for them: when it is night on earth, it is day in the underworld. They can see only in the dark and sleep suspended from the roofs of their houses like bats. But they have their own swiddens, and grow their own crops. The one thing they lack is meat and this they beg from their surviving relatives and friends. They may speak to the latter in dreams, or cause them to fall ill so that their desires are ascertainable only through a medium. In particular, they may demand that any pigs they owned at the time of their death be sacrificed for them. Ghosts are regarded as being especially greedy and possessive in general. Aside from periodic demands for meat, they strongly oppose the remarriage of a surviving spouse. Two women in Ayufay remained unmarried for more than two years for this reason, although they were not yet fifty years old. One of them had been married to a 'Bangun', noted in life for his black magic and aggressive behaviour. The other wanted to marry a man whose wife was the sister of the dead husband of the first woman. There was another case in which a young man was forced to pay compensation to the ghost of his fiancée's dead husband. This marriage was successfully completed as the ghost involved did not have a reputation for jealous behaviour. Some ghosts are regarded as being relatively well disposed toward the living, but not as being a source of positive good. They are merely less of a nuisance than the aggressive ones, and must still be fed.

In summary, ghosts are thought of as putting their own desires ahead of those of the living and of being capable of causing illness and even death to achieve their ends. A ghost is, in fact, a soul which has been deprived of the controlling agency of the mind which recognises social responsibility. It is significant that it intervenes in the world of the living in precisely those areas of communal sharing which form the basis of Buid social solidarity: the sharing of meat and of spouses. Their behaviour represents an inversion of the moral ideal that one should give meat and accept it only as the unsought consequence of someone else's ritual activity. Instead they demand meat and cause rituals to be performed. Rather than simply surrendering a spouse they no longer need, they are capable of causing the death of a living rival.[2]

The minds of adult Buid must control the souls of individuals at all four stages of the life cycle. The souls of the very young think only of themselves, demanding food and attention without being able to offer anything in return. Their minds are incapable of resisting the attacks of the reified emotions. The souls of adults remain a source of violent emotion, which threatens to rise up and cause aggression against their own bodies or those of others. The very old again become dependent on others, and must be fed and clothed while they live, lest their ghost take vengeance after they have died. Finally, the ghosts themselves must be controlled by the minds of adults with the aid of familiars. The soul is both subject to the aggression of the predatory spirits and a source of aggression within the visible world. Its capacity for causing harm to others steadily increases as an individual matures, reaching a peak after death. As we shall see in the next chapter, desire and aggression are thought of as necessary but distasteful conditions of life. Individual needs and desires must be satisfied in a controlled manner, dependent on cooperation with others. This is obviously true in the case of sexual needs, whose gratification is almost by definition social, and which is in any case subject to the intervention of the whole community in *tultulan*. It is also true of the need for food, the production and consumption of which are social acts. This is especially true in the case of meat. In this sense, individual desire, and the soul from which it arises, is always subordinate to and dependent on society and the minds of which society is composed.

The power of speech is characteristic of the mind as the social aspect of the person, while the need for food is characteristic of the soul as the anti-social source of individual needs and desires. This dichotomy is illustrated by the structure of Buid ritual, in that spirit mediumship is based on the mastery of a specialised form of speech, the chant, which allows for heightened communication with the spirit world, while sacrifice is based on the use of food to appease the anti-social desires of the ghosts. With this background, we may now turn to a more detailed consideration of what goes on in a seance.

The seance

Lai are described as spirits with a human form who dwell at the places of the rising and setting sun. The sun must pass through a hole at the edge of the world where the sky meets the earth. This is also the dwelling place of the *afu daga*, the 'owners of the earth', who will be discussed in the next chapter. *Lai* have the power of flight and, like all spirits, the ability to see in the dark. Every medium possesses at least one and possibly four or more *lai*. They are summoned by a chant, also called a *lai*, peculiar to each. The medium himself is called a *fanlaian*, 'place of the *lai*', and the holding of a seance *aglai*, 'to chant'. When a medium says *U e ufwatak lai*, 'I have four *lai*', he may mean equally that he knows four different chants or that he possesses four different familiars. Every medium who chants frequently has a stake lashed to the threshold of his house, with the wing feathers of a domestic chicken attached to it at the top. This is in order to guide the *lai*, as it leaps from peak to peak on its journey from the place of the rising or setting sun to the house of the medium. On important occasions a fresh chicken may be sacrificed, and its wing feathers lashed to the threshold to ensure the appearance of the *lai* in the right house. I will reserve my discussion of this portion of the seance to the next chapter.

All adult Buid men know at least one chant, but some households normally rely on the services of a medium from another household who is known to have a more powerful familiar. Mediums receive no compensation for their efforts on behalf of others, but they must be given a string of white beads about seven centimetres in length. This is hung by the medium on his shoulder bag during the seance and is afterwards taken home and hung on the wall of his house. A medium who is in great demand can be identified by the number of strings of beads hanging on his walls. These strings serve to identify the intended beneficiary of the seance and allow the medium to conduct the seance in his own house if he wishes instead of spending the night away from home. When mediums do chant away from home, the familiar is able to follow these beads back to the house of the medium at the end of the seance. Without this guide, a familiar might become disorientated and remain behind in the house of the beneficiary.

In a settlement the size of Ugun Liguma, i.e. one containing about twenty-five households, someone will be chanting almost every night. Often there will be no specific reason for the seance, a medium merely desiring to have a look round to see if anything dangerous is in the vicinity. In this case, he will chant quietly by himself in his own house, occasionally drifting off to sleep, waking up, and beginning to chant again. A medium begins by calling his familiar with a *kss kss* sound. He sits upright, swaying his body slowly back and forth (*agliglig*). He begins to hum his chant quietly under his breath. I was never able to get a medium to tell me the words of his chant, because, I suspect, each chant can belong to only one medium at a time. Chants are made up of short verses muttered under the breath, followed by longer periods of humming. During the periods of humming, the vocal chords are made to vibrate with each exhalation in such a way as to produce a deep sonorant sound of varying pitch. Less experienced mediums are apt to chant too vigorously and get themselves out of breath, much to the amusement of the more highly practised. A good medium should be able to keep it up for hours on end. It may be quite a while before the familiar actually arrives. Once it has done so, the chant must be continued for as long as the medium is in touch with it. After a while, the medium may lie down and continue in a more relaxed manner. There is absolutely nothing ecstatic or unusual about the behaviour of a medium during a seance. He is neither possessed, nor does he lose hold of his soul or rational faculties. From time to time, he may break off his chanting to inform the others present of what he has seen, where it is, how dangerous it is and so on. When this happens, the others pay close attention, but for the most part they occupy themselves with other tasks, gossip quietly, or simply go off to sleep. Chanting is such a natural part of everyday life that it causes no great disruption in and of itself. Indeed, I believe that the absence of chanting for too many nights in a row would cause greater agitation than does its performance. Anxiety is caused not by chanting, which brings a feeling of security, but by the beings which cause seances to be held. If someone is seriously ill or has recently died, large groups of mediums gather together in the afflicted house. On such occasions, the non-chanters will remain in a state of alertness because of their fear of the evil spirits which are roaming about the neighbourhood.

The mediums describe their experience during a seance as follows. After they have been chanting for a while, they begin to sense the location of their familiar in the distance. Usually they described it as leaping towards them from mountain peak to mountain peak, but I was once told that a familiar was long in arriving because it had to travel down through all the underworlds (there are six levels) and then down through all the upperworlds (six more) before it would reach the house. When the familiar has entered the house, the mind of the medium 'climbs on its back', and together they soar up into the sky. Mediums compare their ability to see in the darkness to the powerful headlights on the lorry of a logging company. The medium scans the ground with these beams until he locates an evil spirit. The beams lock on to the spirit and begin to push it away with an invisible force, likened by the Buid to a strong wind. Only the most experienced mediums are able to see the evil spirits themselves. Younger mediums must be chanting with a more powerful one in order to catch a glimpse of the spirits 'over the shoulder' of the senior mediums. It is said that certain very powerful mediums can see spirits even in the day, but that to chant while the sun is up is extremely dangerous.

A medium faces many dangers, especially when chanting alone. He may encounter a spirit endowed with the power of flight which is able to fly higher than his familiar and to throw a blanket over the latter's head. As the power of the familiar rests on its extraordinary powers of perception, this blinding will cause it to lose control and plummet to earth together with the medium. If such a spirit is encountered, the medium must immediately break off the seance and wait until he can assemble a group of more powerful mediums. The less experienced mediums never chant alone because of the feebleness of their vision, but serve in a supporting role to the more adept. Certain mediums habitually chant together, especially those who stand in a mentor-pupil relationship. A familiar cannot be transferred to a new owner all at once. It takes years before a man and, in rare instances, a woman, has enough control over a familiar to be able to 'see' spirits. It is for this reason that a man often gets his familiar from his father. This is not due to a rule of inheritance, but to the long period of cooperation required for training. A man may instead acquire a familiar from his father-in-law or other close friend of the senior generation if the familiars of his own father are not very powerful. In the case of a woman who has lived for many years with one husband, she may take over the latter's familiar when he begins to lose his senses of sight and hearing. Although no formal training is involved in these cases, pro-longed co-residence seems to be enough in itself to effect the transfer.

I encountered few households in which no one had a familiar. Two such households contained only elderly widows and seven contained young bachelors or newly married couples. There were four house-holds in which old women had gained control of their husbands' respective familiars. Of the remaining seventeen households in Ugun Liguma, each had a resident male medium. Of these, perhaps six could be regarded as master mediums, able to chant and 'see' on their own. Significantly, none of the men in Agaw's cluster (A and B, see Figure 1) could be so regarded. They chanted discreetly on occasion, but seemed to regard chanting as being somewhat incompatible with their innovatory role in the community. They tended to call in other mediums when a member of their household was ill. Three of the master mediums used to chant regularly together. Of these, the two most powerful were part of Cluster F, the cluster which had the least to do with lowland affairs and which seldom expressed an opinion on them in political meetings. Two of the master mediums belonged to Cluster C, the full-sibling group mentioned above (p. 104) which constituted the core of resistance to Agaw's leadership. They tended to chant only for the members of their own cluster.

Large-scale seances are held in the event of serious illness or emotional disturbance, but they are absolutely essential in the wake of a death. In that event up to a dozen master mediums drawn from all the communities in a region will be called together to chant in a series of seances designed to drive off the predatory spirits which have been attracted by the smell of the decaying corpse. As funerary practices are covered in the next chapter, I will confine myself to noting the necessity of large-scale seances as part of them at this point. During one post-mortem seance, mediums from five of the six communities in the Ayufay region attended, including the political leaders of four of them. Twenty different spirits were sighted and driven away in the course of the night. The spirits were attempting to creep down the mountain from the graveyard and attack the living members of the settlement. What was most extraordinary during this, and other large-scale seances, was the fact that all the mediums seemed to maintain a complete unanimity of opinion as to the identity and location of the enemy spirits, without any one of them actually directing the proceedings. To the naive observer, everything appeared to be conducted in perfect anarchy. On closer inspection, however, it became apparent that this unanimity was being constructed in an extremely subtle way.

Large-scale seances begin with much confusion, as mediums from distant settlements slowly gather in the house of the afflicted family, after having eaten in their own homes. Each medium receives a string of beads and attaches it to his shoulder bag. Before getting down to chanting, there is a good deal of joking, gossiping and recitation of poetry, the normal concomitants of any large Buid gathering. The gathering has no spatial focus. Some mediums may sit facing the wall, others may lie stretched out on the floor. Each must call his own familiar individually. They begin to do so one by one, without taking any notice of the fact that late-comers may still be climbing into the house and trying to find a bit of unoccupied floor space. In contrast to the smaller gatherings of mediums, where one individual is usually acknowledged to be the most experienced and acts as seer for the others, the majority of mediums in a large gathering will be able to see the spirits for themselves. They all spend the first one or two hours in making contact with their familiars and only gradually does the commotion settle down as people become preoccupied with the invisible world.

After a time, a medium will spot an enemy spirit, and will pause in his chanting to let the others know what and where it is. If a medium is chanting alone, he may wait until the next day to tell others what he saw the night before. If there is a large group, however, it is important that everyone be informed of possible dangers. A typical interchange might run as follows: '*Sama, uglag labang babuy sem buid.*' '*Ala, sama, adawa kati?*' '*Glaw as Binagaw, daul fag babuy*' – '*Sama*, I see a pig spirit uphill.' 'Yes, *sama*, where is it going?' 'It's walking toward the Binagaw river, it's a big one.' And so on. The location and direction of travel of spirits are of the utmost importance. The mediums are building up a mental map of the current distribution of hostile beings. Buid spirit mediumship does not involve the travel of the medium to a supernatural world. It remains firmly based on the everyday topography of the human world. It is the spirits who are thought to be intruding into the human world from their normal habitats and who must be driven back. Gradually, the group of mediums begin to arrive at a consensus concerning the nature and location of their opponents. While every medium reports to the others what he is seeing, the testimony of the most powerful mediums is given greater weight.

The communication that goes on between mediums in a seance is similar to that which I have described in other social settings. Individuals sit facing away from one another and speak to no one in particular, expecting a response only from those auditors who are in agreement with them. No one is obliged to accept the word of another that a certain spirit is actually in the area, but in the highly-charged setting of a large-scale seance, the other mediums do actually begin to see the same spirits. Working by suggestion rather than command, the senior mediums are able to provide a focus without appearing to do so. The fact that mediums are able to 'see' the same invisible beings lends an air of intersubjective validity to what is occurring in their several minds. It really does seem as if the spirits are walking about out there, lingering by a particular stream or tree that one knows intimately, creeping up towards the house and even biting the soul of someone who is in the room. I shall give an example from my field notes.

Gay-an and Gaynu first sighted a *fangablang*, a giant Christian spirit, behind our house. He was carrying a gun, a tin can, and he had a dog as big as a water buffalo at his side. Their familiar drove him down toward Ikoy's house by the river, then down through his fields, across the river to Celso's house, and up the mountain on the other side. At this point Ruhi, my wife, said that she had seen the spirits since they had reached Ikoy's house, and that the *fangablang* had had difficulty crossing the river because his dog had held him back. After crossing the river, she said that the *fangablang* had paused to decide whether to go down the road toward Nati's house or up into the mountains. Finally, it had gone so far away that she lost sight of it. Gay-an confirmed the fact that the dog had hesitated at the river, and the fact that it had disappeared, but said this was only because it had gone behind a mountain range. Gaynu speculated that it had followed Agaw back from across the river when he returned three days ago from Batangan. Next, they saw a *labang manuk*, a predatory bird spirit, near Mayun-ay's house, and two more *fangablang* near Malam-ay's house. The bird spirit was forced to land in Gaynu's ploughed field, but Ruhi thought she saw it flying toward Ayufay. Finally, a flying spirit was sighted that was too strong for the mediums' familiars. Gaynu and Gay-an abruptly broke off the seance, saying they would need Ligday's help to deal with it.

Chanting normally continues until dawn, and the exhausted mediums spend the next day lounging about at home and napping.

The mediums and their familiars are unable to destroy the evil spirits they encounter. The most they can do is drive them away from a particular settlement, which often has the effect of driving them into a neighbouring settlement. If this happens very often, the mediums of both settlements must get together, to drive the spirits off in another direction (see below, p. 208). The mediums work to construct an invisible wall around each house which the spirits cannot enter. Medicines may be placed around the posts that support the house to provide added protection.[3] None of these expedients provides a permanent defence against the predatory spirits. They require constant reinforcement. It is the sense of constant vulnerability to the intrusion of alien beings which gives a Buid community a sense of interdependence, and a concern with maintaining the spatial integrity of their bodies, houses and settlements. Aside from the intrusive spirits which invade Buid houses and bite their inhabitants, there are other spirits which keep to their own territory and attack humans only when they trespass on it.

The Buid occupy two interpenetrating worlds. The visible world of the daytime is devoted to getting a living, and is populated by humans, animals and plants. The invisible world of the night is devoted to a continuous struggle against the predatory spirit world and is populated by a host of normally invisible beings. Buid religion does not relate to extraordinary events occurring in remote times and places, but to issues of everyday health and well-being. To conclude this description of the Buid seance, I shall briefly list the chief attributes of the predatory spirits most commonly sighted during seances.

Predatory spirits commonly encountered during a seance
Perhaps the most common spirit visitor is the *labang taw*, or ghost, which I will discuss in the next chapter. Other spirits with a human form are as follows:

1   *Taw ugbut*, 'little men'. These are the agents of witchcraft. They are said to be about 15 centimetres in height and to operate in pairs.
2   *Malawan*, 'those who walk'. These live in springs in the deep forest, away from all human habitation, and generally keep to themselves. Attacks by them are relatively rare and occur when a human invades their territory by accident. They harm their victims by stabbing their soul with a bush knife. This is nearly always fatal. Chanting against them may have to be reinforced by a *saysayan*, 'swinging pig', ritual (see Chapter 7). They are described as ugly and aggressive beings 'like the Bangun'.
3   *Taw gubat*, 'jungle men'. These also live in the deep forest, ambushing their victims at night on the trail. Their stab wounds are fatal and are blamed for many deaths. They are also likened to the Bangun.
4   *Fangablang*, 'those who are encountered'. These are the most

common, and the most feared of the predatory human spirits. Unlike the *taw gubat* and the *malawan*, they are cannibals who do not merely attack their victims, but eat their souls and desire the flesh of their corpses. They go in search of prey and will come right up to people's houses. They attack with bush knives, stick or fists. They live mostly in graveyards. There is a myth which describes their origins.

Long ago the earth was so thickly populated one couldn't sleep for the noise made by one's neighbours. In those days the *fangablang* were visible just like ordinary men. They were transformed into cannibals when a great flood came and extinguished their cooking fires and they were forced to eat their meat raw. Two human brothers, Kasinan and Kulindas, returned home one day to find that the *fangablang* had eaten all their children. Kulindas retaliated by imprisoning most of the *fangablang* beneath the roots of the giant fig tree (*baliti*). The rest he surrounded in a field of spear grass, to the perimeter of which he set fire. All the *fangablang* perished except for two small children, which he trapped in an *ufitan* (chicken cage). He carefully left it in his house, but it was near some embers which burnt a hole in the side, allowing the captives to escape. From this pair of children all the *fangablang* are now descended, except for those freed by the felling of fig trees. Kulindas was killed in the end by *fangablang*. His brother Kasinan was afraid, so he summoned his five *lai* familiars. Together they picked up his house and flew away with it. They flew for five days, travelling first to the east, then to the west, then to the north, until finally they flew out of the world altogether. Since that time, the *fangablang* have been visible only to the *lai*.

Fangablang are described as being giants, two metres tall and as resembling ugly and ferocious Christians.

5 *Bulaw*, 'shooting stars'. These live in mountain peaks, and are also cannibals. A shooting star is said to be a *bulaw* flying from one mountain peak to another, lighting its way with a torch made from a human bone. They are very fierce and afraid of no one. They are also very beautiful, especially the women, who may entrap their victims by appearing to men in the forest and luring them deeper and deeper into it, until they grab them and eat them. The *bulaw* are said to be 'like Christians'.

In addition to spirits with a human form, there are a number of animal spirits, the most common of which have the form of those wild animals which regularly invade human territory. These are:

6   *Labang babuy*, 'spirit pig'. Spirit pigs prey on the souls of humans. The physical symptoms of such attack are a wasting away of the body, caused by the pig's gnawing on the victim's soul.
7   *Labang manuk*, 'spirit bird'. These cause illnesses of the upper body, such as influenza and headache. They have the form of a bird of prey, of the type which carries off domesticated chickens.
8   *Labang imuk*, 'spirit monkey'. These cause both deafness and kleptomania in their victims.

Along with the *fangablang*, these spirit animals tend to congregate in large numbers in graveyards when they are not on the look-out for living victims. The Buid say that all the spirits which regard humans as food gather together to feast on the corpse of a recently-dead Buid. *Manga taw ka babuy an labang* – 'Humans are the pigs of the predatory spirits.' Several more exotic types of animal spirit were sighted during one large-scale seance after a death. These included the *labang* of three Christian domesticated animals: a water buffalo, a horse and a cat. I shall go into the significance of Buid animal categories as they relate to spirit beliefs in the next chapter.

I have already mentioned the formless spirits which represent reified emotions. It was sometimes unclear to me whether these were always distinct from the spirits listed above, or whether another type of spirit, particularly the *taw ugbut*, could also be referred to by the emotional ailment it caused. For example, I was once told that a child had been bitten by a *fangugyab*, 'that which causes crying', which was in fact a *taw ugbut* sent by the *labang taw*, 'ghost', of its grandfather. The potential complexity of a diagnosis can be seen from this case. This is an important point, for it means that spirit mediums enjoy a great deal of freedom in their diagnosis of the cause of an illness. Anticipating the argument of Chapter 8 somewhat, it may be said that spirit mediums are able to reinterpret accusations of witchcraft in order to transfer culpability from a human to a neutral spirit source which represents an equal threat to the members of both factions in a quarrel. The imaginary function of mediation which spirit mediums perform in relation to the spirit world can become a real function of mediation within the human community. Their role has become increasingly distinguished from that of political leaders, and it is their very neutrality in political disputes which allows them to bring about a reconciliation between opposing factions by manipulating their contact with the spirit world. This role differentiation may be brought out more clearly by comparing the Buid medium with the Taubuid shaman, who combines the role of shaman with that of political leader, and who does not hesitate to use witchcraft to gain his ends.

Shamanism among the Taubuid

While there is a rough hierarchy among Buid mediums, power as a medium confers no prestige on an individual outside the context of a seance. Up-river Buid have a reputation for great control over the invisible world. Exaggerated stories circulate concerning the ambiguous powers of 'Bangun' mediums. Some are said to be in possession of certain white stones which they have found in mountain springs. These give them the power of *tarubung*, the ability to enter mountain peaks through springs and to travel by the subterranean paths of the *andagaw*, covering enormous distances in an instant.[4]

According to Pennoyer: 'The neighbouring tribes recognize that the Taubuid possess strong cursing abilities and if a person dies while a Taubuid is visiting their area, the visitor is generally accused of the death' (1980b: 706). This was certainly true in Ayufay, where several deaths were blamed on Taubuid men thought to be in control of witchcraft, or on the ghosts of 'Bangun' men and women. I shall go into these particular accusations in Chapter 8. Bangun mediums certainly play on the fears aroused by their reputation for black magic. Both Kikuchi (1971) and Pennoyer (1975) report the existence of hereditary leaders of Taubuid hamlets called *magurang*, 'elders'. They are said to possess the rights of usufruct over an area of land initially cleared by their ancestors. 'There may be several hamlets in such a local territory and the occupants are all related to the hereditary leader or have chosen to be subordinate to him' (Pennoyer, 1975: 93). He can demand a share of his followers' crops, that they work on his fields, and he is often the only person who speaks Tagalog.

> He may also be a powerful shaman who has a large ritual practice and enforces his edicts through fear and witchcraft.
> Traditionally, the overseer probably acted as the *balianan* [shaman], and his family functioned as the repository of certain ritual knowledge, e.g. witchcraft, which could be implemented by

them as a protective device for the whole group when strangers approached or used to maintain the *balianan's* control over his subordinates. (ibid.: 97)

I bring up the case of the Taubuid for two reasons. In the first place they provide a strong contrast to the egalitarian values and organisation of Buid society, and so help to illuminate the latter. In the second place, they are the neighbours of the Buid, and the Buid themselves define their values in opposition to those of the Taubuid. While one must treat with caution some of the statements of Pennoyer's informants, given that they were recent converts to Christianity anxious to play up the evils of the 'pagan' past, one does gain an overall impression from his material of a society deeply divided by fear of outsiders, spirits and witchcraft.

While the Taubuid are afraid of strangers from the lowlands, they are also apprehensive about other Taubuid, including the members of their hamlet. In a sense, this is a fear of the *bara* ['eternal spirits'] which humans can order to assassinate other people. Most of the *famalabag* [protection] rituals, such as the spirit trail blocks, also double as devices to ward off curses and send back the *bara* to the one who is attempting the curse. (Pennoyer, 1980b: 707)

Now, the Buid also believe that certain people are in possession of what they call *taw ugbut*, 'little men', a sort of perverted spirit familiar, which allows them to cause illness or death to others by mystical means. Some examples of such accusations are given in Chapter 8. But the accused are almost always from up-river and have strong Taubuid connections. It is a kind of power thought to be contrary to all Buid norms of conduct. Accusations are made when social relations are strained, and are usually withdrawn when good relations are restored. At that point, an alternative, socially neutral explanation is put forward (see Chapter 8). Taubuid mediums, on the contrary, play up their reputation for sorcery, as we have seen in the case of Miun, and use it to coerce others (see Chapter 5).

This leads us to the heart of the contrast between the two groups. The Taubuid appear to have always had a hierarchy of leaders who combined both mystical and political powers, and who used the former to back up the latter.

While each hamlet may still have a hereditary overseer, these are subordinate to the territorial leader and act as his henchmen. The territorial big men are generally overseers who through their ability as shamans or spokesmen have extended their influence beyond their local hamlet. Among the Eastern Taubuid there are six or seven such men and boundaries are fluid as each seeks to enlarge his sphere of influence by attracting new members. . . . Sumsumagang claims to be the leader of all the Taubuid and his orders are carried out by his underlings; his power reaches from the interior to the lower Taubuid hamlets. (Pennoyer, 1975: 94)

Pennoyer describes Taubuid shamans (to use his term) as 'proud persons with a strong desire for power that borders on megalomania' (1975: 96). By contrast, the most powerful mediums in Ayufay were shy and retiring men who took little part in community politics. A Buid medium gains respect by helping others without displaying any self-interest. Taubuid shamans boast of their ability to practise witchcraft and sorcery, while the Buid regard such practices as the most shameful thing imaginable (Pennoyer, 1980b: 706).

It is difficult to know from Pennoyer's material just how much real power the interior 'shamans' in fact possess over their subordinates, or how long they have had it. One sometimes has the impression that the edicts of the shaman living 'two mountain ranges, a big river and many kilometers away' were merely used as an excuse by Taubuid who did not wish to cooperate with the anthropologist anyway (Pennoyer, 1978: 53). Similar stories have been told by other Protestant missionaries in Mindoro (Stickley, 1975: 87, 210). However, the shamans do seem to attempt to monopolise all contact with the outside world, including all trade and wage labour (Pennoyer, 1975: 93; 1978). In contrast to the current situation among the Buid, where the leader with the most contact with the lowlands has the most power, among the Taubuid it appears that the most powerful man is the one in the interior with the least contact. A power hierarchy appears to be an integral part of Taubuid society, and it is one of the reasons why the Buid fear and despise them so much. As the Buid say of themselves *kebi mi dye gurangun*, 'in past times we had no great men'. So while some mediums are known to be more powerful than others among the Buid, they do not use their mystical power to advance their material situation. The hierarchy which is now growing up in Buid society has an entirely different basis. In Ayufay there is, for the time being, a rough balance between those who have power through their contacts with the spirit world and those who have power through their contacts with the lowland world. It is easy to see, however, the way in which two sorts of power might come to be identified in areas where the influence of the lowland world is less significant.

It is very rare for a Buid to seek the help of a Taubuid shaman because of the ambiguous nature of the latter's power. Normally one seeks help from the most powerful medium in the community, or, if that proves unsuccessful, in the region. When outside mediums are called in, they are always joined by a group of local mediums. The collective nature of large-scale seances serves to dilute the prestige which attaches to any individual who participates in them. Strength comes from numbers, and this is made evident following a death when the predatory spirits are present in great numbers and only a multiplicity of familiars can drive them all away. The unique features of Buid spirit mediumship stand out even more sharply if they are placed within a wider, regional context.

Shamanism in Southeast Asia

There is a vast body of literature on shamanism in Southeast Asia. The Taubuid word for shaman, *balianan*, is clearly cognate with the word for shaman among the Hanunoo of Mindoro (Conklin, 1955a: 235); the Tagbanuwa and Palawan of Palawan (Fox, 1954: 213; Macdonald, 1973: 11); the Sulod of Panay (Jocano, 1968: 31); the Tiruray and Subanun of Mindanao (Schlegel, 1970: 24; Finley, 1913: 33); the Malays and some Negrito groups of the Malay peninsula (Endicott, 1970: 17; Evans, 1937: 190); and the Ngaju, Tempasuk Dusun, Maloh and Melanau of Borneo (Scharer, 1963: 43; Evans, 1953: 43; King, 1976: 129; Morris, 1967: 198). Clearly we are in the presence of a deeply-rooted institution found throughout the central Malaysian area, almost as characteristic as bilateral kinship. My intention here is not to conduct a systematic comparison between the forms and functions of shamanism in all of these societies, but to place the Buid within a regional context. Most of the features commonly attributed to the institution of shamanism in Southeast Asia are absent among the Buid. This suggests that Buid religion has undergone a specialised transformation in which mystical power has come to be equally dis-tributed among adult males. The reader may have remarked that I have carefully avoided applying the term 'shaman' to the Buid *fanlaian*, the most commonly used label in the literature for those who have regular and controlled contact with the spirit world.

One of the earliest writers to use the term in a Malaysian context was Winstedt, who explicitly compared Malay seances with those performed by Siberian shamans:

> The main tasks of the Siberian shaman are healing and divination. His familiar spirit or spirits, possessing him their medium, descend at a *seance* to cure the sick, foretell the future or answer enquiries. By auto-suggestion the shaman falls into a trance and is possessed by spirits who speak through his mouth. All these are features of the Malay *seance*, which resembles that of the Mongol shaman even in the details of ritual: the beating of a tambourine, wild singing, the rustle and voices of invisible spirits, the expulsion or sucking out of the spirit of diseases, the medium on return to consciousness oblivious of what has passed, the offerings made to spirits. (Winstedt, 1925: 96)

This is an admirably succinct account of a prototypical shamanistic ceremony, in which trance, or, as another author puts it, ecstatic behaviour, appears to be a key element (Lewis, 1971). This definition according to trance, or an altered 'psychic state', is followed by Jensen writing on the Iban *manang* (Jensen, 1974: 142). Firth, on the other hand, does not see trance as essential, so long as the shaman 'is thought to control spirits by ritual techniques'. He is a 'master of spirits' (Firth, 1964: 248). Firth is followed in this definition by Morris in his account of the Melanau *a-bayoh* (Morris, 1967: 198). Lewis develops Firth's emphasis on shamans as masters of spirits, and sees them as individuals who have gone through an initial period of involuntary possession, only to reach an ultimate understanding with their possessing familiars:

> the shaman's vocation is normally announced by an initially un-controlled state of possession: a traumatic experience associated with hysteroid, ecstatic behaviour. This, I think, is a universal feature in the assumption of shamanistic roles and is even present, though in muted form, when they pass from one kinsman to another. Thus, in the case of those who persist in the shamanistic calling, the uncontrol-led, unsolicited, initial possession leads to a state where possession can be controlled and can be turned on and off at will in shamanistic seances. (Lewis, 1971: 55)

There is some evidence for this kind of scenario in Southeast Asia, but most of the evidence points towards a deliberate attempt by would-be shamans to acquire familiars through the practice of austerities (Atkinson, 1979: 135–8; Evans, 1953: 43; Jensen, 1974: 143; Endicott, 1970: 15; but see also Macdonald, 1981 for an account of unsolicited possession among the Palawan, and Scharer, 1963: 133 for such possession among the Ngaju). The authors emphasise that while one may seek, few are chosen, and the emphasis in most societies possessing *balianan* or their equivalents is on the special nature of the communication which occurs between the shaman and the spirit world, a communication from which most members of society are excluded.

In line with the special status accorded to the shaman, seances tend to be characterised by the construction of a special sacred place, and the ritual by a set of initial and concluding rituals which mark out a special sacred time. The audience is given evidence of the shaman's contact with the spirit world in the form of the latter's erratic and abnormal behaviour when in trance. Malay shamans are associated with tigers, as 'the two creatures hold similar positions in their respective societies, one being the most powerful (or dangerous) of men, and the other the same for the jungle beasts' (Endicott, 1970: 22). At a certain point in the seance,

> the shaman begins to twitch and then rises up, 'possessed' by the tiger-spirit. Growls are heard, and the [shaman] begins to scratch the floor, leap around, and lick up the rice on the floor. He then stoops forward and licks the body of the patient all over, as a tigress might lick her cub. (Endicott, 1970: 163, quoting Skeat; see also Karim, 1981: 179; and Winstedt, 1925: 98, 100)

The shaman may be compared to a king – 'one being supreme in relations with the supernatural and the other in relations among men' (Endicott, 1970: 13) – or to 'low-level functionaries in a hierarchy of cosmic administration ultimately under Allah' (Kessler, 1977: 322). Many of the other societies I have mentioned also attach importance to the privileged nature of the shaman as seer of the invisible, manifested in public as an ability to go into trance (Macdonald, 1973; Jocano, 1968: 262–3; Atkinson, 1979: 119; Jensen, 1974: 149; Evans, 1953: 45; 1937: 194).

In my description of the Buid seance, I have tried to stress the extreme simplicity of the ritual paraphernalia, the lack of abnormal behaviour on the part of the spirit mediums, and the matter of fact manner in which seances are conducted. Buid are not initiated into mediumship either through unsolicited possession or illness, mediums are not set apart from their fellows as beings endowed with unique gifts or personalities, and they do not experience dramatically altered states of consciousness. As these features are so widely associated with what has been described as shamanism in Southeast Asia, I have thought it better to refer to Buid *fanlaian* simply as mediums. According to Firth's definition, they are shamans in that they do have mastery over certain spirits: but since this is true of most adult men, to call them all shamans would do violence to Firth's intention of identifying by the term only those having 'prime authority' in ritual proceedings (1967: 199). No one in Buid society has such authority. Each medium controls his own familiar and is able to control adversary spirits only with the help of other, equal, mediums.

The Buid are familiar with the term *balianan*, but say that it describes a phenomenon found only among the Taubuid. They clearly associate the excessive power of Taubuid shamans over the invisible world with their ability to control men through the practice of sorcery. A similar ambiguity in attitudes toward the power of shamans is also found among the Melanau of Sarawak and the Wana of Sulawesi (Morris, 1967: 204; Atkinson, 1979: 120). The Buid associate sorcery with a distinct type of familiar, the *taw ugbut*, whose possession is normally attributed only to those with Taubuid connections. The *lai* familiars are believed to be incapable of being used to harm other humans, and draw their power from the spirits of the earth, which are wholly good.

The closest parallel to the Buid system of spirit mediumship that I have found in Southeast Asia is that presented in Endicott's description of the Lebir Batek of Malaya.

For the Lebir Batek, being a shaman is not a special status but merely a potentiality which is more or less developed by every individual . . . most of the adult men and many of the women are considered shamans to some degree. The role of shaman is just one of many social roles played by the average mature Batek; it does not set one off as a special type of person. . . . The shaman or his assistant sings of the exploits of the shaman's shadow-soul and the rest of the people sing along, following his lead. They vicariously participate in the experiences described in the song, and some people claim that the shadow-souls of everyone on the platform accompany that of the shaman on its journey. In this way the imaginary experience of visiting the *hala' 'asal* is shared by the whole group. (1979: 129, 131, 154)

Significantly, the Lebir Batek are also the most egalitarian of the societies I have been discussing, and this point brings us to the subject of the last section of this chapter: the nature of religious authority in Buid society. As Kessler has pointed out, Malay shamans operate within the context of a world religion, which draws its primary authority from a sacred text, and of a hierarchical political tradition, which provides the dominant symbolism of power for ritual practitioners (Kessler, 1977). In the non-literate, non-centralised societies of Borneo, which are nevertheless characterised by an internal stratification into aristocrats, commoners and slaves, ritual authority derives from oral tradition, from the memorisation of long sacred chants, legends and rites (Scharer, 1963: 40–54; Evans, 1953: 50–3; Morris, 1967: 190, 207; King, 1976: 127, 129). The difference between shamans in these stratified societies and priests is that the former are also believed to derive at least some of their knowledge and power from direct personal experience of the supernatural. They legitimate their position not only by their knowledge of tradition, but also by their demonstrated ability to achieve an altered state of consciousness, and to express that ability in public performances. In societies where shamanism is the province of the few, such external signs of authenticity are required. The question of authenticity does not arise in the same way among the Buid. Everything happens as if the mediums view a shared supernatural reality which is potentially accessible to any male interested enough in acquiring a familiar. Women also have this opportunity under certain conditions and they are never excluded from observing the external actions of a seance.

The egalitarian legitimation of belief

The core of Buid religion is made up of the collectively validated experiences of the several participants in ritual activities, of which the most frequent is the seance. The necessity for creating a consensus among a large group of mediums, none of whom has a qualitatively different kind of access to the spirit world, leads to a relative simplicity in Buid representations of its inhabitants. All are closely modelled on empirical beings and inhabit the same physical terrain as the humans they attack (see below, pp. 194–200). Shamanistic 'trips' in other societies frequently involve the shaman in an extended journey through a mythological terrain and a series of encounters with fabulous creatures, which are related to a passive audience either during or after the shaman's trance. Buid mediums communicate with one another and with those who are not themselves chanting during a seance in order to help the former see and fight what they are seeing and so as not to exclude the latter from participation. They do not seek to emphasise the uniqueness of their own powers, nor do they represent themselves as controlling all access to the spirit world. Buid mediums do not serve as vessels through which the spirits speak to a larger audience, for they are not 'possessed' by alien powers. Because they are held to remain in full control of themselves throughout a seance, they are given no licence to behave in an unusual, much less anti-social, way. Seances may be used as a neutral forum for the resolution of social tensions not because the mediums become dissociated from their ordinary selves, as has been argued by Kessler for the Malays, and by Lewis more generally, but because they achieve a consensus of opinion which transcends factional affiliation. I shall return to this point in Chapter 8. Indeed, as I have shown in the first part of this chapter, ecstatic trance would be completely out of place in a Buid seance, given their view of the soul and emotions as the source of aggression and vulnerability to aggression by spirits. Seances are intended to re-establish control by the mind and society over the unruly behaviour of ghosts, cannibalistic spirits and wilful souls.

It is not simply the egalitarian values of Buid society which limit competition and exhibition among mediums, but the fact that it is a society which believes itself to be under constant siege by predatory spirits. Collective vigilance and action is the only defence against spirit-induced illness and death. The intervention of the spirits in the human world is not restricted to special occasions, nor is it mediated by a special category of persons. Contact occurs every night and is only intensified by exceptional events such as a death in the community. Seances do not construct a special 'sacred' time and place within which contact with the spirit world takes place: they seek to control a contact which is always already there. Buid mediumship is as much concerned with prevention as with cure, with the protection of the community as with the treatment of individuals.

I have argued that the Buid attempt to minimise their dependency on specific others through the practices of sharing and personal autonomy in the choice of companions. But Buid society is not composed of an aggregate of atomised individualists. Just as the practice of sharing leads to the physical dependence of the individual on an undifferentiated social whole, so the collective nature of Buid ritual leads to the mystical dependence of the individual on the whole. Buid ritual calls for the collective participation of all members of society, especially following a death. In this context, the entire community is at risk from predatory spirits and all the adult men in it must gather to combat them. Just as rituals in hierarchical societies tend to focus on the social relationships which carry the strongest rights and obligations between individuals, so the collective rituals of Buid society focus on the relationship between the individual and the whole, for it is only towards the whole that the individual has the obligation to give, and only from it that he or she has the right to receive in sharing.

Constant participation in obligatory collective ritual, in which the legitimacy of religious belief derives from personal experience of the spirit world, and not from tradition as interpreted by elders or specialists, from a sacred text, or from the privileged experience of a charismatic figure, provides the Buid with a shared core of belief and a deep conviction of the reality of invisible powers. While many Buid expressed scepticism to me as to the truth of statements concerning the effects of breaking certain taboos, or as to the accuracy of mythical stories, no one ever questioned the reality of predatory spirits, their role in causing illness and death, or the efficacy of seances in repelling them. Knowledge of the rituals and spirits which I discuss in this and the next chapter is universal among adult Buid. Even those Buid who have nominally converted to Christianity in Batangan continue to believe in these spirits, only claiming now to have found a more effective means of repelling them in the collective rituals of the Christian church, which invoke the aid of the Holy Spirit (translated by the missionaries as *Fiya fag Falad*, 'Good Soul'). As I noted in Chapter 1, the Buid were initially suspicious of me because they assumed I was a missionary who had come to tamper with their rituals. This caused real fear among them.

In contrast to the deep conservatism which surrounds Buid attitudes toward their ritual practices, the Buid exhibit a remarkable freedom in relation to more esoteric religious doctrines. The core of belief in invisible powers which is formed in ritual serves as a springboard for individual speculation on metaphysical issues. Such speculation is not thought to be of great practical importance, and fulfills an essentially intellectual function. Everyone is free to believe what they like, so long as they contribute to the collective rituals. Stories concerning the origin and structure of the universe and various things in it, and stories about the exploits of culture heroes concern events which occurred in the remote past. They serve the purpose of making human existence intelligible at an abstract level. Not all Buid feel an equal need for this sort of understanding, and so mythological knowledge is unevenly distributed. Certain wise old men know these stories in detail and in abundance and such authorities are well known in each community. A Buid who remembers only a truncated version of the original story will usually refer the enquirer to the authority from whom he first heard it himself. Ordinary Buid are likely to express some doubt as to the literal truth of these stories in their particulars, but do not often doubt that they contain a good deal of truth as a whole. Buid are not socialised into accepting statements from authority and feel free to speculate about anything lying beyond their direct experience, or that of their immediate and trusted companions. Those Buid who showed an interest in listening to the stories of the 'old ones' showed an equal interest in listening to alternative accounts of the origin of the universe, whether derived from Christian mythology or from Western science. Adam, Eve, Noah and *Diyus* (from *Deos*, 'God') make their way into a number of stories, coexisting with indigenous mythical personages without friction. It turned out that I had been quite wrong to worry about asking the Ayufay Buid for clarifications concerning the missionaries' translation of the New Testament into Buid, given their hostility to Christian interference in their ritual. They were in fact eager to hear passages from John and the Acts of the Apostles. Speculation on the ultimate nature of reality is a matter of individual interest. It is not seen as a threat to communal survival, as is tampering with ritual practice.

In the Buid seance, there is an overwhelming concern to establish and maintain a series of barriers between the human and the predatory spirit worlds. Earlier in this chapter, I stated that the soul is the source of all aggression within human society and the object of all aggression originating from the spirit world. Aggression must be controlled by the mind and by rational speech, whether in the context of the *tultulan* 'collective discussion' or in the context of the seance, which uses a specialised form of speech and heightened mental perception to counter external aggression. Because of its connections with exploitation and hierarchy, aggression is associated with the exterior of Buid society. The Buid employ the idiom of eating in describing the attacks of the predatory spirits. The relationship between the eater and the eaten represents an extreme form of hierarchy. No communication is possible between men and the spirits which bite their souls. In the next chapter, I will be discussing the parallel relationship between humans and animals, in which men become the predators. Again, no communication is possible between the two types of being. One of the strongest taboos is that against speaking to animals in human language. The Buid dogmatically state that domesticated animals cannot be taught to respond to verbal commands, and were quite shocked to hear that it was done in my homeland. They have a set of distinctive, inarticulate sounds appropriate to each species of domesticated animal which are used to attract the animals' attention or to drive them away. The Buid do not like to be reminded of their similarity to animals: men *awang*, 'speak', while animals *uni*, 'emit inarticulate noise', and, as I mentioned in Chapter 4, the words for sexual intercourse among humans and every species of domesticated animal are different.

If relations of predator and prey define a non-social relationship, then commensality defines a social relationship. If humans desire to enter into communication with a non-predatory spirit, they must sacrifice an animal and share its meat with that spirit. In this chapter, I have been dealing mainly with the hostile predatory spirits. In the next, I shall be concerned with the ritual means by which the Buid make contact with their spirit allies, and with other spirit types which do not regard men as their food. The rituals which involve the manipulation of animals must be presented in their totality before the full significance of animal sacrifice can be determined. The importance of establishing mystical barriers which has taken up much of this chapter may then be placed in relation to the equally important necessity of establishing and maintaining links with the spirit world which will be described in the next chapter. We have already seen that virtually every household possesses a spirit ally in the form of a familiar and that great care is taken to ensure that the familiar remains anchored to a specific house. We must now examine the means by which relations are established, maintained and broken off between human households and a variety of other spirit types.

7 Animal Sacrifice

By sacrifice in the context of Buid society, I mean the ritual manipulation, killing and commensal consumption of a 'sacred' animal. These animals are felt to be sacred because they serve as mediators between the human and spirit worlds, and because they contain a source of vitality which can be tapped by humans. Under the heading of sacrifice, I include all rituals which involve the use of animals as mediators and in which animals are killed in order to prolong the lives of humans. Buid sacrifice can be used either to bring about a disjunction between humans and undesirable spirit types, or to bring about a conjunction between humans and desirable spirit types. The object of the first part of this chapter will be to explain why domesticated pigs and chickens are felt to be appropriate mediators in the first place. This can only be done by placing them within the entire system of animal classification. I then give a brief account of the various means by which the vitality of the animals is concentrated and transferred to humans before turning to the rituals themselves. The first ritual to be described represents an intensification of the seance described in the last chapter, in which animals take over the role of the spirit familiars in chasing away evil spirits. The second ritual concerns the payments made to the spirit 'owners' of wild pigs. This ritual helps to clarify the nature of pigs as mediators between the human and non-human worlds. My account of Buid ideas concerning wild game will serve as an introduction to the fourth part of the chapter, which deals with the more central sacrifices involved in mortuary rituals and their aftermath. The ultimate aim of Buid mortuary practices is to establish and maintain a disjunction between the society of the living and the society of the dead. It does this primarily through the offering of meat and other items to ghosts during periodic rituals termed *fanisik* or *fansuguan*, 'sending away'. Finally, I turn to the rituals designed to re-establish a conjunction between the human world and the forces of fertility and regeneration constituted by the spirits of the earth and the spirit familiars. In this last type of sacrifice, we shall find a clear expression of the ultimate social values of sharing, giving and communal solidarity. We shall also receive confirmation of the significance

151

of mediation in Buid sacrifice in the symbolism associated with the threshold.

Buid animal classification

We may make an initial division between those animals recognised by the Buid as a potential source of food and those not so recognised. As we shall see, this is very much a matter of social recognition, for the Buid are aware that the Christians eat many kinds of animal which they do not.

Inedible animals

In the first place, there are animals regarded as being 'too close' to men, the prime example of which is the dog. Most Buid households keep a dog as a pet. As such, they live inside the house with their owners, share their food, often off the same plate and, most importantly, share the meat of other animals with them. By contrast, dog meat is regarded as a great delicacy by the Christians, who serve it on social occasions such as christenings or as an accompaniment (*pulutan*) to the consumption of alcohol. The Buid do not avoid dog meat because it is thought to be ritually 'unclean', but because dogs are in some sense companions to humans. When a dog dies, its body must be disposed of far from human habitation, because the smell of its decaying flesh is thought to attract evil spirits in the same way as does a human corpse.

In the second place, there are animals regarded as being 'too remote' from men to be edible. The animals in this category include primarily those traditionally domesticated by the Christians but not by the Buid. They include cattle, water buffalo and horses. All these animals are eaten by the Christians, normally only after they have died from natural causes, as they are too valuable to be slaughtered and usually belong to patrons in any case. If a Buid is offered the meat of such an animal, he will reject it, saying *midwanyayum udi*, 'we just are not accustomed to it'. Conservative Buid will say the same thing of any tinned food, especially corned beef. These foods again are not regarded as being ritually dangerous, but merely as unfamiliar and associated with Christian custom. Goats provide an interesting borderline case. They were traditionally raised by the Hanunoo (Conklin, 1957: 11) but not by the Buid. In recent years they have been adopted by the Buid as a source of cash income from sale to the

Christians. As domesticated animals they should be slaughtered only for a sacrifice, by analogy with pigs and chickens. Because they have no place in the ritual system, however, the Buid seldom eat them, but use them to pay debts to Christians. The Buid do not sell their pigs and chickens to non-Buid and only lend them to other Buid on the understanding that they will be repaid in kind. The Buid often seem not to know what to do with their goats. Of some twenty goats owned by the inhabitants of Ugun Liguma when I first arrived, more than half had either died of neglect in the bush, or had been stolen by Christians when I left two years later. None had been eaten by the Buid themselves. There was a clear contradiction between their roles as individual property in the cash economy and their character as domesticated animals which could only be eaten in the context of a communal sacrifice.

Edible animals

Of the animals recognised as edible, an initial distinction may be made between those with and those without ritual associations. Wild animals which live a completely independent existence from humans and never invade human territory, are regarded as edible without ritual impediment. This category includes riverine animals such as fish, crustacea and frogs, and animals of the forest such as bats and civets. They may all be characterised as distant but indigenous beings.

Animals with ritual associations are of two types: those domesticated by humans and those which live in the wild but make periodic incursions into human territory and attack human property. Generally speaking, the former have a positive religious significance and the latter a negative one. Intrusive wild animals include wild pigs, monkeys and birds of prey, which carry off chickens and even small pigs. As I noted in the last chapter, predatory spirits in the form of these animal types are some of the most commonly encountered adversaries in seances. They are all responsible for specific illnesses. It is only following a death that the spirit counterparts of Christian domesticated animals put in an appearance, when the emphasis is on the extreme vulnerability of the whole community to the totality of the spirit world. All animals which have no positive role to play in Buid society become, during this period of polarisation, adversaries, on the principle of 'what is not for us is against us'. Wild animals which are regarded as responsible for causing depredations in human territory embody a principle of anti-fertility, and as such can be controlled only by the agents of fertility, the spirits of the earth. One of the chief supplications addressed to the latter in the fertility rituals described below, is that they control the incursions of mice which can destroy most of a crop. The spirits of the earth are also thought to be able to talk to the spirits of wild animals and persuade them to cease their incursions.

Wild pigs and monkeys are only trapped and eaten by humans when they have damaged human crops. Although the Buid sometimes speak of all wild animals as having invisible human owners, such that fish may be said to be the 'pigs' of the *afu safa*, 'river spirits', in practice the Buid are only concerned with the reactions of the owners of wild pigs, the *andagaw*, to the hunting activities of humans. There are several reasons for this attitude. In the first place, pigs are regarded as the paradigmatic form of meat, as shown by their frequent use in metaphor. Men are said to be the 'pigs' of the predatory spirits and fish are the 'pigs' of the river spirits. In the second place, the boundary between domesticated and wild pigs is not clear, and always reversible (see above, p. 43). Men must deliberately domesticate every generation of pigs if they are to be prevented from going wild, and wild pigs, if caught young, can always be domesticated. Wild pigs which stray from their spirit owners into human cultivation are bringing about a potentially dangerous conjunction between the human and spirit worlds. In the third place, domesticated pigs serve as the primary mediators in Buid ritual and it is not surprising that a greater ritual significance is attached to the consumption of their wild counterparts than is attached to the consumption of other wild species which have no domesticated counterpart in ritual.

Finally, we come to domesticated pigs and chickens. Their importance as social mediators was discussed in Chapter 3, where their life cycle was characterised as involving an outward movement from an initial period of domestication within the house, to maturity outside, but in close proximity to, the house, to their final death and distribution among the members of other households. Their function as mediators between the human and non-human worlds, between cultivation and the bush, was also described. But they also possess more specific characteristics which suit them for their role in sacrifices to particular spirit types. Chickens, as we have seen, are used to mediate between mediums and their familiars. The latter are identified with their powers of leaping from one mountain peak to another, a mode of displacement strongly reminiscent of the flight of chickens.

But chickens resemble familiars not only in their ability to mediate between the sky and the earth, but also in their more specific ability to mediate between the interior and the exterior of a house. Mature chickens roost in the branches of trees which overhang the roof of a house and lay their eggs in baskets attached to the outside of a house's walls. They thus serve as a convenient link between the household of a medium and his aerial familiar. In the sacrifices to the familiars which precede a seance we are confronted, then, with a series of mediations. Those parts of the chicken's anatomy which allow it to mediate between the earth and the sky, its wing feathers, are attached to a stake which is lashed to the threshold of the house. These stakes are called *famana*, 'arrows', which they closely resemble. Spirit familiars may also be called *famana*. Just as wing feathers give the power of flight to chickens and to arrows, so familiars give the power of flight to mediums. The 'arrow', then, draws the familiar into the house, mediating between the medium and his familiar. The familiar, in turn, mediates between the medium and the spirits of the earth by another series of identifications to be discussed below.

Pigs mediate in another direction, for they live beneath the house, root and wallow in the soil as well as walking on it, thus mediating between the human world and the spirits of the earth. When humans desire to make contact with the spirits of the earth, a pig is laid across the threshold of the house and sacrificed. They serve to draw the spirits of the earth into the house and so re-establish the fertility of its occupants and their crops. Houses, then, are surrounded above and below by 'sacred' animals which serve as a point of potential contact with the beneficial spirits of the earth and the air.

	Inedible	Edible Only in ritual contexts		Edible Without restriction	Inedible
Social	'Too near'	Intermediate		Distant but familiar	'Too remote'
Type of animal	dog	chicken pig	bird of prey monkey wild pig	bats civets fish, etc.	water buffalo horse cattle
Relation to spirit world	none	mediate with good spirits	mediate with ambiguous spirits / attack men in spirit form	none	attack men in spirit form
Relation to human world	domesticated			wild	alien

Figure 7 Buid animal classification.

This discussion of Buid animal categories is summarised in Figure 7. The significant oppositions are those between edibility and inedibility; domestication and wildness; degree of social distance from humans, and association with good and evil spirit types. Because attempts at making correlations between animal categories and social categories, particularly those which relate to degrees of marriageability, have become common in the anthropological literature, it may not be out of place to comment on the utility of such an attempt as regards my Buid material (see Leach 1964; Bulmer, 1967: 20; Douglas, 1973: 36; Tambiah, 1969: 442). Since kinship categories receive little symbolic elaboration among the Buid, who are far more concerned to play down internal divisions than to pay them undue attention, it would seem at first futile to try to correlate them with animal categories. One can, of course, discern functional parallels between human and animal types. For example, there is a certain similarity between children who are raised in one household only to be shared in marriage with other households when they mature, and pigs and chickens, which are raised in one household and shared in sacrifice when they mature. But the logic of the arguments presented by the authors in question rests on a global parallel between two, or rather three, series: animals classified according to edibility; humans classified according to marriageability, and space classified according to degrees of social distance. The symbolic role played by Buid animals derives, on the contrary, from their relationship to the invisible world and cannot simply be read off from their metaphorical association with divisions internal to human society in accordance with the approach developed by Durkheim and Mauss (1963). The Buid define themselves not according to a series of internal social divisions, but in opposition to a variety of human, animal and spirit types external to their society. It is perhaps because internal social distinctions are so weak among the Buid that they attach so much importance to the habits and attributes of their visible and invisible neighbours. A full discussion of this issue must await the analysis of the spirit world in general and its articulation with the visible world.

Domesticated animals, then, serve as both social and ritual mediators. But there is another, equally important aspect of animal sacrifice. Sacrifice involves an act of aggression, a deliberate taking of the life of another being. In this sense, the Buid may be regarded as no better than the predatory spirits which take the lives of humans. The Buid make the parallel explicit when they say that 'humans are the pigs of the evil spirits', and that the death of a human provides the evil spirits with a feast in the same way as the killing of a pig in sacrifice provides humans with a feast. Both humans and predatory spirits are thus dependent on the appropriation of the vitality of beings at a lower level in the food hierarchy. The cosmic order is viewed as an exploitative system in which the stronger prey on the weaker. But while the predatory spirits respect no boundaries, attacking humans even in their homes, the Buid are careful to kill only those animals they have themselves nurtured, or to pay compensation to the 'owners' of those they have not. The Buid are morally justified in killing their domesticated animals, for the latter owe their lives to their owners in the first place. The Buid also kill their animals in a responsible and controlled fashion, while the evil spirits bite and begin to consume their victims while they are still alive.

Sacrifices, then, involve the controlled appropriation of animal vitality. They are performed when the vitality of men is under direct threat of appropriation by predatory spirits, and they are used to counter that threat. From the human point of view, animals represent a source of continuing life and growth, while the predatory spirits represent a source of death and decay. In certain rituals, the vitality of animals is brought into direct opposition to the forces of death. The controlled release of that vitality is said to frighten the predatory spirits away. In other rituals, the vitality of animals is shared with the spirits of fertility. In this case, the controlled release of animal vitality brings men into contact with the benevolent spirits. The association of animals with vitality is not the product of an abstract mental operation. It derives in part from the feeling of physical satiation which follows the consumption of even a small amount of meat when one is living on a diet low in fats and protein. As I know from personal experience, one really does feel revitalised following a sacrifice. Buid children in particular approach a state of near euphoria following a pig feast. They walk about the settlement rubbing their stomachs, smacking their lips and grinning from ear to ear. The unmistakable affection Buid show for their pigs is linked to the knowledge that one day they will eat them.

In the rituals which are about to be described, various devices are employed to concentrate the essence of a pig's vitality in order to transfer it to those members of the community most in need of a supplement, that is, to children and nursing mothers. The most common method is boiling. A myth concerning the culture hero Litaw recounts how he brought his father back from death by pouring five cauldrons of broth extracted from a single enormous pig over his father's corpse. Other methods include the systematic diminution of the whole pig by cutting off bits of meat from every part of its anatomy and cooking them together in a pot; the careful distribution of the head meat, which is associated with the soul, or vital element of the pig; and the manipulation of the blood and the wound through which the life of the pig escapes when it is slaughtered.

The swinging pig and chicken ritual

Saysayan babuy, 'swinging pig' rituals are performed to dislodge especially tenacious spirits which have become rooted to a specific place in human territory, such as a house or swidden. On one occasion, a child, who had been throwing tantrums for several weeks in succession, was diagnosed as having been bitten by a *fangugyab* (see above, p. 138). After an unsuccessful attempt to rid the child of this spirit, it was determined that all the hollow places in his house were infested with evil spirits. The affected child and all the other children living in his house or in neighbouring ones were assembled one night in a corner of his house. A live pig was bound and suspended from the rafters above them. One of the five mediums conducting the seance slowly swung the pig back and forth over the heads of the children chanting *sugu sugu, faglagyu wa fagayu fag labang*, 'depart depart, run away now all you spirits'. I was told that the swinging of the pig performed the same function as the swaying of the medium during a seance. It constitutes a controlled indication of animation which frightens the predatory spirits. The pig's throat was then cut where it hung above the children, its death struggles providing a further cause for alarm to the evil spirits. Finally it was taken down and laid in a corner to be butchered later on.

Next, two chickens were grasped by the legs and swung over the heads of the children, accompanied by the chanting of the same invocation as in the case of the pig. The chickens were then bound to the floor by one leg and their throats cut. They were left to flutter freely about until they died. The medium said that by now all the evil spirits would be so thoroughly alarmed that they would be fleeing from the house in all directions. The directions in which the beaks of the chickens finally came to rest would indicate to the mediums in which directions the spirits had fled, allowing them to be pursued later on during the seance. The pigs and chickens were then chopped up and boiled, and the broth was fed to the children in greatest danger from the spirits. The mediums spent the rest of the night chasing the evil spirits back to the graveyard whence they had come.[1]

Discussion

The opposition between the predatory spirits and animal life is clearly stated in this ritual. The spirits fear the swaying of the pigs and chickens and their final struggles. Animals normally live on the boundary between the human and non-human worlds. In a sense, they define that boundary at both the spatial and conceptual levels. In this ritual, they are brought inside the house in order to re-establish the mystical barriers which have been breached by the invading spirits who have taken up residence in human space. The extent of their penetration was indicated by the fact that they had invaded not only the house but the enclosed spaces within it (pots, baskets, bamboo inter-nodes, etc.). Only the sacrifice of a pig and two chickens was sufficient to dislodge them. It was not that the animals was being used as a substitute for the children. The Buid specifically denied that any meat would be offered to the evil spirits. In this ritual the vitality of the animals would be wholly appropriated by the children. This vitality was transferred to the children both by their consumption of the broth and by the swinging of the animals over their heads.

It may be noted that the sacrifice involved a spatial inversion, for the pig was sacrificed near the roof and the chickens near the floor of the house. In rituals which aim to establish contact with benevolent spirits, pigs are associated with the earth and chickens with the sky. They are used to create continuities between the interior of the house and the spirit allies which dwell above and below it. By contrast, when it is desired to create a discontinuity between the interior of the house and its exterior, the animal which is associated with the bottom of the house is placed at the top, and the animal associated with the top is placed near the bottom, thus effectuating a double discontinuity.

Traditionally, a place which has become associated with evil spirits is avoided and, in the case of a house, abandoned. This is no longer so easy to do in the context of a large-scale settlement, although it sometimes happened in Ugun Liguma. The settlement site was littered with the remnants of houses after only two years' occupation, as their inhabitants shifted to new sites built only yards away from the old ones (see below, p. 163).

Paying for wild pigs

While domesticated animals may be used to define the boundaries between human and non-human space, the wild counterparts of those animals threaten to blur the boundaries. The Buid rarely set out to hunt wild pigs and monkeys, for they are believed to belong to a category of spirits called *andagaw*. When one of these animals strays into a swidden, however, and damages the crops, action will be taken to trap it. Even then, capturing a wild animal and bringing it back to one's house is a dangerous business, for it intensifies the transgression of human space already initiated by the intrusive animal. When a wild pig is captured, the Buid say: *Aw nu dwagbayad andagaw, taktaban emu sas daga lutuk*, 'If you do not pay the *andagaw*, they will take you away beneath the earth'. Payment is less often made for monkeys, although they too belong to the *andagaw*. In a sense, the intrusion of a wild animal into a human's swidden constitutes the first phase of a series of exchanges, which ends either in the creation of a dangerous state of companionship between men and the spirits, or in the payment of compensation designed to terminate that companionship.

The Buid say that the *andagaw* are *taw yadi*, 'also men', except that they happen to be invisible. The *andagaw* belong to a parallel society which normally avoids contact with human society. Their *balay*, 'houses', are under mountain peaks and their doorways are springs, caves, or other *sakbawan*, 'openings', into the earth. Humans must be careful to respect these thresholds. For example, one may bathe in a stream which originates in the spring of an *andagaw*, but one must not laugh or behave inconsiderately in it. If one does, the *andagaw* will give the offender an invisible blow to the head, causing it to become hot and painful. A person so afflicted is said to be *gandagaw*.[2] The real danger to men from the *andagaw* is not, however, aggression, but its opposite, over-friendliness. One of the basic aims of the *andagaw* is to lure men into their houses and integrate them into their society. They use their animals as bait in pursuit of this aim.

When a wild pig is caught, it is carried back to the house of the person who owns the swidden in which it was trapped. There it is chopped up and set to cook. Meanwhile the owner of the swidden places an offering consisting of five fathoms of red beads, of the sort traditionally used in divorce settlements, on a stick which is thrust into the thatch just over the threshold inside the house. Next to it is placed the jawbone of the pig and a bush knife. By this time most of the settlement will have heard of the catch and will have assembled in the house to await their share of the meat. They all begin to call out *mi sumali wa*, 'we are paying now'. The older mediums name aloud all the important mountain peaks in the area, notifying their occupants that a pig has been caught and requesting the owner to come and receive payment. Eventually, the owner of the pig is said to approach the house and to stop at its threshold. It should be noted that the owner is not invited inside to share the meal, but is expected to reach in through the doorway and take the payment without entering the house.

The relationship between humans and the *andagaw* is equal but distant. They eat the same kind of food, but they do not share it with one another. While the *andagaw* is left standing outside the doorway, the community of humans inside the house is busily sharing out the meat in exactly equal portions. The broth and the head meat are consumed on the spot, while the remainder may be taken away to be consumed at leisure.[3]

Humans recognise their equality with the *andagaw* by addressing them in human language and by offering them compensation in the same way that they offer compensation to other humans when they desire to break off a social relationship. This simultaneous recognition of equality with, and separation from, the *andagaw* may be demonstrated more clearly if we examine exactly what happens when compensation is not paid. The *andagaw* are said to appear to humans in the form of one of their habitual companions of the same sex. There is no way for an unsuspecting victim to tell the difference between the *andagaw* and their real friend. The *andagaw* then invites the individual to go off on some sociable enterprise such as a fishing expedition. The *andagaw* leads the victim away from human territory and eventually conducts him or her under the earth. I was told that this had actually happened to one woman known to my informants, and that she had spent five nights in the realm of the *andagaw*. During this time, the spirit mediums had engaged in a protracted series of *tultulan* with her captors, finally agreeing on and paying a sum of compensation to secure her release. The woman had been led through a series of underground passageways to a point several kilometres distant from her point of entry into the earth.

Buid beliefs concerning the *andagaw* express in symbolic form the ambiguity of the boundary between the human and non-human worlds in a regime of shifting cultivation. The forest is an integral part of the swidden cycle and is regularly incorporated into the sphere of human activity just as swiddens regularly revert to forest. Domesticated animals may go wild, just as wild animals may be domesticated. The Buid represent these transformations as a social process of exchange between themselves and the invisible owners of the forest. The boundaries between the human and non-human worlds are prone to blurring. This is represented as a desire on the part of the *andagaw* to draw men into relations of co-residence, sharing and companionship which must be opposed by a respect for the thresholds of the *andagaw* by men and of the thresholds of men by the *andagaw*; by the denial of commensality; and by the holding of *tultulan* and the payment of compensation designed to terminate social relations.

Unlike the spirits described in the last chapter, the *andagaw* are not associated with the savage Bangun or with the cannibalistic Christians with whom no communication is possible. They are compared, rather, to the Hanunoo and said to be exceedingly beautiful and cultured. They wear their hair long, in the traditional Hanunoo style. The relationship between humans and the *andagaw* is not one of entrenched hostility, but of carefully balanced exchange. The potential transformations between the world of men and the world of the *andagaw* may be represented as follows:

If offerings to the *andagaw* are designed to prevent their intrusion into the houses of men and the luring of men into the houses of the *andagaw*, offerings to the ghosts are designed to expel ghosts from the houses of men and to prevent them from drawing men into the houses of the dead, i.e. into graves. Humans must prevent the relationship of equal exchange with the *andagaw* from developing into a more intense form of sharing and companionship. In the case of ghosts, humans must break off a pre-existing companionship with the dead and prevent it from developing into a one-sided relationship of exploitation. This is the object of the mortuary rituals described in the next section.

Mortuary rites

Buid mortuary rituals have a familiar tripartite structure beginning with the initial separation of the dead person from the society of the living, followed by a liminal period in which the ghost is wandering about and presents a danger to the survivors, and ending with the reintegration of the mourners into human society and of the ghost into the society of the dead. Actually, matters are not quite so simple, as the society of the dead is incomplete and remains forever dependent on the society of the living. The ghosts have everything they need in the underworld except for domesticated animals. They must return and beg them from the living in order to satisfy their craving for meat. The separation of the ghost from human society is never finally completed, but has to be continually reproduced in a series of rituals which recall the initial mortuary rites on a reduced scale.

The object of the first part of the mortuary cycle is to remove the corpse of the deceased from the house in which he died and to place it in a specially constructed spirit house, or grave. A house in which someone has died becomes *li*, 'cursed', and must be abandoned. The smell of decaying flesh attracts hordes of predatory spirits which gather to feast on the corpse, which must be removed as far as possible from human habitation. Anyone who is in the house at the time of death becomes contaminated and subject to spirit attack as well. They are kept in a state of quarantine in the house for a period of five or ten days (cf. Lopez, 1981: 182) before they are allowed to mix freely with others. The Ayufay Buid will sometimes flee a house just before death occurs in order to avoid contamination. They claim that the Bangun, or Taubuid, abandon moribund individuals in enclosures built in the forest so as not to have to abandon the houses in which they die. This is corroborated by Pennoyer (1975: 117). Among the Buid, the cursed house is burnt down after the burial.

The spirits which caused the death may be trapped on the house site by planting a special banana tree on it.[4] The fruit of such a tree is called *fagliun*, 'cursed', or *baybayun*, 'prohibited'. Because of its associations with death and the spirit world, only powerful mediums dare eat it and women avoid it entirely. Any house which has remained uninhabited for more than a few weeks is suspected of being haunted. Unless a house is constantly protected by a medium, predatory spirits will invade it. Before entering an empty house, it is considered a wise precaution to build a fire, the smoke of which will drive the spirits away. There are many localities thought to be haunted by the pre-datory spirits. These places are called *takalabangan*, 'place of the evil spirits', or *takabaya*, 'forbidden area'. Mediums are able to detect such localities and warn others against approaching them. The most dangerous of these localities are the graveyards, where a number of Buid have been buried close together. The mortuary rituals attempt to root the ghosts to the sites of their graves and to prevent them from wandering about human territory. It is for this reason that the ghosts of suicides are so dangerous, for their bodies have never been buried, but are simply left to decompose where they lie in the forest. Having no resting place, the ghosts of suicides roam the earth looking for companions.

According to Lopez, the person who carries the corpse becomes heir to the deceased in Batangan. This custom has acquired a great deal of importance there now that so much wealth in land and money has been accumulated. There is often considerable competition among the survivors to take on the task (Lopez, 1981: 224–6).[5] In Ayufay, it is not undertaken with much enthusiasm, because of the mystical contamination it brings to the corpse bearer. I received no indication from the Ayufay Buid that the personal effects of the deceased went to the corpse bearer. They seemed to be divided among the closest companions of a person at the time of the death and not to go by right to specific kinsmen. In one instance, an old man died who had no surviving relatives. His corpse was carried to the graveyard by his wife's brother, but it was the widow who inherited most of the dead man's money.

The corpse is placed in a foetal position and bound inside an old sleeping mat. The one who is to carry it places it in a sling suspended on his back by a rope passed around his shoulders and chest in the same manner as baskets of produce are transported from a swidden. The corpse is carried from the house straight up the mountain side to the graveyard. It is preceded by a group of men who hack out a new path through the underbrush. Like the house site, this path becomes *li*, 'cursed', and must thenceforth be avoided. Its presence is marked with bamboo signs where it crosses established trails. Arriving at the graveyard, the helpers set about selecting a grave site. Two large trees growing at the same level on the slope are required. A trench is dug uphill to the trees to a depth of about one metre. Meanwhile, the other helpers are busy cutting and trimming saplings to form the floor of the grave. This is covered with a sleeping mat, and the corpse is laid on top. It is placed on its side, with its head on a pillow, in the typical posture of sleep. The dead person must then be provided with all the requisites of existence in the underworld. A bush knife, the all-purpose hand tool that a Buid is never without, is pressed into the hand. A tin of water and some cooked staple (*fafa*) provide sustenance. Finally, some torch resin, for fire and light; some glass beads; and a few coins are added. When everything has been properly arranged, small branches are inserted into the walls of the trench and covered with leaves, forming a roof over the corpse, and completing the last necessity of 'life', a house. This house is designed to contain the spirit of the dead person, to protect it from the attacks of evil spirits and to prevent wild animals from getting at the body.

Two logs are then placed against the tree trunks standing downhill from the trench, and earth is filled in on top of the grave in such a way as to form a level surface above it (see Figure 8a). A second house is then constructed on top of the grave. More saplings are laid lengthwise along the grave and lashed into position to form a second floor. A roof is built above this floor out of sticks and leaves. In future, the grave may be identified according to the species of trees against which it is built. Around it the remains of previous graves are clearly visible. One has the feeling, in a Buid graveyard, that one is in a miniature Buid settlement. The Buid say that they bury their dead close to one another so that they will have companions and will not feel the need to haunt the living.

The completion of the surface house marks the end of the burial. It is accomplished as rapidly as possible. The helpers set out for home through the forest, avoiding established trails in order to confuse any pursuing predatory spirits. On their way, they pause to build a fire out of damp leaves and bathe themselves in the smoke. They do this in order to remove the sensation of cold induced by contact with death and to frighten the evil spirits. Both before and after the burial, care is taken not to provide the spirits with a direct path back to the dwellings of the living. For the next few months, one of the primary tasks of the spirit mediums will be to confine the predatory spirits to the graveyard, where they are busy consuming the flesh of the corpse and to prevent them from creeping down the mountain into human habitations.

There now follows a series of three offerings to the ghost, performed at monthly intervals, and increasing in scale until the final ceremony. During this time, the community of the living is under constant threat from the predatory spirits and from the ghost itself which has not yet accepted its separation from its erstwhile companions. A group of local mediums gathers nightly to keep the predatory spirits at bay, but the offerings to the dead are made the occasion for inviting mediums from neighbouring communities to perform large-scale seances. The whole region shows its solidarity with the household of the survivors by sending representatives to chant

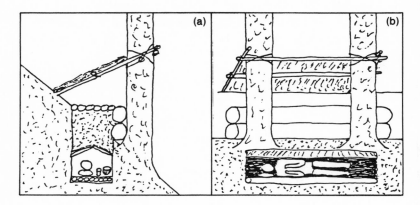

Figure 8 Side and front cross-sections of Buid grave.

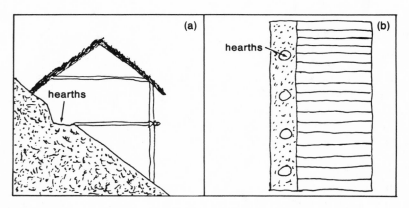

Figure 9 Cross-section and floor-plan of guest-house for mourning ritual.

for them and the afflicted household expresses its solidarity by sharing the meat of its domesticated animals with the visitors. A smoky fire is kept burning throughout the seances to provide added protection from the evil spirits. A description of these seances was provided in the last chapter.

For the sake of brevity, I shall provide a detailed account only of the final and most elaborate offering to the ghost. In preparation for it, one or two temporary houses will be constructed near the place where the death occurred. Members of all the neighbouring communities will be invited to take part in the feast. For most of them, the offering will be

Figure 10 Mourning ritual and ordinary spirit houses.

the least significant aspect of the occasion, as it also provides an opportunity for gossip, flirtation and the promise of meat. Many of the younger generation wear their special 'town' clothes. Everyone takes a hand in the preparations, which involve weaving bamboo eating trays, making bamboo water tubes, gathering firewood and putting the final touches to the temporary houses.

For the close associates of the deceased, however, the feast is a more serious business, for they will be brought into close contact with the ghost once again. The ghost is invited to take part in the feast, but it is not allowed to enter the houses in which the rest of the community is assembled. A friend or relative of the ghost builds a special spirit house about one metre square and one metre in height. It is carefully thatched and provided with a floor of split bamboo. This spirit house reproduces, on a diminished scale, the house which was built above the grave, which was itself a small-scale replica of a typical Buid field house (compare Figures 8 and 10a). The next step is to prepare the offering for the ghost. A medium lays out several strings of white beads, of the type used in seances, on a winnowing tray. These beads are always strung on long loops of thread, a fathom in length. Next to them, the medium places several seven-centimetre strings of white beads, which have been used already in a seance to mediate between the human and spirit worlds. From the latter, he makes up about twenty rings of beads, containing ten beads each. I was told that the ghost would accept each of these rings as being equivalent to a fathom of beads. The equivalence is established by the rings being placed in contiguity with the real fathoms on the same tray. Several small coins are then added to the tray, totalling one peso in value. This sum is said to be accepted by the ghost as being equivalent to one thousand pesos.

The pigs and chickens are now made ready for slaughter. While the first two offerings involve only a single small pig, on the third and final occasion two large pigs are provided. They are laid out on either side of the spirit house with their legs pointing in towards it and their heads pointing uphill toward the graveyard. The pigs are stabbed in the heart and their blood collected in a pot. The chickens are strangled. When there is a large group of people attending a ceremony, a general division of labour emerges. Adult men take responsibility for slaughtering and butchering the pigs, young boys attend to the chickens, adult women prepare the rice and other staples, and young girls clean the intestines of the animals in the river and fetch water. The men first quarter the carcasses of the pigs, and then carefully remove bits from the ears, jaw, snout, hind legs, tail and each of the internal organs. The boys remove bits from the wings, beak, and internal organs of the chickens. All these bits are placed in a small pot together with some rice and water, and set to stew. This is the only occasion on which rice is cooked with anything else. While the men and boys continue to chop up the rest of the meat, the women begin to cook vast quantities of rice in rotation on the hearths inside the temporary houses (see Figure 9). As soon as one pot is ready, its contents are emptied into a basket lined with banana leaves. It is then refilled and set to cook again. As many as eight pots may be cooking at one time.

While these preparations are going on, the individual who carried the corpse slips away. He returns some time later with a basket stuffed with old leaves on his back. Dressed only in a loincloth made of old sacking, and leaning heavily on a staff, he walks about among the other participants in imitation of a very old and feeble man who can barely stay on his feet. His behaviour and appearance recall both his role as corpse-bearer and the dead person just before he died. His entrance marks the arrival of the ghost on the scene, preparatory to the final offering. He behaves in an extremely intrusive manner, jostling and sliding into people. He deliberately brings them into physical contact with death in a provocative way. This performance constitutes a dramatic enactment of the stereotype of ghosts as aggressive, unwelcome intruders. The liminal period, which is now drawing to a close, has been dominated by the image of the dead person's decomposing body and of the predatory spirits which have been consuming it (cf. Bloch and Parry, 1982: 25).

By this time, the stew mentioned above will be fully cooked. The bits of meat are fished out of the pot and an even smaller bit cut from each of them. These are placed on an eating tray together with some of the cooked rice. This is the ghost's share of the feast and is the result of a sort of double distillation of the sacrificed animals. It should be noted that the same process of quantitative diminution was applied to the beads and money earlier on.[6] The remainder of the stew is fed to small children and nursing mothers. The food tray of the ghost is then placed on the floor of the spirit house together with the prepared beads and money. To these items are added: a 'blanket' (some old piece of sacking), an article of clothing (some cast-off garment), a 'rice mortar' and 'pestle' (a bamboo internode with a hole cut in the side and a stick), a bush knife, and some salt and sugar. These items reproduce those placed in the grave with the corpse, and constitute a sort of inventory of the provisions required for the ghost to lead a self-sufficient life.

As each item is placed in the spirit house, it is held up for public appreciation. The onlookers comment loudly to one another on their high value and quality. This is to convince the ghost of the generosity of the living. On one occasion I remarked to a small boy that the chickens being offered to a ghost were in fact only day-old chicks. He told me, dead pan, that they were the largest chickens he had ever seen. Given their lack of a mind, ghosts are treated as being rather gullible and stupid. They are addressed in a loud tone of command, of a sort rarely heard used between the living. Once the offering has been completed, the ghost is told in no uncertain terms to be off, and not to trouble the living any longer.

Those most closely associated with the dead person mark their separation from it in an emphatic way. A small platform is built on the hillside out of bamboo, and they take turns stamping on it while turning around three times in a clockwise direction (cf. Needham, 1967). The closest associate, for example, the widow of a dead man, then removes a leaf head-dress and adds it to the other items on the floor of the spirit house. It is only now that the community of the living is free to retire to the temporary guest houses and to enjoy their feast without fear of mystical intrusion. Banana leaves are laid down the centre of the floor space and covered with a long continuous mound of cooked rice. The guests sit facing one another and eat together. This is one of the few occasions on which people belonging to different households share *fafa*, 'cooked starch staple', together, and their solidarity is further emphasised by the fact that the *fafa* is not divided into distinct portions, but constitutes one enormous helping. The meat, on the other hand, is carefully divided into exactly equal portions, which are placed in front of each guest. The feast is followed by a final large-scale seance, in which the most powerful mediums from all the communities in the region take a hand in driving off the ghouls which have just finished consuming one victim, and are now in search of another.

During the liminal period immediately following a death, the totality of the predatory spirits organise themselves into a compact mass by gathering at the grave to feast on the corpse. It is not only humans who express their solidarity through commensality. After three months, when the corpse has been wholly consumed and the feast of the ghouls is over, the community of the living gathers to reassert its own solidarity in opposition to the forces of death and decay. In this communal feast, the normal internal social divisions between households, the sexes and children and adults are overcome. In the large-scale seances, the mystical power of the whole region is concentrated and directed against the massed forces of the predatory spirit world. The ghost itself is firmly dissociated from the community of the living. It is provided with a new and separate house of its own and a new set of companions in the underworld. Although it is fed, it is prevented from entering the same house as the living, and from eating with them. The continuing desire of the ghosts to return to the society of their former companions is never fully overcome because of a fatal flaw in the constitution of the underworld. Ghosts do not have domesticated animals of their own to share with one another and they do not have minds with which to control their individual desires. They remain forever dependent on the living for meat. They may appear to their former associates years after their death, demanding meat. They must be fed, for fear of their causing serious illness to those who refuse them.

The offerings made to the ghosts of those long dead resemble the ones just described in most detail, but are performed on a much reduced scale. First, a spirit house is built out of a tripod of sticks, with a handful of grass to represent a roof and some bits of wood to represent a floor (see Figure 10b). It is built at the edge of the cleared area which surrounds the house, standing half in the wild vegetation. The meat of both a chicken and a pig, however small, is always included in the offering, and items representing tools, clothing and valuables are usually included as well. It is because ghosts may demand meat at any time that a household must keep a stock of pigs and chickens constantly on hand. The object of the sacrificers is to comply with the minimum demands of the ghosts and to get rid of them as quickly as possible. Offerings to ghosts of the long dead are the most frequent reason for killing domesticated animals and distributing their meat throughout the community. In a sense, inter-household ties are continually being asserted in opposition to the world of the dead. The boundary between the two worlds is always in question and must be redrawn whenever the ghosts intrude into the world of the living.

The living are forced to accede to the demands of the ghosts, because of the mystical power of the latter to harm them. They use this power without compunction to satisfy their desires. Offerings to the dead may be seen as a symbolic commentary on the difference between sharing and extortion. In the former, one gives without asking anything in return. In the latter, one takes without offering anything in return. Offerings to the ghost may be compared to trade with the Christians. In both cases, one is making a calculated deal with a superior power in which one suffers a material loss in order to avert an even worse outcome. One does not regard the exchange as establishing a moral tie between giver and recipient, for the recipient is not regarded as being endowed with any moral scruples. The exploitative nature of the transaction is recognised by the giver, who consequently feels justified in resorting to deceit in order to minimise his loss. One is barely on speaking terms with such trading partners: indeed, there is a very close parallel between the abrupt manner in which the Buid address ghosts and the abrupt manner in which the Christians address Buid. Above all, one does not invite either ghosts or Christians into one's house, although they often force their way in and remain until they have been given something.

I once observed a striking instance of this parallel between the behaviour of ghosts and of Christians. The Buid had sacrificed a pig for a ghost in the settlement of Ugun Liguma late one night in order to avoid detection by the meat-hungry Christians. Buid never demand meat during a sacrifice, but quietly await their share. The Christians used to turn out in force whenever there was the hint of a Buid sacrifice in the air and cluster around begging for a share. This is exactly like the behaviour of a ghost. On this particular occasion, three Christians happened to be returning home late at night when they heard the squeals of the dying pig. They crept up to the spirit house and stood in the shadows behind it, pleading for a portion. The children had great fun mimicking their wheedling tone, while the adults did their best to ignore them. Eventually, after the Christians had followed us back to the house in which the pig was to be butchered, the Buid handed over a slab of raw meat in disgust to be rid of them.

The three types of ritual described so far in this chapter all involve the use of animals to overcome internal social divisions between separate households, through the widespread sharing of their meat, and to maintain the mystical divisions between the human and spirit worlds. These divisions concern the opposition between mystical predators and human prey, between the world of the forest and the world of human cultivation, and between the world of the living and the world of the dead. In all of them, the human world is symbolised by the house, which contains and protects its inhabitants from hostile external agencies. In the swinging-pig ritual, predatory spirits are expelled from a house they have invaded through the violent release of animal vitality. In the offerings to the dead, ghosts are provided with a new house, in which they may receive their share of meat without having to enter the houses of the living. In the payment for wild pigs, the *andagaw* are prevented from entering human houses by being paid compensation on the threshold, cancelling the ties of companionship initiated when humans first took one of their pigs. I am now going to describe a ritual in which humans deliberately invite a spirit into their house, and in which the opposition between the human and spirit worlds is deliberately overcome.

Sacrifices to the spirits of the earth

Afu means 'source', 'owner', 'master' or 'essence'. It is in this sense that *andagaw* are sometimes referred to as *afu fungsu*, 'owners of mountain peaks', and the spirits of the river as *afu safa*. But while the *andagaw* have a clear and vivid form, being 'also human' like the spirit familiars and the ghosts, beliefs concerning the *afu daga*, 'spirits of the earth', are more inchoate. They are invisible even to the most powerful mediums, who can only sense their presence and hear their voices. [7]

They are usually said to consist of a pair of spirits: one male, dwelling at the place of the rising sun, and one female, dwelling at the place of the setting sun.[8] They thus exist at the margins of space and time, and constitute an eternal source of fertility which is not subject to corruption and decay. It is from their dwellings at the places of the rising and setting suns that the spirit familiars are said to come when they are called by the mediums. The spirits of the earth themselves provide a more general and diffuse sort of protection. While the familiars are used to drive away specific evil spirits, the spirits of the earth supply a blanket protection which is only withdrawn if they are angered. They have the ability to communicate with the wild animal spirits and with *Ama Dalugdug*, 'Father Thunder', who punishes the breach of certain taboos. There is no room to go into these taboos in detail here. They are basically concerned with ensuring that certain categories are kept separate, and range from the incest taboo to the mixing of certain types of food. The spirits of the earth are able to mediate when these taboos are broken because they stand outside all classificatory structures. It is partially because of their transcendent nature that they are so difficult to categorise. In myth they are spoken of as a duality, in ritual they are often treated as if they constituted a simple unity or as if they were made up of a multiplicity of spirits.

The spirits of the earth are angered by the violation of certain agricultural taboos (see above, p. 48), by the existence of discord within a household, and by the marriage of those who are too closely or too distantly related (see below). They express their anger by withdrawing their protection from growing crops and children, and a sacrifice must be performed to regain their benevolence. Buid notions of vitality and fertility are focused on growth rather than on implantation. Humans are responsible for the latter, the spirits of the earth for the former. Sacrifices to the spirits of the earth are usually made only after a child is born or the crops are in the ground.

Sacrifices to the spirits of the earth are called *fanurukan*, 'making the house post', or *fanfukfukan*, 'hatching the eggs'. The spirits of the earth are thought of as providing the mystical foundations of the house, just as its physical foundations are provided by its wooden posts. Both sorts of foundation must be kept in good repair. Buid will state as a general rule that it is necessary for every couple to sacrifice five pigs to the spirits of the earth to secure the growth and survival of their children. The couple undergo no mystical danger themselves if they neglect these sacrifices. In practice, they tend to be made one by one at irregular intervals when a child falls sick, or is thought to be at risk because the spirits of the earth have been offended. Normally, one pig is sacrificed when a couple establishes a household with the intention of having children. In two types of situation, however, it is said to be advisable to sacrifice two pigs straight away. The first type is when first cousins marry, a union which borders on incest. The second type concerns a union between individuals belonging to different regions, especially if one is a potter and the other a basket-weaver. Frequent quarrelling is thought to be very likely in such cases, and quarrelling between spouses is highly offensive to the spirits of the earth. The fact that one man had been lazy in making the proper sacrifices despite being married to his first cousin was given to me as the reason for the low survival rate of his children. It is not always the case, however, that the welfare of the children is of paramount concern in a marriage. The *fanurukan* is not a marriage ceremony but a fertility ritual. The fact that all five pigs have been sacrificed by, and that a number of children have been born to, a couple makes no difference to the ease with which they can divorce. These sacrifices are intended solely to ensure the growth and well-being of children, not to reinforce the marital relationship. On the other hand, however, most *fanurukan* are performed after the resolution of a marital dispute in a *tultulan* as a sign to the spirits of the earth that harmony has been restored, and that they are not to endanger the lives of the children any longer.

In certain myths, the universe is explicitly compared to a house, with the sky as roof, the earth as floor, and the places of the rising and setting suns as doorways. The spirits of the earth dwell just outside these thresholds and are able to enter and leave the world by means of them. In myth, they provide the culture heroes with a means of passage to the spirit world, allowing them to reach it by climbing on to the moon as it rises through them on its way from the underworld to the upperworld. A *fanurukan* begins at sunset when the sun provides a link between the interior and the exterior of the universe. A bamboo platform is then constructed just outside the threshold of the house, touching the floor inside. In the ritual which follows, the house becomes a microcosm and the spirits of the earth are brought into close proximity with humans by being invited to sit on this platform just outside the house.

In order to draw the spirits into the house, a pig is bound and laid across the threshold with its head resting on the platform outside. Pigs mediate between the house and the earth, and between the human and

spirit worlds. While the rituals described above were primarily concerned with preventing the intrusion of unwanted spirits into the
house, the *fanurukan* is intended to facilitate the passage of the spirits
of the earth across the threshold. This use of an animal as a mediator
on the threshold recalls the practice of attracting spirit familiars by
means of a chicken's wing feathers.

The pig is stabbed in the heart, which lies directly above the
threshold. The blood is collected in a pot. A red cacao fruit is dipped
in the blood and placed, along with the bloody banana leaves on which
the pig was lying, in the thatch above the doorway. The cacao fruit is
later planted in a swidden to increase its fertility. These offerings may
be compared to those placed in the same position when payment is
being made for wild pigs. In this case, it is the life of the pig and not a
substitute for it which is being offered. I was told that the flesh
immediately surrounding the wound is the share of the spirits of the
earth. It is through this aperture that the life of the pig is released to
the spirits of the earth. In return, humans expect the spirits to release
their vitality through the aperture of the house.

The meat of the jaw and neck is chopped up and set to cook. The
rest of the meat is divided equally between the respective local communities of the husband and the wife, to be redistributed among their
members later. The cooked meat of the jaw and neck is shared out
immediately and consumed on the spot, as is the broth in which it was
cooked. Part of the cooked meat is set aside for the spirits of the earth
and placed on a tray. The medium who has taken charge of the
proceedings positions himself next to the threshold and begins to strike
a china plate with an iron nail. The most highly valued plates are those
which give off the brightest, clearest sound when struck. I was told that
it was this ringing sound which attracted the spirits of the earth to
come and sit on the platform. It signifies the arrival of the spirits and
the conjunction of the human and spirit worlds (cf. Needham, 1967).

When the medium senses the arrival of the spirit (or spirits), he
begins to speak to it (*agdarangin*). Unlike the chanting of the spirit
mediums during a seance, which is unintelligible to the other
participants, *darangin* are spoken in ordinary language in a normal,
conversational tone of voice. The spirits are asked to acknowledge the
fact that the members of the household and community are once again
united, that all internal divisions have been healed. They are asked to
restore their protection to the crops and children of the whole community. At this point, anyone in the house may address a specific

request to them concerning their crops and children. They are asked to bring on the gentle monsoon rains which nourish the crops and to prevent the depredations of field mice.

When the speeches to the spirits are over, the medium places the tray containing their share of the cooked food on the threshold. The husband and wife sponsoring the sacrifice each light a cigar and place them on the tray, allowing the smoke to rise up through the doorway. After the tray has been left on the threshold for an interval, the medium cuts off a bit of meat from each chunk on the tray and places them in a basket with the cigars. The basket is hung next to the other offerings above the threshold. Finally, the medium and the married couple cover their eyes with one hand and slowly draw the tray back into the house with the other, as if afraid to disrupt the contact with the spirits of the earth that has just been established. The remainder of the meat is then divided among all who are present and carefully consumed.

Discussion

If the offerings demanded by the ghosts represent a form of extortion and the payments made to the *andagaw* represent a balanced exchange, the offerings to the spirits of the earth constitute a form of sharing. The Buid integrate the spirits of the earth into their households in a communal meal just as they integrate the members of other human households. In accordance with the fundamental social value of sharing, the spirits of the earth give to humans without demanding anything in return. The *fanurukan* is not, as might appear at first sight, a calculated transaction in which humans acquire life for themselves by substituting the life of a pig. The spirits of the earth provide protection to humans as a matter of course. It is withdrawn only when the latter have quarrelled among themselves and it is restored when they have resolved their differences. The object of the *fanurukan* is to re-establish the relationship of companionship between humans and their spirit allies. In order to understand the full implications of this sharing with an external power, we must go back and pick up the thread of the argument in Chapter 4.

The Buid construct their social groups on the basis of shared social space and activity. The integrity of larger social groupings is threatened by the existence of smaller groups within them whose members share with one another on a more intensive scale. In particular, the unity of the community is threatened by the existence of potentially exclusive household units. This exclusiveness is broken down by the periodic redistribution of individuals among different households. The high rate of divorce creates an expectation in every individual that a household may come to be shared with virtually any other member of the community at some point in time. The unity of the community as a whole is positively asserted in collective ritual activity. In seances, for example, mediums belonging to different households gather under one roof to bring their collective power to bear against an external threat. The consensus created among mediums in a seance is extended to the whole community in animal sacrifice. The sharing out of sacrificial meat decomposes the separate households into their constituent individuals and recreates a larger social group in which all distinctions of age, sex and separate residence are overcome. Confronted with an external threat to one of its members, a household must dissolve its identity into that of a larger collectivity by sharing the meat of the domesticated animals with which it is identified with the whole community.

The identity of a social group among the Buid is defined in opposition to the type of threat it faces. The greater the threat, the larger the group needed to combat it. In some cases, the nature of the threat requires the cooperation of neighbouring communities. This is true when an individual has actually died and the totality of the predatory spirit world is on the offensive and when seances in one community only succeed in driving a predatory spirit into a neighbouring community. On such occasions, really large-scale seances must be held. External threats are countered through an intensified cooperation within the relevant social unit.

As a corollary to the need to call larger groups into action against a common threat, divisions within social groups allow hostile external agencies a point of entry. The community must act to contain social divisions within its component households, and between the members of different households. The traditional source of such divisions lies primarily in disputes over spouses. The community defines these disputes as a quarrel between two members of a single household and acts either to segregate them from one another or to reconcile them. It is the existence of a division within the community rather than the continued integrity of a particular household which is of paramount concern. In any case, too great a continuity in household membership is to be avoided because it would strengthen the household in relation to the community. The ideal image of the household consists in a tranquil but temporary state of voluntary cooperation between its adult members. This image constitutes a model for all social relationships. Any attempt to assert exclusive rights over another individual, through the expression of jealousy or possessiveness, is condemned. Quarrelling within a household threatens not only the mystical well-being of its children, but its links with the rest of the community. In the *fanurukan*, a household re-establishes both its internal unity and its unity with the community as a whole.

In the *fanurukan* we can also see that the unity of the community has a mystical as well as a concrete expression. Just as the spirit familiars may be taken as a mystical expression of the mental faculties of perception and speech, and of the ability of individuals to transcend their selfish desires in social interaction, so the spirits of the earth may be taken as a mystical expression of the community itself, of the dependence of the individual on the community. Spirit familiars protect the smallest social group, the household. They are individuated and identified by the unique chant with which each is associated, and they may only be called to a particular house by a particular medium. The spirits of the earth, on the other hand, protect the whole community. They are not individuated, but constitute a formless source of vitality which may be drawn upon by any household. The mystical unity of the community, which is created in collective rituals, is perceived by the participants as deriving from an external source of power.

The *fanurukan* makes explicit the relationship between internal social division and external attack, on the one hand, and the need to maintain internal unity within the household and external alliances with more powerful external forces, on the other. Unity is expressed through sharing, in which each part of the whole gives to every other part of the whole without reference to past transactions. Fertility itself derives from the solidarity of the community. A man and a woman can, on their own, share a house and engage in sexual intercourse. But they cannot produce healthy children without the sanction of the spirits of the earth who embody the values of sharing and companionship. I shall return to this theme in the final section of this chapter.

In summary, then, we can say that the offering to the spirits of the earth represents a symbolic statement concerning the value of sharing within human society. Not only does it hold the human community together, but it attracts the support of a powerful mystical ally. If the extortion practised by the ghosts is the transactional equivalent of death, isolation and decay, the sharing practised by the spirits of the earth is the transactional equivalent of life, solidarity and growth. The moral implications of different types of exchange is one of the dominant themes of Buid ritual. I would like to briefly develop this theme, and its theoretical implications for the interpretation of animal sacrifice, before concluding this chapter with a summary of Buid ideas concerning vitality and death.

Theories of animal sacrifice

Evans-Pritchard saw the essence of Nuer sacrifice as the expiation of a sin. A guilty individual appeases the wrath of God by offering Him the life of an animal in exchange for his own life. The sacrificer indentifies himself with the victim by rubbing ashes on to its back with his right hand (1956: 262). This interpretation was later taken up and generalised by Lévi-Strauss, for whom the fundamental principle of sacrifice is substitution (1966: 224). Now, we have seen that the notion that human life and animal life may be regarded as somehow equivalent is at complete variance with Buid ideas concerning the cosmic hierarchy of predator and prey. The only mystical beings which desire to take the lives of men are the predatory spirits, and for them the life of an animal is no substitute. In the swinging-pig ritual, the pig is not offered to the spirits at all. Its vitality is assimilated by humans in order to drive off the predatory spirits. In the case of the ghosts, which are on the same level of the food hierarchy as are living humans, the relationship between the sacrificer and the victim is more complex; the ghosts attack humans because they desire the flesh of an animal. In this case the human victim is initially a substitute for the animal which eventually replaces him. The *andagaw* desire the lives of neither humans nor of their animals. They offer their own animals to men in order to create a social bond. Men offer them a social form of compensation, the beads used in divorce payments, as a substitute for the life of the wild pig they have taken. Finally, when humans share the life of an animal with their spirit allies, they do so in order to maintain a bond of companionship with them. It is the sharing which establishes the tie between humans and their spirit allies, not the offering of a gift to the latter which must be reciprocated by some counter-prestation.

This brings me to my next point. If animals cannot be seen as substitutes for their owners, neither can they be seen as gifts to the spirits. There is a sort of continuum in Buid rituals ranging from relations of extreme hostility and separation from certain spirit types at one pole to relations of absolute alliance and virtual fusion at the other. These relations are expressed in terms of the dominant mode of transaction between humans and each of the spirit types. The predatory spirits occupy one end of the continuum. They are engaged in a process of unadulterated exploitation. They continuously take from humans without offering anything in return. It is their nature to do so, and humans can only try to limit their contact with them as much as possible. Because they stand at different levels in the food hierarchy, humans cannot eat with the predatory spirits, nor engage them in any sort of communication. The predatory spirits are the cause of all discontinuity in social life, bringing about the extinction of the minds of humans in death and the removal of their souls to a separate society in the underworld.

The predatory spirits are opposed by the spirit familiars, who occupy the other end of the continuum. They are engaged in a process of unadulterated generosity. They continuously give to humans without asking anything in return. It is in their nature to do so, and humans try to maintain as much contact with them as possible. Because they stand on the same level of the food hierarchy, humans can share their food with them and engage them in a sort of perfect communication. In a seance, the common possession of a specialised idiolect, the chant, by a medium and his familiar, brings about a near-fusion of their minds and perceptions. The spirit familiars are one of the primary means by which continuity is maintained in social life, as they are passed on from one generation of mediums to another. The cooperation between spirit mediums is one of the main means by which the society of the living maintains its internal unity.

In between these two poles of absolute antagonism and absolute companionship lie the relations between humans and the ghosts, *andagaw*, and spirits of the earth. Humans engage in social relations of varying degrees of intensity with each of them. The ghosts are engaged in a process of extortion from humans only slightly less severe than the exploitation practised by the predatory spirits. Like the latter, they are continually taking from humans without offering anything in return. Because of the one-sided nature of the exchange, humans try to limit their contact with the ghosts by driving them off with the aid of their spirit familiars and by buying them off with gifts of food. The fact that they do eat the same foods means that humans are able to engage in a minimal form of communication with the ghosts. The content of this communication is limited to demands on the part of the ghosts and commands on the part of humans. On both sides, it is a language of hostility, but it is still language. The ghosts belong to an external society of their own, but it is one which is dependent on human society, as a parasite is dependent on its host.

The *andagaw* are engaged in a process of balanced reciprocity with humans. They offer their animals to humans on condition either that they receive appropriate compensation or that they are enabled to recruit the recipients into their own society. Humans try to limit their contact with the *andagaw* through the use of rational discussion and the negotiation of compensation. Humans are able to talk to the *andagaw* because they stand at the same level of the food hierarchy and they are able to converse as equals because neither is dependent on the other for food. While ghosts are kept away from human habitation and made to eat alone, the *andagaw* are invited to the threshold of the house to hear the speeches of humans. They are then asked to receive the proffered compensation and retire to their own houses in the forest. Humans and *andagaw* address one another in a language of mutual respect, which simultaneously implies distance. The *andagaw* belong to an external and independent society of their own. The relations between humans and *andagaw* as exemplified in the ritual payment for wild pigs constitutes the mid-point in the continuum of Buid relations with the spirit world.

The spirits of the earth are engaged in a process of generosity only slightly less unconditional than that practised by the spirit familiars. Like the latter, they are continually giving to humans without asking anything in return. As the sole conditions for their help, they ask that humans continue to live harmoniously and that they respect the integrity of the earth on which their subsistence is based. In the *fanurukan*, humans share the meat of their domesticated animals with the spirits of the earth, and so are able to communicate with them. While the ghosts and the *andagaw* are prevented from entering the house, the spirits of the earth are invited to do so. They are addressed in a language of friendship and solidarity. The spirits of the earth are part of human society. In a sense, they are that society, for they embody the values of sharing and companionship on which it is based. Humans are dependent on the spirits of the earth as an individual is dependent on the group to which he or she belongs.

The different modes of transaction between humans and the spirit world may be summarised as follows:

exploitation	predatory spirits
extortion	ghosts
balanced reciprocity	*andagaw*
sharing	spirits of the earth
fusion	spirit familiars

At the beginning of this chapter, a somewhat idiosyncratic definition of sacrifice was adopted which contained two elements: the use of sacred animals as mediators with the spirit world, and the ritual manipulation of animal vitality. The utility of this definition for the analysis of Buid religion has now been demonstrated. It allowed the full range of Buid rituals to be placed in the same conceptual framework. The more usual definition of sacrifice as a gift to spiritual beings, in which the life of an animal is substituted for the life of a human, has little relevance to Buid religion. But if Buid sacrifice involves neither a substitution nor a gift, some alternative theoretical framework must be found. I would like to concentrate, for the time being, on the *fanurukan*, in which animals are used to establish a relationship of contiguity between the human and spirit worlds. This is one of the primary objectives of many of the rituals described as sacrificial in the literature, and will serve as a convenient point of comparison.

Despite his hostility to the theories of Robertson-Smith, Evans-Pritchard has provided a useful summary of his views on animal sacrifice. This summary will be quoted in full, before a point by point examination is made of it as it relates to Buid sacrifice.

> Briefly, his theory was that primitive sacrifice, and particularly early Semitic sacrifice, was a feast in which the god and his worshippers ate together. It was a communion or act of social fellowship – not a gift, not a tribute, not a covenant, not an expiation, not a propitiation. All these ideas were either much later or, if present in the earliest forms of sacrifice, were secondary or even merely germinal. Moreover, the sacrificial victim was a sacred beast, not in virtue of being set apart or

consecrated for sacrifice, but intrinsically. (Evans-Pritchard, 1956: 273, cf. also 1965: 52)

Evans-Pritchard then goes on to describe a rather more questionable part of Robertson-Smith's theory, which I will come back to later. Now, the notion that the god and his worshippers eat together in an act of communal fellowship seems to describe the *fanurukan* quite well. The point can be made even more explicitly by quoting directly from Robertson-Smith:

> By admitting man to his table the god admits him to his friendship; but this favour is extended to no man in his mere private capacity; he is received as one of a community, to eat and drink along with his fellows, and in the same measure as the act of worship cements the bond between him and his god, it cements also the bond between him and his brethren in the common faith. (1907: 265)

This quotation serves to draw attention to the fact that it is not only the bond between an individual and the spirits of the earth which is recreated in the *fanurukan*, but the bond which unites the members of the community as well. To continue: the offering is not a gift, for a gift implies the creation of a debt and imposes an obligation to repay. The idea of a gift appears only in the offerings of wild pigs by the *andagaw* to humans. The offering is not a tribute: given the egalitarian nature of Buid society, one would not expect the benevolent spirits to demand gifts by right of their superior power (cf. Robertson-Smith, 1907: 346). The idea of tribute appears only in the offerings made to ghosts, and it is represented as a form of illegitimate extortion. The offering is not a covenant in the sense intended by Robertson-Smith, for it does not, in itself, bring two separate parties together, but reinforces a pre-existing bond between them (ibid.: 319). The offering is not an expiation or propitiation. It is held to celebrate the restoration of the spirit of communal harmony only after all disputes have been resolved by other means.

Finally, the animals which are offered to the spirits of the earth are felt to be appropriate mediators because of their intrinsic characteristics. Domesticated pigs are set apart, as a species, for their ritual role. They do not need to be individually 'consecrated' on each ritual occasion. Pigs are intimately associated with the household that raised them. They begin life in the house, are fed by hand with human food, and live underneath the house when they mature. They provide a link between the human world and the earth.

Robertson-Smith's communion theory of sacrifice has fallen into disrepute largely as a result of the explanation he put forward to account for the sacred character of domesticated animals. Again, this explanation is best summarised by Evans-Pritchard:

> [The sacrificial victim] was the totem of the clan and hence of the same blood as the people who slew and ate it. But in a sense it was also the god himself, for the god was the ancestor of the clan and therefore kin to both his worshippers and their totemic victim. By sacramentally eating their god, the anthropomorphic and theriomorphic victim, the worshippers acquired spiritual strength. (Evans-Pritchard, 1956: 273)

Robertson-Smith began by assuming that kinship, which he defined as the literal sharing of 'a common mass of flesh blood and bones' (1907: 274), constituted 'the only recognised type of permanent friendly relation between man and man' in the earliest stage of society (ibid.: 51). It therefore followed that the relationship between man and god had to be framed in terms of shared substance as well. This argument is not really so bizarre as the insistence on kinship as shared physical substance makes it appear. The general point that humans conceive of their relationship with spirits in the same terms as they conceive of their relationship with other humans is widely accepted. Where kinship provides the dominant idiom of social relations, it often also provides the dominant idiom of religious discourse. In Buid society, however, 'the only recognised type of permanent friendly relation between man and man' is that constituted by shared activity and companionship. The Buid represent their relationship with the spirits of the earth in just these terms. Where Robertson-Smith went seriously astray was in making a further identification between the substance of the gods and the substance of the animals with which they were associated in ritual (ibid.: 288). From here it is but a short step to asserting that 'kinship between families of men and animal kinds was an idea equally deep-seated' (ibid.: 289). He presents little evidence for either of these two assertions.

I have attributed the 'sacred' character of Buid domesticated animals to the fact that they serve as spatial, social and spiritual mediators and to the fact that they constitute a source of vitality under human control. Indeed, the Buid may be said to recognise a sort of social solidarity with their household animals. A pig or a chicken which has formed an especially close tie with its master, such that it will accompany its master on a trail through the forest without straying, is called *batiti*, 'pet', or perhaps, 'animal companion'. Although it is taboo to address pets with human language, animals do share a specialised form of speech with humans. Humans do not kill their animals merely to satisfy their hunger for meat. They are used as a source of food only on collective ritual occasions. The controlled manner in which animal life is taken contrasts with the uncontrolled predation of the evil spirits. Aggression is viewed as a necessary but distasteful aspect of the struggle for existence. Given all the above qualifications, a certain amount of insight may be discovered even in Robertson-Smith's assertion of a certain kinship between humans and their animals: 'the beasts are sacred and kindred beings, for they are the source of human life and subsistence. They are killed only in time of need, and the butchers are unclean, which implies that the slaughter was an impious act' (1907: 296). In concluding this chapter, the link between aggression and vitality in the context of Buid cosmology as a whole will be examined.

The Buid world view

The Buid view the cosmos as containing a hierarchy of predators. The higher up this hierarchy one goes, the more unpleasant and aggressive are the beings. Pigs eat only plants, which do not struggle against their fate but accept it passively. Humans eat pigs, but only those they have raised themselves or 'bought' from their rightful owners, the *andagaw*. Humans kill their victims in a 'humane' manner, cook them, and carefully respect the limits of their own domain. The predatory spirits invade human territory and begin to consume their victims while the latter are still alive and prefer to eat flesh rotten and uncooked. The very worst spirits are those in human form which consume human victims. They bring about a confusion between levels, transgressing not only spatial but conceptual boundaries. This hierarchy is a hierarchy of illegitimate power, in which the stronger exploit the weaker. It is, by Buid definition, anti-social and immoral.

At the bottom of the hierarchy are the plants which provide the major source of subsistence for both humans and animals. There has been little occasion in my discussion of Buid religion to mention plants, but this should not blind us to the central role they play in Buid life and thought. They constitute the background against which the activities of animals, humans and spirits stand out in contrast. While the night is devoted to the struggle with the forces of death and aggression, the day is devoted to the cultivation of plants. Like the Hanunoo to the south, the Buid are keen botanists. The former, according to Conklin, are able to identify over 1,600 distinct plant types in their environment, and assign a cultural significance to 93 per cent of them (1955: 249). This figure appears to be near the upper limit of the capacity of the human brain for remembering folk taxonomies in non-literate cultures (Lévi-Strauss, 1966: 154). Because of my different interests, I did not conduct a similar ethnobotanical study among the Buid, but on the basis of casual observation I suspect that their knowledge of the plant world is of the same order of magnitude. Now, such a tremendous interest in the plant world cannot be explained on utilitarian grounds alone. The Buid are fascinated by plants for a deeper reason.

The autonomous growth of plants, indeed, their apparently inexhaustible capacity for spontaneous regeneration in the humid tropics, provides an example of a life form in which struggle and aggression are unnecessary. Plants are exploited by other life forms without seeming to suffer from it. They continually give life without having to take it. They serve as an apt symbol of the moral ideal of sharing. Despite their ritual concern with animals, the Buid are primarily horticulturalists in outlook. In opposition to the immoral hierarchy of predation, there is an inverse hierarchy of morality, in which the beings at the bottom of the food chain constitute a source of continual regeneration for those at the top. Just as the predatory spirits constitute an exaggerated image of humans as parasites on the plant and animal worlds, so the spirits of the earth constitute an exaggerated image of plants as the source of all growth and vitality.

The spirits of the earth embody the moral ideal of sharing in that they can give without having to receive. Being wholly self-contained, they realise the value of autonomy. They are able to escape from all the problems of exploitation, aggression and thwarted desire experienced by humans, who are dependent on an external source of vitality and who must cooperate with one another to obtain it. In a perfect world, humans would not have to resort to aggression, nor would they have to depend on their fellows. As it is, humans are caught in a contradiction between their nature as individual organisms with a need for food and sex, and their nature as social beings who can only meet those needs through cooperation with others. A compromise is achieved by directing all aggression outside human society toward animals, on the one hand, and toward predatory spirits, on the other, and by diffusing the dependency of the individual on to the social whole. Buid morality stresses the danger of the individual desires which arise in the soul, but it also recognises the necessity of providing an institutionalised means of fulfilling them. The integration of Buid society is based on the proper handling of the desires for meat and for sex. If conflicts did not arise within households, spouses would not be shared between them. If animals were never killed, meat would never be shared between households.

In their religious beliefs and practices, the Buid show themselves to be obsessed with the themes of hierarchy and exploitation. Death and disorder are believed to originate from an external source which is beyond the influence of human values. These negative forces can be controlled to a certain extent by the spirit mediums with the aid of their spirit allies. These mediums are almost always men, who are associated with the maintenance of the external boundaries of human space. Life and the social order are also believed to derive from an external source which embodies the highest ideals of human society. Fertility is associated with the spontaneous growth of plants and of children and is produced by communal harmony. The power to generate vitality is not appropriated by the holder of political or ritual office, as in so many hierarchical societies. The significance of this point can best be brought out by contrasting Buid religion with the religion of a society based on kinship and descent.

> In these societies, the kind of authority and right here at issue is generated and exercised through social relations created by kinship and descent. Jural authority vests in a person by virtue of kinship status or of office that, in the last resort, depends on descent. Ancestors symbolise the continuity of the social structure, and the proper allocation, at any given time, of the authority and right they have transmitted. Ancestor worship puts the final source of jural authority and right, or to use a more inclusive term, jurisdiction, on a pedestal, so to speak, where it is inviolate and unchallengeable, and thus able to mobilize the consent of all who must comply with it. (Fortes, 1966: 137)

By contrast, in Buid society mortuary practices are wholly directed toward the exclusion, first of the corpse, and then of the ghost, from the social group. To the extent that ghosts try to exert a continuing influence on the affairs of the living, they are evil and the carriers of further misfortune.

Bloch and Parry have argued that the aleatory events of biological birth and death constitute a threat to the continuity of a social system based on traditional authority. The holders of authority in such systems must be able to assert an ideological control over these events, turning the death of an elder into a source of continuing vitality for the group. Authority is legitimised by being associated with fertility and by invoking the deepest emotions, beliefs and fears of people everywhere (1982: 41). A dead person is de-individualised and integrated into the eternal society of the ancestors. In terms of ritual, this often involves the removal of the parts of the corpse which are subject to decay and the careful preservation of the bones in a tomb (ibid.: 36).

By contrast, the Buid do not construct an image of an eternal, ossified society of the dead to provide a model for the continuity of social groups. The dead have no legitimate right to intervene in the society of the living and they are not used to bolster the authority of the holders of political or ritual office. Continuity in social life is provided by the uninterrupted solidarity of the community of the living and of humans and their spirit allies. It is only the ritual communion of humans and these spirits which ensures the growth of crops and of children. Buid mortuary and fertility rituals serve to legitimate an egalitarian social order in which no one individual has authority over another. Life, as well as death, derives from a socially neutral, external source. It is in the balance between these external agencies, between the spirits of the earth and the predatory spirits, that the perpetuation of the community is assured.

In this chapter, I have examined the way in which traditional Buid values were expressed in their religious beliefs and practices. They are imbued with the need for maintaining a rigid separation between the human and the predatory spirit worlds, and with the need for maintaining a rigorous internal solidarity to combat the latter. Now, the Buid have been surrounded for centuries by hostile societies of incalculably greater power. They have been able to maintain their autonomy only by rigorously excluding foreign economic, political and ideological influences, and by maintaining a remarkable degree of internal solidarity in their dealings with outsiders. In the next chapter, the parallels between the world of empirical experience and the imaginary world of collective representation will be further examined. Buid religion continues to be affected by recent changes in the nature of the threat from the lowlands and to influence the Buid response toward that threat.

IV

Religion, Society and History

8　Belief and Experience

The relationship between Buid religion and society will be examined on two levels in this chapter. In the first place, there is a correlation between Buid representations of their human and of their spirit neighbours. The Buid inhabit a highly diversified social environment in which they are engaged in a continuous struggle to preserve their social and cultural integrity. There is a correlation between the fact that the threat from neighbouring societies is far greater than that from the natural environment, on the one hand, and the importance in Buid cosmology of 'human' spirit types, all of which have empirical counterparts among the neighbours of the Buid, on the other. The characteristics attributed to these spirits represent Buid attitudes toward their neighbours in a simplified and exaggerated form. Buid collective representations of the invisible world have been conditioned by their long history of persecution by and resistance to the lowland world. During this period they have come to see themselves as embedded in a larger structural system in which relations between members of neighbouring societies are dominated by mutual hostility. The Buid define their identity and moral values in opposition to those of their human and spirit neighbours. The high value placed on egalitarianism and personal autonomy is balanced by an equally strong need to maintain internal solidarity against a common external threat.

In the second place, there is a correlation between the social processes employed to maintain the internal cohesion of Buid society and the ritual processes employed to maintain the cohesion of humans and their spirit allies. The two sorts of process are, in fact, mutually reinforcing. While the form of ritual activity has remained largely unchanged in recent years, its content has been affected by the emergence of a corporate community and of disputes over land and political leadership. The necessity of collective ritual activity for combating the predatory spirits has helped to keep these disputes in check by diverting attention away from the disputes and towards a common external threat. A number of case histories are given to illustrate this process. In the final analysis, however, the actual state of dependency of the corporate community on its internal leaders and on its external patrons is undermining the unity of its members. As the members of different households come to enjoy differential rates of success in exploiting the cash economy and political system of the lowlands, their interests will begin to diverge. There is a growing pressure on the more successful to question the relevance of the traditional religion for the attainment of their own goals and to consider the alternative path of acquiring a lowland education for themselves or their children.

The structure of the human spirit world

The most important spirit types are said to be *taw*, 'human', except that they are invisible and have customs and characteristics peculiar to themselves. In Chapter 6 the Buid concepts of mind and soul were elucidated by considering them in the light of their beliefs concerning ghosts and spirit familiars. In Chapter 7, a consideration of the predatory animal spirits was used to elucidate the nature of animals as mediators between the human and spirit worlds. In this section, the same method will be employed with regard to the remaining spirit types, in order to elucidate Buid attitudes toward the members of neighbouring human societies.

Human classification
According to one myth, all humans are descendants of Adan and Iba, who were the only survivors of a flood that wiped out the rest of humanity. Adan and Iba had four (or five) children. One of them, the ancestor of the Buid, remained in the place where he was born. One moved uphill and became the ancestor of the Bangun. One moved downhill and became the ancestor of the Mangyan patag. The fourth left the island altogether, his descendants returning only after many generations, and became the ancestor of the *luktanun* (Christians). A fifth child is sometimes introduced in order to account for the existence of 'Americans', who are usually considered to form a class of humanity distinct from the *luktanun*. Some Buid even hesitate to consider them properly human at all and speak of them as a type of *aswang*, 'witch'.

As the myth implies, the Buid see themselves as occupying a central position in the cosmos, with neighbours living uphill and downhill from them, and a third group intruding from across the sea. Those living uphill are generally despised and held to represent all that is uncouth in social behaviour. 'Bangun' is, in itself, a derogatory term which no one accepts as applying to himself. The Buid as a whole define themselves in opposition to the category of Bangun, but the content of the category is relative. Down-river Buid regions generally consider the members of up-river regions to be Bangun, while the members of up-river regions deny this and assert that the *Bangun arungan*, 'true Bangun', live even further up-river. The Buid of Ayufay are thus considered to be Bangun by the Buid of Batangan (cf. Lopez, 1981: 189), while the former speak of themselves as Buid and reserve the term Bangun for the inhabitants of Alid and beyond. The characteristics associated with the category 'Bangun' by all Buid are those which emphasise crudity. The Ayufay Buid were fond of telling 'Bangun stories'. In them, Bangun are represented as being physically ugly, infested with ringworm, impervious to pain and unkempt. In particular, they are thought to be dirty. This belief may be not unconnected with the Taubuid practice of blackening their faces with ash or pitch to make contact with the spirit world (Pennoyer, 1975: 77). In terms of behaviour, the Bangun are accused of being selfish, aggressive, gullible and unreliable. They are possessive of their spouses, threatening violence to rivals rather than accepting compensation. Such behaviour contradicts the Buid values of personal autonomy and communal solidarity based on the sharing of spouses. Bangun shamans are said to practise sorcery to advance their own interests. They are said to abandon their ageing relatives in the forest before they die out of fear of the predatory spirits. Now, it is implicit in much of Buid behaviour that fear of the dead and jealousy over spouses are emotions they feel strongly, but suppress in the interests of communal harmony. The Bangun are represented as being incapable of controlling these emotions and thus as being anti-social.

Anecdotes relating to specific instances of Bangun savagery are recounted with relish. They are said not to chew their food, but to swallow it whole. One Buid claimed to have seen a Bangun swallow a bone the size of his fist. They are able to pick up glowing embers with their bare hands and calmly light their pipes without showing any signs of discomfort. Above all, the Buid find the characteristic drawl of Bangun speech highly comic, and imitations of it are sure to provoke gales of laughter. In short, the Bangun are represented as epitomising all that is inept, if not downright malevolent in social behaviour. The Buid of Ayufay were all the more eager to differentiate themselves from the Bangun because they are associated with them by the Buid of Batangan.

Downhill live the Mangyan patag, or Hanunoo. The Buid of Ayufay are not in frequent contact with them, so their image is less detailed and more idealised than their image of the Bangun. For the Buid, the Mangyan represent the peak of cultural achievement among the indigenous highlanders of Mindoro. They produce embroidered cloth, decorative baskets and bamboo containers covered in written verse. They are held to be physically beautiful and graceful, wearing their hair long and clinging to the traditional style of dress. They represent an aesthetic ideal. There is a distinct tendency for cultural borrowing to proceed in an upriver direction from the Mangyan to the Buid. The Batangan Buid have adopted many Mangyan techniques, and their relative superiority to the Ayufay Buid in terms of the traditional value system stems partly from this fact. The northern Buid obtained most of their cotton loincloths and skirts from the southern Buid, who had learned how to make them from the Hanunoo.

The categories of Buid, Bangun and Mangyan may all be classed together as Buid in opposition to the category of *luktanun*, 'lowlander'. In this usage, the term Buid has a positive connotation. The Christians for their part refer to all non-Christian highlanders as Mangyan or *sandugu*. On their lips, the term Mangyan is decidedly derogatory, connoting all that is 'uncivilised'. These two cover terms indicate the presence of a sharp social divide, each side of which adheres to a different system of values. 'Buid' or 'Mangyan' in these usages refer to all those who wear loincloths or tubular skirts, practise shifting cultivation and residence, and have a shy and unaggressive disposition. These characteristics all carry a positive connotation for the highlanders and a negative one for the lowlanders. *Luktanun* wear long trousers or skirts, know how to cultivate wet rice, even if they are too poor to do so, and have a violent and aggressive disposition. These characteristics all carry a positive connotation among the lowlanders and a negative one among the highlanders. But the attitude of the highlanders is complicated by a certain envy of the greater wealth and power of the lowlanders. The social norms of the *luktanun* are condemned without reservation, but their material culture provokes a certain amount of admiration.

Human spirit classification

The human spirits belong to societies of their own which exist in parallel to human society. The two spirit types which are in closest contact with the Buid are the spirit familiars and the ghosts. They represent certain aspects of the Buid themselves in magnified form. The spirit familiars are associated with the positive side of the human personality, with its rational, social and communicative mind. In the seance, they serve as a model for the cooperation of individuals against a common, external threat. The ghosts are associated with the negative side of the human personality, with its emotional, individualistic and inarticulate soul. In the offerings to the ghosts, the ghosts serve as a model of the threat posed to the community by the selfish desires of its members. The society of humans is dependent on the spirit familiars and tries to integrate them into itself. The ghosts are dependent on human society and try to remain integrated with it. This opposition between ghosts and familiars is expressed in ritual by the provision of a separate house for ghosts, on the one hand, and in the invitation of the familiars into the house, on the other.

The society of the ghosts stands in moral opposition to the society of the familiars. Together they serve to define the nature of human society, caught between the conflicting demands of the minds and souls of its members. This theme receives a further elaboration in Buid representations of the spirit types which are less closely identified with the Buid, such as the *andagaw*, the jungle men and the cannibal spirits.

Like the spirit familiars, the *andagaw* operate on human minds. But they do not refine and intensify human perceptions, they confuse and distort them by appearing in the guise of a companion of the same sex and by offering the social gift of pigs. They manipulate the values of trust and sharing in order to lure humans into their own society. In the ritual payments for wild pigs, the *andagaw* portray the deceit which is an inevitable potentiality in all social interaction and the danger of being lured into a debt relationship. They belong to an autonomous society, but seek to draw humans into it; they are morally ambiguous in that they give to humans, but impose conditions on them; but they do not desire to harm humans. They are a threat because they are, as it were, over-social. So long as they can be prevented from entering the houses of humans, or from luring humans into their houses all is well. They are associated with the Mangyan, belonging like the latter to a parallel society which is aesthetically attractive but morally suspect. They are to be respected, and avoided, as equals.

Like the ghosts, the *taw gubat*, 'jungle men', operate on the souls of their victims. Unlike the ghosts, they desire nothing from humans, except to be left alone. They portray the dangers of anti-social and aggressive behaviour in a pure form, for they are wantonly destructive. They live deep in the forest, away from human habitation. They are associated with the Bangun, being savage, ugly and anti-social. Since they desire neither to eat or communicate with humans, there is little ritual contact with them. They are blamed for the occasional death, but are not viewed as predators.

The *andagaw* and the jungle men represent further exaggerations of the values embodied by the spirit familiars and the ghosts. They are associated with the non-Christian neighbours of the Buid as beings similar enough to occupy the same level of the food hierarchy. So long as humans respect the social space of these spirits, they have nothing to fear from them. But there are two other categories of human spirit which consistently invade human space, and which place themselves at a higher level of the food hierarchy, regarding men as their pigs.

Like the spirit familiars and the *andagaw*, the *bulaw* operate on the minds of humans. They do so by appealing not to the higher social impulses of companionship, but to their sexual passions. They appear to humans in the form of beautiful youths or maidens of the opposite sex, luring them into the forest to eat them. Here the ambivalent attitude of the Buid toward sex comes to the fore. It constitutes a primary social bond between spouses, but it is also relatively uncontrollable. A Buid lives with the constant awareness that his or her spouse may develop a passion for another and that the solidarity of the household may thereby be destroyed. Sexual desire is only fully socialised in the context of a household whose members are under the protection of the spirits of the earth. The negative aspect of sexuality as the gratification of sexual desire is embodied in the *bulaw*, who carry it to the point of eating the partner. While the *andagaw* desire human companionship, the *bulaw* want to possess them completely, to physically incorporate them. Now, eating is a metaphor for exploitation among the Buid. It involves a hierarchical activity in which the will of the victim is completely subordinated to the will of the predator. It is opposed to speech, which is a symmetrical and equal activity. Because the Buid are eaten by *bulaw*, they are unable to communicate with them. The *bulaw* are said to be like Christians in that they employ cunning and deceit to get their way. They occupy the same mountain peaks as the *andagaw*, but the *andagaw* regard them with the same distaste as the Buid regard their human neighbours, the Christians. The *bulaw* are part of the predatory spirit world, which is dependent on human society in the same way as humans are dependent on their pigs.

Like the ghosts and the jungle men, the *fangablang* operate directly on human souls. But they do not bite human souls in order to obtain something else as do the ghosts. They attack their victims in order to kill them and eat their flesh. They do not keep away from human territory as do the jungle men, but enter human settlements in search of victims. They are the most feared of predatory spirits, being huge, ugly and vicious. As cannibals, they are the epitome of evil perversion. The Buid are obsessed with the idea of cannibalism. They are firmly convinced that there are groups of actual human beings who adhere to the practice of eating their fellows, if not in Mindoro, then somewhere across the sea. I was often asked to show them on my map where the true cannibals, *fanggamat*, 'those who grab', lived. From news broadcasts heard on their transistor radios, they are aware of the various wars being fought in different parts of the world and are apprehensive about their spreading to Mindoro. It is assumed that all wars are fought for one purpose: to eat the flesh of the adversary. They support this belief with accounts of cannibalism practised by Japanese soldiers during the war. The idea of human cannibals carrying off their children and devouring them seems to appeal strongly to their collective imagination. The *fangablang* embody a distilled cultural nightmare in which elements involving the superior power and rapacity of the Christians loom large. The more conservative Buid claimed that there was a strong correlation between the proximity of Christian settlers and the frequency of attacks by the *fangablang*. This belief contributed to Agaw's problems in keeping the settlement of Ugun Liguma together.

The spirits associated with the 'Bangun' (Taubuid) and the 'Mangyan' (Hanunoo) play a relatively small part in Buid life. They serve more as symbolic images which define the limits of proper Buid behaviour than as real threats. Buid religion is far more preoccupied with the spirits which are correlated with aspects of their own personalities, on the one hand, and with the spirits which are correlated with intrusive animal and human types, on the other. The structure of collective representations concerning the invisible world is ordered along three axes grounded in empirical experience. 1) The Buid are engaged in relations of fusion and dependency with the spirit familiars and ghosts associated with the house; in relations of separation and equality with the *andagaw* and jungle men associated with the forest; and in relations of predator and prey with the *bulaw* and *fangablang* who are associated with the deliberate transgression of boundaries. 2) The first pair of spirits is associated with the Buid themselves; the second pair with the neighbouring Mangyan and Bangun; and the third pair with the alien world of the lowlands. 3) The spirit familiars, *andagaw* and *bulaw* operate on the minds and perceptions of humans; the ghosts, jungle men and *fangablang* operate on their souls. Standing outside all these oppositions are the spirits of the earth, who are both one and many, exist both beyond the edge of the universe and within the house, and understand human speech but cannot be 'seen'. These relationships are summarised in Figure 11.

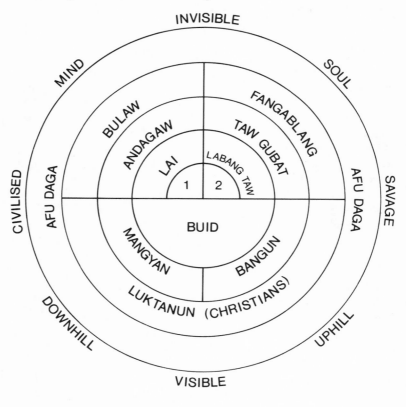

1 - FANGAYUFAN (MIND)   2 - FALAD (SOUL)

Figure 11 The structure of the human spirit world.

The social significance of Buid religion

The attributes of the various Buid spirits are grounded in empirical experience. The deepest moral and existential concerns of the Buid are embodied in a set of imaginary beings which are collective representations in the fullest sense. These representations would never achieve the same degree of internal consistency and elaboration if they were the products of the imagination of a single individual. The 'reality' of their existence is brought home to every individual in the context of a concrete social process: the collective rituals which constrain the imaginations of their participants to develop in a definite, homogeneous direction. Collective representations, once formulated, take on a life of their own. But if they are to retain their vigour they must continue to help in the interpretation of the vicissitudes of everyday life. This point was made by Lienhardt in his examination of the collective representations of a very different type of society:

> I have suggested that the Powers may be understood as images corresponding to complex and various combinations of Dinka experience which are contingent upon their particular social and physical environment. For the Dinka they are the grounds of those experiences; in our analysis we have shown them to be grounded in them, for to a European the experiences are more readily understood than the Powers, and the existence of the latter cannot be posited as a condition of the former. . . . With the imaging of the grounds of suffering in a particular Power, the Dinka can grasp its nature intellectually in a way which satisfies them, and thus to some extent transcend and dominate it in this act of knowledge. (1961: 170)

The Buid are able to share food with certain spirit types and so subsume them within their own moral code. With the aid of these spirit allies, humans are able to exert some control over their own mortality and so they need not feel themselves completely at the mercy of an unintelligible natural order. Proper moral behaviour within the community is a precondition for attracting the support of these mystical allies. The Buid solve the problem of unmerited suffering by attributing malevolence to a group of invisible beings which lacks a moral code and by attributing benevolence to a group of invisible beings which realises the moral code of humans completely. They do not, for the most part, regard illness and death as the product of their own transgressions, although those may play a contributory role, but as the product of unalterably hostile external forces. Their religion teaches them that these forces can be controlled only by engaging in continuous collective action.

The particular social and physical environment which gives rise to Buid images of good and evil finds a close parallel in Borneo. And, indeed, there is a great deal of similarity between Buid religion and the religions of the indigenous inhabitants of that island.

> The Melanau, then, look on spirits and other non-human beings as members of foreign societies, so to speak, all of which make up the world or cosmos. Every creature has its appropriate place and mode of life; so that every creature and each part of the World is governed by its own particular *adat*. . . . It is as if the Melanau thought that the World and the different beings in it formed a kind of loose composite or 'international' society knit together by a commonly held idea of a 'rule of law' (*Adat*), and by certain practical arrangements for avoiding or resolving conflicts that arise between beings subject to different *adat*. . . .
>
> The Melanau of Sarawak live, and apparently always have lived, in a highly diversified social environment in which many cultural and linguistic groups are interspersed with and closely related to one another. In so far as this environment forms a system it is a composite or plural one. The model of the World which the Melanau use for thinking about themselves indicates this state of affairs. Furthermore, the view that all human and non-human societies constitute a field of diplomatic relations, so to speak, is one they share with many of the other peoples of Borneo. (Morris, 1967: 214, 216)

Now this account fits the case of the Buid quite well in so far as their relations with other highland groups, and the spirits associated with them, are concerned. But the presence of the Christians means that the whole system cannot be regarded as an 'international society governed by a rule of law'. The Buid do not regard themselves, and are not regarded by the Christians, as belonging to the same social system governed by a shared set of values. Neither the Christians nor the predatory spirits respect the limits of Buid territory. Rather than a field of diplomatic relations existing in Mindoro, there is a situation of cold war, periodically breaking out into open conflict.

To the demands of the external social environment must be added those of the internal social environment. The internal values of homogeneity and equality in communal life are defined in opposition to the hostility of the spiritual, social and physical environments in which the Buid live. The aggressive and predatory behaviour of their human and spirit neighbours serves to cement the members of an internally undifferentiated society together. The common threats to which all the members of society are exposed act as a brake on the uncontrolled expression of personal autonomy. The representation of the spirit world as a source of unremitting danger unites the human community in a way that the extremely limited economic interdependence of households does not. In the final analysis, Buid society is held together by its collective representations and rituals.

The close connection between social and religious processes can best be demonstrated by examining a number of concrete instances of spirit attack and the response to them. It is in the response to particular instances of spirit attack that the effects of the changing political and economic environment on Buid religion can be most clearly seen.

Case histories of spirit attack

The case histories which follow are meant as illustrations of the political implications of spirit attack. They turn on the rivalry between Consejal Agaw and two ambitious competitors for political leadership, Tanay and Abun. They demonstrate the tactical attribution of responsibility for illness and death to different mystical agencies, and the necessity of joint ritual activity by opposing factions to ward off spirit attack.

Case 1

One of the main contestants for political leadership in Ugun Liguma is a 'Bangun' from Alid called Tanay. Tanay is the only Buid I ever encountered who had been married to a Christian. He had even served for a time as an assistant to the police and had developed a boastful (*buagun*) and aggressive (*maisug*) manner as a result. He was for these reasons highly distrusted in the settlement. It was rumoured that he was in possession of *taw ugbut*, the 'little men' used in sorcery. Tanay often clashed with Agaw in political meetings and is reported to have threatened him with mystical attack on one occasion. Shortly after this incident, one of Agaw's children and one of his brothers died. The issue came to the attention of Yaum in Batangan, and is recorded by Lopez (1981: 189). By the time I arrived, a year later, an alternative explanation of these deaths had gained general acceptance in Ugun Liguma. This was that Agaw's relatives had in fact been killed by the ghost of a distant relative of Tanay, Yumaynan.

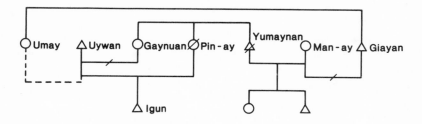

Figure 12 Links among those involved in case histories of spirit attack 1 and 2.

Case 2

Yumaynan was also a 'Bangun' from Alid. He had married into the local community of Fayagnun, as had his sister Pin-ay. Another sister, Gaynuan, tried to take Pin-ay's husband from her. Pin-ay reacted violently, threatening Gaynuan with a bush knife, and eventually forcing her to leave the husband, Uywan. Shortly afterward, Pin-ay died and gained a reputation as a malevolent ghost, due in part to her violent behaviour in life. Uywan continues to live in fear of her ghost. Although he has long desired to marry Umay, he is afraid of the ghost's jealousy. A year later, Yumaynan died, and he is believed to have since caused the death of his own father for not making sufficient offerings to Yumaynan's ghost.

Yumaynan had moved to Ayufay shortly before his death, and his widow, Man-ay, was living there with their two children when I arrived. The community is of the opinion that her presence continues to attract the malevolent attentions of her dead husband's ghost and she tends to be avoided as a result. As I have said, the deaths of Agaw's relatives were blamed in the end on this ghost. Man-ay has no relatives in Ayufay and leads a miserable existence. She suffers from chronic malaria, tuberculosis and ringworm, and has two small children to bring up by herself. Because of the reputation of her husband's ghost, she has few prospects of remarrying. Her isolation from the rest of the community and her inability to supply her own needs have forced her into dependence on one of the local Christian families, which hopes to acquire her land when she dies. Her dead husband's nephew, Igun, is also trying to acquire this land and to force Man-ay out of the settlement altogether. He is being assisted in this by Umay, the woman who wants to marry his father. Both of them refuse to do anything to help Man-ay, to take responsibility for her children, or even to bury her when she dies. Man-ay is obsessed with the idea that all her misfortunes are being caused by Yumaynan's ghost. She believes that the latter will not rest until his children are assured of their inheritance and that their future will be secured only if Igun will agree to take them on as foster children and to sacrifice a pig to Yumaynan's ghost as evidence of his good intentions. This Igun refuses to do. Such was the general background to the events which followed.

20 September 1980: After dreaming about Yumaynan, Man-ay decided that she must make an immediate offering to him. She succeeded in borrowing a chicken and a pig for the purpose. During the offering, she was assisted by Tanay, Umay and Giayan (the brother of Umay and a former husband of Man-ay).

21 September: There was a meeting in the barrio hall to discuss what should be done about Man-ay's land. Umay proposed that Man-ay return to her closest surviving relations, some first cousins, in Sigaw, and that she, Umay, would then purchase her land. Man-ay replied that she had no intention of leaving, and that since the only people who were prepared to help her were the Christians, the land would go to them when she died. Agaw opposed both proposals. He does not want to see Buid land going to Christians, but neither does he want one of his followers to be forced out of his settlement. The meeting ended inconclusively.

29 September: It was determined during a seance that Yumaynan had 'bitten' Man-ay three weeks previously as a warning. The Bureau of Forest Development had at that time been conducting a Forest Occupancy Survey (see Chapter 3). Igun had told the surveyors that Yumaynan's land belonged to him. Man-ay told me that if Igun would only give her a pig to sacrifice to Yumaynan, she would split her land with him, retaining only the portion she had under cultivation. She said, however, that Igun did not care whether or not the ghost killed her, he wanted to steal the land at all costs. Another informant told me that if Igun really had honest intentions, he would begin to take care of Man-ay's children. Yumaynan's surviving sister is also supposed to provide a pig, but has refused to do so. Man-ay had to make do with the sacrifice of one small chicken, the only animal she had.

30 September: For the third night in succession, a seance was conducted in Man-ay's house to drive off the ghost of Yumaynan, but the ghost proved so strong it was able to turn the tables and chase the familiars both on the ground and in the air. It has become angry with the entire settlement and no longer believes in its good intentions. A large pig must be sacrificed before it can be dislodged from Man-ay's house.

1 November: A pig was finally obtained and immediately sacrificed. But Igun and Gaynuan have continued to refuse to cooperate. Man-ay said that she will die within two weeks unless they give in. Although public opinion was on Man-ay's side at this point, nothing could be done to compel Igun and Gaynuan to cooperate.

23 November: Yet another pig was killed and the community was beginning to lose patience with Man-ay. The mediums in particular considered any further effort on their part to be futile without the cooperation of Igun and Gaynuan. People began to say that Man-ay was becoming greedy for meat and that they were tired of her incessant requests to be loaned pigs. In the end she was forced to go to join her

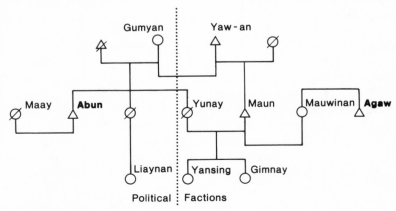

Figure 13 Links among those involved in case history of spirit attack 3.

relatives in Sigaw. Even there, people were said to be afraid that the ghost of Yumaynan would follow her and begin to haunt their settlement in turn.

Case 3

This case turns on the power struggle between Agaw and Abun. Abun is a much stronger candidate for leadership than Tanay, is more aggressive than Agaw, and is more familiar with the Christians. Unlike Tanay, he is not a 'Bangun'. When he failed to gain the leadership of the Ayufay Buid, he moved across the Bongabon river to a small settlement in Hagan. He remains closely involved in the affairs of Ugun Liguma through his relatives there, among whom are his nieces, Yansing and Gimnay. Abun's sister, Yunay, had two daughters by Maun before she died. Maun then married Agaw's sister, Mauwinan, and had several children by her. Mauwinan brought up Yansing and Gimnay from an early age, and they continue to live near her and their father in Ugun Liguma. Their father is a close friend and ally of Agaw, and so the two younger women find themselves in the ambiguous position of supporting the brother of their stepmother and opposing the brother of their real mother. To complicate matters further, Abun's mother, Gumyan, is now married to Maun's father, Yaw-an, making Maun and Abun stepbrothers as well as former brothers-in-law. Abun lives with Gumyan and Yaw-an in Hagan. They often come across to visit in Ugun Liguma. When Gumyan visits, she tends to interfere with her granddaughters, Yansing and Gimnay, and is much resented. Such was the background to the following rather complicated events.

4 October 1980: Abun's current wife Maay died, so Maun and his older daughters went across to Hagan to help with the funeral. Gumyan and Yaw-an, their grandparents on their mother's and father's sides respectively, decided to leave Hagan and move to Ambuan. Such a decision is not unusual following a death in a settlement. Maun brought them back to Ugun Liguma, which is on the way to Ambuan, and they spent a few nights in Yansing's house.

13 October: The sons of Yansing, Mauwinan and Gimnay all fell ill with similar symptoms. The illnesses were blamed on *taw ugbut* sent by Gumyan. This accusation could be correlated with the political division between those associated with Abun, and the members of his family who were allied with Agaw. Gumyan was a likely source of mystical attack because of her resentment against Yansing and Gimnay for rejecting their mother's relatives and assimilating themselves wholly to the family of their stepmother. Five mediums conducted a seance to drive off the *taw ugbut*, beginning in Yansing's house and then continuing in Mauwinan's house. The seances went on for four nights.

29 October: The children of Yansing, Gimnay and Liaynan were all ill at this point. Now, Liaynan is also a niece of Abun by another of his sisters, and lives near him in Hagan. It was determined that the cause of her children's illness was the same as that of the children of Yansing and Gimnay. This diagnosis made the attribution of responsibility to Gumyan untenable, as she would hardly attack a co-resident granddaughter's children in this way. A different diagnosis had to be found, and Gumyan herself began putting around the theory that the attacks were in fact due to the ghost of her daughter, Yunay. Yunay had died young, killed, it was said, by a jungle man while returning from a fishing expedition late at night. The shift in attribution was tacitly recognised by Agaw and Yansing when they went to help Gumyan harvest Abun's cassava in Hagan. It received official recognition when the households of Yansing and Gimnay performed a joint sacrifice to the ghost of their mother, Yunay.

16 November: A young man in Ugun Liguma was attacked by a *fansungun*, 'spirit of depression'. His father, a powerful medium, conducted a seance, during which the spirit was driven across the river to Abun's settlement in Hagan.

29 November: News arrived that the *fansungun* had now attacked Liaynan and her son, so the three most powerful mediums in Ugun Liguma went across to help expel it. They succeeded in doing so, but the spirit flew straight back to Ayufay.

30 November: A large-scale seance was held in Maun's house. It was led by his father, Yaw-an, who was now living in Ugun Liguma. He was helped by Maun, the husband of Maun's daughter, and the father of the boy who had originally been attacked by the *fansungun*. This time the spirit was driven off in a direction opposite to that of Abun's settlement. Many other spirits were sighted and chased away in the course of the seance, most of which seemed to be congregating around Yansing's house.

6 May 1981: A sacrifice was performed for Abun's dead wife Maay, who had died seven months earlier (see above). The immediate cause of the sacrifice was the fact that Maay's ghost demanded a pig she had bought from Yansing, but which she had not received before she died. Yansing and her daughter had fallen ill as a result. By this time, Abun had remarried, and his current wife and her children came to Ugun Liguma to participate in the offering of the pig. Also participating were Yansing, Gimnay and Liaynan (Abun's nieces) and one of Maay's sisters. When the ghost arrived to receive its share of the pig, it was addressed in turn by Abun, its sister, Liaynan, and Yansing's husband. It was told to leave everyone alone, now that it had received its pig.

Many past conflicts were implicit in this last sacrifice. There was a fear that the ghost might be jealous of Abun's new spouse and there was the continuing tension within Abun's kindred between those who supported him and those who supported Agaw. The fact that all of Abun's affinal and consanguineal relations rallied round in a show of unity against this mystical threat was highly significant.

Discussion

The first point to note about these cases is the crucial role of the mediums in defining the source of mystical attack and their consequent ability to mediate in political disputes. All the seances which occurred during the events described above involved mediums who had no direct stake in the running political battles. In Chapter 6, the way in which a group of mediums achieves a consensus during a seance was described. The power they have to extend that consensus throughout the community is displayed in these cases. This power rests on certain commonly held beliefs: first, that certain spirits are believed to attack individuals belonging to opposed factions; secondly, that the only way to repel such an attack is for the members of both factions to cooperate with one another; and thirdly, that the spirits are believed to attack the weakest members of the community, especially small children and nursing mothers. The continuation of conflict between factional leaders puts innocent victims at risk. Public attention shifts from the disputants to the victims and moral pressure begins to build on the rivals to cooperate. Agaw's relatives were attacked on two occasions by *taw ugbut* sent by the members of opposing factions

(Tanay and Gumyan). In each case, the diagnosis was subsequently revised by the mediums and blamed on a ghost, which, while being more or less closely related to the person originally accused of sorcery, was held to be acting out of its own motives. As regards Case 1, I have no way of knowing whether the revised diagnosis was ever completely accepted by Agaw's faction, or whether they continued to harbour doubts about Tanay's possession of *taw ugbut*. I rather suspect that they do, but that they publicly profess a belief in the guilt of Yumaynan's ghost in the interests of communal harmony. Yumaynan had already been held responsible for several other deaths, including that of his own father, and so served as a plausible scapegoat. In Case 3, a ghost was found which was equally related to members of both factions, thereby forcing them to engage in cooperative ritual activity. A hungry and determined ghost, as shown in Case 2, cannot be driven off by spirit mediums alone. Ghosts appear to have a relatively restricted target population, but the same is not true of the *fansungun*. It was batted back and forth between the respective settlements of Agaw and Abun before the combined power of mediums from both drove it off in a third direction.

In summary, then, the spirit mediums can exert their authority to redefine misfortunes as being indirectly caused, or at least prolonged, by conflicts within the community. The joint rituals they prescribe can be used by political rivals as a face-saving device for re-establishing amicable relations. Joint ritual activity can also serve as a neutral medium in which political compromises achieved in other settings can be given formal recognition. The mediums cannot always bring about a resolution, however, as is indicated by Case 2. Both factions must be interested in resolving a dispute; they must feel themselves equally at risk from the same mystical agency; and they must be subject to the same public opinion before a resolution can be achieved. This was not true in Man-ay's case. Igun lived in Akliang and had backers of his own there, while Man-ay was relatively isolated in Ugun Liguma, despite the measure of public sympathy she enjoyed. This sympathy was somewhat qualified by the belief that the ghost of her husband was implacable and that she was putting everyone in danger by her presence. If a member of Igun's faction had fallen ill at a crucial time, they would perhaps have been more amenable to the suggestions of the mediums that a joint sacrifice to the ghost was necessary, as well as some provision for the future subsistence of its children. As it was, they all remained in perfectly good health, and saw no reason to interfere with a ghost which seemed bent on victimising only their rivals. The one drawback to their wait-and-see approach was that if Man-ay were to die they might become subject to the attacks of her ghost as well. It was a risk they were prepared to take. Igun had attended several years of primary school and was relatively Christianised in outlook.

The second point to note about these cases, especially Case 2, is the light they shed on Buid notions of land tenure. Despite their partial acceptance of the concept of private landownership, they do not regard land as subject to free purchase or sale. Aside from the members of Igun's faction, everyone in Ugun Liguma held that whoever took over Man-ay's land would also have to take over responsibility for raising her children should she die. Even the Christians admitted this linkage and played on it for their own ends. Land continues to be regarded as a source of subsistence to which every Buid has an equal right and should not be treated as a source of exchange value or object of accumulation. Igun already had plenty of land in Akliang and the community in Ugun Liguma regarded him as grasping and selfish in trying to get hold of Man-ay's miserable portion, even for a 'fair' price. The Buid possess no traditional method for dealing with disputes over land, because it was never regarded as a scarce resource. It is now regarded to some extent as the corporate property of the community as a whole and rights to pieces of land within the communal territory are subject to communal control. Disputes over specific plots are aired in political meetings. One of the fundamental rules regarding land is that it should not leave the community. In order to strengthen his claim on his uncle's land, therefore, Igun built a house in Ugun Liguma, but continued to spend most of his time in Akliang. As a member of the community, Agaw was concerned to protect Man-ay's rights to her plot, and above all to prevent it from falling into Christian hands. One of Abun's worst political mistakes while I was in the field was his taking of a land dispute with another Buid straight to the Christian barrio captain of Lisap without first submitting it to a Buid political meeting. Since the main sanction against the behaviour of individuals like Abun and Igun is public opinion and the threat of boycott, there was little the community could do against them, as they lived in other settlements. Igun won a temporary victory in that Man-ay was forced to retreat to Sigaw for a while, but the community held her land in reserve until her return.

Political and religious transformations

It is now possible to draw together some of the various themes treated in this book. In Chapter 4, I described the way in which the community intervenes in domestic quarrels through the institution of the *tultulan*. Traditionally, the household was the one semi-corporate unit in society. It provided a model of cooperative activity between autonomous individuals, who share food, labour and sex within its confines. But it was also the only unit within which it was impossible for quarrelling individuals to avoid one another. While disputes between the members of different households could be resolved through simple avoidance, disputes within a household could only be resolved through the formal dissolution of the unit. It is for this reason that the household could also provide a model of social conflict. The traditional method of dispute resolution, the *tultulan*, defined all conflicts over spouses as being confined to the members of a single household. The *tultulan* provided a forum in which individuals could articulate their grievances and receive compensation for them. By restricting disputes to the smallest social unit, the community as a whole was able to preserve a sense of its overall unity. Although there was no one with the authority to impose a particular settlement, the combined weight of public opinion was brought to bear on the quarrelling couple until some sort of resolution was achieved.

The centrality of the household received symbolic recognition in the belief that it was the social solidarity of a married couple which was responsible for the fertility of humans and of crops, and not their sexual and agricultural activities. The importance of this solidarity is underlined in the periodic sacrifices made to the spirits of the earth. In Chapter 7, I described the danger to the continued growth and health of the children in a household when their parents quarrelled. The quarrelling causes the spirits of the earth to withdraw their protection and allows the predatory spirits to attack. Internal division and external attack are directly linked. Resistance to external spirit attack is futile so long as those being attacked lack internal solidarity. The belief that those sharing a household share a common liability to spirit attack as a result of their quarrelling, and in the particular vulnerability of their children, provides a mystical incentive for them to resolve their differences one way or another. The *fanurukan* draws all the members of the community together in a display of unity which serves notice to the spirits of the earth that humans are once again worthy of their protection and to the predatory spirits that humans are now prepared to drive them off. The *tultulan* and the *fanurukan* are mutually reinforcing processes on the visible and invisible planes, both tending toward the re-establishment of harmonious social relationships within the household and community.

If we turn now to the cases described above, it will be seen that behind all of them lie disputes over land or political leadership. As I argued in Chapter 5, inter-household disputes have become much more frequent over the past few years as the community has acquired an increasingly corporate character. In the first place, most of the Ayufay Buid now live in a single large settlement and can no longer avoid one another by building new houses elsewhere. In the second place, land has become a scarce resource subject to communal control. In the third place, the accumulation of economic wealth and political power is now possible due to the growing involvement of the Buid with the cash economy and lowland patrons. Members of different households who are in conflict can no longer avoid one another and there are many more opportunities for conflicts to arise. These conflicts are resolved in political meetings which include all the members of the community. As in the case of traditional divorce discussions, an attempt is made to confine disputes within the smallest relevant social unit and to prevent them from spilling over into a larger social arena. Skilful orators like Agaw constantly remind their adversaries of the common threat everyone is under from the Christians and of the necessity for resolving disputes within the community so that a united front may be presented to external aggressors. Such orators do not have the power to impose a specific resolution to a quarrel, but they marshal the forces of public opinion against those causing internal division. They reiterate the basic principles of communal solidarity and equality over and over again in their speeches. As in the *tultulan* the selfish passions of quarrelling individuals are submitted to the moderating influence of protracted rational debate. Eventually, a compromise is reached, if only after months of talks. The indirect nature of Buid speech allows for the emergence of an acceptable solution without it being clear who originated it. The political meeting provides a forum in which individuals can articulate their grievances, and in which a consensus of opinion as to how to deal with the Christians can be achieved. Those with a recognised expertise in lowland affairs naturally have a greater influence on policy than others, but they must always explain their reasons for advocating a particular course of action. This is true even of Yaum, who spends half his time in making speeches to the various communities over which he exercises some influence.

The skilful politcal leader must play on the external threat posed by the Christians, while at the same time demonstrating a familiarity with their customs. It was Agaw who initiated the construction of a fence around Ugun Liguma to serve as a symbolic barrier against Christian intrusion, but it is also Agaw who conducts negotiations with the Christians on behalf of the community. There is a close parallel here with the actions of the spirit mediums, who construct invisible walls around settlements to keep out the predatory spirits, but who also negotiate with the more articulate spirit types. Mediums and political leaders both claim a relative expertise in dealing with external agencies of aggression. In relation to the group's internal affairs, they are treated as equals. In relation to its external affairs, they receive a certain amount of deference, but they must still operate within the constraints of collective decision-making, whether in the context of the large-scale seance or of the political meeting.

In Chapter 6 I described the way in which spirit mediums arrive at a consensus of opinion concerning the nature of the spirits which are attacking a settlement. No medium is powerful enough on his own to repel these attacks. He must work in conjunction with his colleagues to buid up a picture of the current state of affairs in the invisible world and to drive off spirits which might overpower him if he acted on his own. In a large-scale seance, there will be several mediums with the ability to 'see' the same spirits and the assumption is that all the mediums will eventually be able to 'see' the same spirits. The authenticity of a diagnosis is established by mutual agreement and is legitimised not by the privileged experience of any one individual, but by the group of mediums as a whole. The threat to the community is especially grave when one of its members has recently died, or when the members of several different households fall ill simultaneously. Certain spirits, such as the Christian cannibals, pose an equal threat to all Buid, while others, such as the ghosts, pose a more specifc threat. Even in the latter case, however, it is expected that unrelated mediums will help out in the spirit of *tarugbungan*, 'mutual assistance', without asking for any compensation. The mediums in a seance shift back and forth between their individualised chants, intelligible only to themselves and their familiars, and normal speech, which connects them with the experiences of the other mediums. In this way the collective power of the community is brought to bear against the external agencies which subject it to a collective liability. As the community has acquired an increasingly clear definition on the ground, so the mystical interdependence of community members has received more frequent recognition in large-scale seances.

The ability of the Buid to organise their communities on corporate lines is in part a product of their traditioinal religious system which stressed the mystical interdependence of community members. However, the emergence of corporate communities has also led to a transformation of their religious system. The spirit mediums are now able to exert a mediating influence on contenders for political leadership, as illustrated in the cases discussed above. In this they play a role complementary to that of the orators who speak in the communal interest. Added to the threat posed by the attacks of the Christians is the threat posed by the mystical attacks of the predatory spirits. The mediums speak for the community in a more indirect manner than do the orators, for they deal with invisible agencies which pose a threat to everyone without discrimination. Just as open quarrelling between the members of a single household poses a mystical threat to its weakest members and so puts pressure on them to resolve their differences, so quarrelling between the leaders of different factions within a single community poses a mystical threat to the weakest members of both factions. And just as the display of ritual unity in the *fanurukan* is a necessary prelude to efficacious action against the spirits which have attacked the children of a divided household, so is a display of ritual unity in large-scale seances and offerings to the dead now seen as a necessary prelude to the repulsion of spirits which have attacked the relatives of rivals for land or political leadership. The large-scale seance and the political meeting have come to be mutually reinforcing processes on the invisible and the visible planes, both tending toward the re-establishment of harmonious relationships within the community.

It is possible, then, to discern a broad parallelism between the traditional *tultulan* and *fanurukan*, on the one hand, and the political meeting and large-scale seance, on the other. Buid religion has been able to transform itself so as to take account of a corporate unit larger than the household. It continues to provide a mystical rationale for the maintenance of internal solidarity despite increasing internal divisions and external pressures. The source of this adaptability lies, I would argue, in the egalitarian nature of Buid religion and society. The correct interpretation of visible and invisible danger is arrived at through collective participation in a number of formal processes, of which the four just discussed are the most important. The political meeting is a recent innovation, but it is firmly grounded in the traditional *tultulan*. In both cases, beliefs concerning the predatory spirit world act as an effective incentive toward cooperation and compromise between autonomous equals.

9   Summary and Conclusions

In this concluding chapter, I will first summarise the argument of the book, and then go on to examine at a more theoretical level one of the key features of Buid social life, that of sharing. It is argued that sharing as practised by the Buid has a fundamentally political, and not economic, significance. In order to understand its meaning, Buid society must be placed within a larger socio-historical context, in much the same manner as Leach was led to interpret the political systems of highland Burma in the context of their contact with the Shan states. I conclude, then, with some reflections on the need for further ethno-historical research in achieving a proper assessment of the political values of highland groups in Southeast Asia.

Summary

The central concern of this book has been to elucidate the fundamental principles and idioms according to which the Buid organise their social life. It has been my contention that Buid religious beliefs and practices are no less essential to the constitution of Buid communities than are their beliefs and practices relating to the economy, politics and the conduct of proper social relations. A more peripheral concern which runs throughout the book is the relationship between the historical experience of the Buid and their current system of social organisation. It has been argued that the Buid have been subjected to a set of pressures from the lowlands for many hundreds of years, and that the Buid have been able to maintain their economic, political and cultural autonomy only by systematically resisting these pressures.

It was shown in Chapter 2 that the Buid were caught between the competing forces of the Spanish empire and the Sulu sultanate in their struggle for hegemony in the Philippine islands. This struggle led to the depopulation of the coastal region of Mindoro, and to a resultant delay in the integration of Mindoro into the world economy. During this period, the principal threat to the survival of the Buid and other highland groups as autonomous societies was their recruitment as

217

slaves by the Sulu and as tributaries by the Spanish. During the post-war period, the primary threat to the Buid has come from pressure on their land, due to the population explosion on neighbouring islands and to the opening of government lands to pioneer settlements.

In Chapters 3, 4 and 5, an account was given of the traditional economic, social and political systems of the Buid as they are still practised among the more isolated groups of the interior, and of their transformation among the more exposed groups forced to live in close proximity to Christian settlers. The traditional value system stresses the absolute equality and autonomy of all adults and the need for collective solidarity in the face of external aggression. The idioms which dominate social life are those of community, companionship and sharing as opposed to the idioms of descent, kinship and reciprocity usually found in other noncentralised societies. The first set of idioms implies a free association of equals in the present, while the second implies an involuntary and permanent status hierarchy inherited from the past. Local communities are bound together by the sharing of speech, food, labour and ritual between the members of different households and by their potential sharing of residence and sex. Social relations are based on the temporary bonds created by the sharing of social space and activity, as opposed to the enduring bonds created by the sharing of a common origin or substance. A constant circulation of individuals between different households accomplished by frequent divorce and a constant flow of goods and services between them, accomplished through collective ritual activity, serve to create an over-arching social whole to which every individual owes allegiance, as against specific individuals. The continuous redistribution of person-nel between the component households of a community prevents the emergence of cohesive kinship groups, while collective liability to mystical attack and collective responsibility for repelling it makes every individual dependent on and responsible to the local group.

This traditional system is under threat at all levels in the areas where Christian settlement is putting pressure on Buid land. The Ayufay Buid, who fled their valley to escape the effects of the Second World War and a subsequent smallpox epidemic, have succeeded in reoccupying their territory only by drastically modifying their social and religious institutions. The local community has been transformed into a semi-corporate group with a recognised leadership, policy-making process, corporate property, membership and identity. They have successfully adapted themselves to the growing of cash crops and are able to use their consequent economic power to bargain with lowland patrons. In return for the protection of their land, the Buid sell their crops to these patrons at a lower price than the patrons would have to give to the Christian settlers, who are dependent on their cash crops for their subsistence. The Buid continue to gain most of their subsistence from their root crops and can spend most of the money they receive from their cash crops on luxuries and taxes. But although a certain degree of equality is maintained within the semi-corporate community, a few individuals have been able to accumulate a dispro-portionate amount of material wealth and political influence. These leaders are now attempting to consolidate their position in the com-munity by manipulating ties of kinship and affinity within it and by monopolising all contact with the lowland world through their position as spokesman and brokers.

Chapters 6 and 7 described Buid ritual activities. They showed that the Buid believe themselves to be under constant attack by a host of predatory spirit types, and that the only way to contain this threat is through the collective power of the spirit mediums, on the one hand, and through the appropriation of animal vitality and the acquisition of powerful spirit allies, on the other. The values of equality and auton-omy are present in both seances and sacrifice, for no individual is strong enough to combat the spirit world alone, but must rely on the support of the whole community. In ritual, the house becomes a symbol of the community. A threat to the occupants of one house is a threat to the whole community. The Buid are engaged in relations ranging from absolute hostility to absolute solidarity with the different types of being which make up the spirit world. These relations are expressed in the same idioms as those employed in the conduct of social relations, that is, in the idioms of companionship, community and sharing. In animal sacrifice, humans simultaneously establish solidarity between the members of different households, and between themselves and their spirit allies, through the sharing of the meat of domesticated animals. Domesticated animals serve as spatial, social and mystical mediators. Certain spirit types are invited into the house to share meat, some are invited only to its threshold, some are fed in a separate house built on the margins of the forest and others are kept away entirely. Buid religion not only embodies the same values as Buid society, it enters into the very constitution of that society.

In Chapter 8, it was shown that the structure of the spirit world constitutes both a model of and a model for the larger social system in which the Buid are embedded. The various spirit types represent Buid moral values in an exaggerated and magnified form. At one extreme are the relations of permanent hostility between the Buid and the Christians, parallelled on the mystical plane by the permanent struggle between the spirit familiars and the predatory spirits. At the other extreme are the relations of mutual help and sharing within the Buid community, parallelled on the mystical plane by the solidarity between humans and the spirits of the earth, who give fertility without asking for a return. Life ultimately depends on the maintenance of solidarity within the human community, which is a prerequisite for the maintenance of solidarity with the spirits of the earth.

Sharing versus reciprocity

One of the key principles of Buid social organisation is that of sharing, which I identify as the denial of reciprocity in the strict sense. Buid sharing is characterised by a radical disconnection between giver and recipient. In sharing, there is an obligation to give, but there is no obligation to receive from, or to repay, a particular individual. The giver does not indebt the recipient, for the recipient is not individuated from the mass. Everyone present receives a share, whatever the past history of the relationship between giver and recipient. Woodburn has summed up the principle involved nicely: 'Entitlement does not depend in any way on donation' (1982: 441). The recipients of words, labour and meat are merged with the undifferentiated community. Dyadic exchanges are avoided because they are seen as inherently competitive or unequal: one must emerge from them as a winner or loser, as a creditor or debtor, as a patron or client.

Polanyi attempted to formulate three types of primitive economy, which he characterised as being organised according to the principles of reciprocity, redistribution and householding, respectively (1944: 55). He later simplified his system, and included householding under the heading of redistribution (1957). Sahlins has taken this simplification even further, treating reciprocity and redistribution as easily discriminable points on a single continuum which ranges from 'generalised' through 'balanced' to 'negative' reciprocity (1972). Under the heading of generalised reciprocity, Sahlins places both the mutuality expected among close kinsmen and the redistribution from the centre characteristic of centralised chiefdoms (1972: 194). What the two have in common is a vagueness in the obligation to repay a prestation. Now, I think that this is a gross oversimplification. There is a qualitative difference between the obligation to give to a specific social superior in a chiefly system and the moral obligation to give to a close kinsman in time of need. Apart from muddling two distinct forms of social interaction, the scheme suffers from an uncritical use of the concept of reciprocity. Its use is only appropriate for what Sahlins calls balanced and negative reciprocity, in which what is exchanged between two parties is qualitatively similar and so commensurable, whether the goods involved be pigs, woman, or deaths. I bring these points up because it is the presence of an ideology of balanced reciprocity which is often taken to indicate the presence of egalitarian values in a society. The segmentary lineages of certain African pastoralists and the competitive feasting of New Guinea big men are cases in point. Forge has, I think, made a much more satisfactory attempt to theorise the political implications of this kind of exchange, in the context of Highland New Guinea: 'The principal mechanism by which equality is maintained [in these societies] is equal exchange of things of the same class or of identical things. Basically all prestations of this type are challenges to prove equality' (1972: 534). This is as good a definition of reciprocity as I know. Forge goes on to note that reciprocity can be used as a means of maintaining a social relationship only on condition that a perfect balance between partners is never achieved. One or the other must always be in debt and obliged to reciprocate. 'Equal exchange is, in fact, a system of alternating seniority' (ibid.: 535). The Buid, who view themselves as 'balancing-up' a relationship at divorce through the payment of compensation, in order to terminate it, illustrate this principal by way of negative example.

Among both African pastoralists and New Guinea highlanders, social relations between adult men are expressed through a complex network of reciprocal debts and claims. Social advancement is achieved through the clever manipulation of dyadic obligations. With skill and luck, one can quickly build up a large herd of cattle or amass a fortune in prestige (see H. Schneider, 1981; A. Strathern, 1971). But good fortune can vanish with equal rapidity, and it is the long-term balancing of fortunes which results in a secular trend toward equality. Rather than viewing equality as a desirable final state, these societies appear to possess an ideology of equal opportunity in a competitive process leading to relative success or failure. New Guinea big men have rather more success in achieving lasting recognition of their prestige than do wealthy Nuer, but this is because the Nuer attach the greatest importance to success in feuding and raiding: their ideology is closer to negative than to balanced reciprocity. 'Skill and courage in fighting are reckoned the highest virtues, raiding the most noble, as well as the most profitable occupation' (Evans-Pritchard, 1940: 50).

Perhaps the most significant difference between the Buid and acephalous societies throughout Africa is the importance attached to kinship ties in organising society among the latter.[1]

Whatever property rights are invested in the descent group, control over its women is of paramount importance. It was Lévi-Strauss who noted the particular value of women as objects of exchange in creating enduring ties between social groups which were not linked by a division of social labour. They unite the exchanging units for at least their lifetimes. According to the formula of restricted exchange, an alliance based on reciprocity can be maintained without resorting to the alternating debt imposed by the exchange of more perishable articles (Lévi-Strauss, 1969: 481). But this solution merely shifts the locus of inequality from inter-segmental relations to the interior of each segment. In the first place, women must be subordinate to men if they are to be used as exchange objects. In the second place, unmarried men are made dependent on those already in control of women for access to wives.

African societies operate according to a more subtle rule than that of restricted exchange. They make good the loss of a woman to one group by acquiring a woman from another group with the wealth obtained from the first group. The principle of reciprocity still applies: the gift of a woman requires a repayment which can be used to replace her with another. Douglas (1963) and Wilson (1950) have well described how control of bridewealth objects, be they raffia cloth or cattle, bolsters up the prestige of the elders who control them and makes junior men dependent on them. Hierarchy in acephalous African societies is most noticeable in relations between the sexes and generations. But the principle of bridewealth can also lead to a differential accumulation of wealth which can be invested in more women. Such accumulations lead to a temporary inequality between polygynists and poor bachelors, but, as Goody points out, these inequalities tend to be evened out in the next generation due to the greater number of heirs fathered by the polygynist (1973: 13).

The dominant idiom of exchanges with political implications in Highland New Guinea and among acephalous African pastoral societies is one of balanced reciprocity. Dyadic reciprocity is either potentially or actually unequal. One must be able to prove one's credit-worthiness in a host of social situations. The exchange of women between descent groups and the consequent inequalities between the sexes and generations, and the competitive struggle to *achieve* and *maintain* equality in these societies all stand in marked contrast to the ideologies of personal choice of marriage partner and of sharing among the Buid.

Going back to Mauss, I would argue that in systems of mechanical solidarity, when each segment is producing the same type of goods as every other, exchange must be interpreted as having more to do with the expression of social relationships than with the acquisition of economic advantages. What is being expressed by sharing is an axiom of social equality: it is primarily a political phenomenon and must be treated as such. Any explanation of its presence as the dominant form of exchange in a society must be sought in terms of that society's political situation. I would argue that the noncompetitive egalitarianism of the Buid is the result of their specific cultural response to enclavement within more powerful societies which were unable to incorporate them due to the Buid's occupation of a mountain habitat unsuitable to the economy of the lowlands. Thoroughgoing egalitarianism in all aspects of Buid life is the consequence not of a simple economy or of an undeveloped division of social labour, but of a culture's rejection of the political values of a neighbouring hierarchical system. This argument can be made more clearly by comparing it with that advanced by Leach in *Political Systems of Highland Burma*.

In that work, Leach asserted that 'It seems to me axiomatic that where neighbouring communities have demonstrable economic, political and military relations with each other then the field of any useful sociological analysis must override cultural boundaries' (1954: 292). Now, Leach described the situation in highland Burma as one in which

> persons who speak a different language, wear a different dress, worship different deities and so on are not regarded as foreigners entirely beyond the pale of social recognition. . . . In this context cultural attributes such as language, dress and ritual procedure are merely symbolic labels denoting the different sectors of a single extensive structural system. (ibid.: 17, see also pp. 280–1)

In other words, there was an integration of political values between the members of neighbouring societies, which allowed them to understand each other's social systems, even if they did not always approve of them.

Leach further emphasised that the societies of the lowland, or at least of the flat areas capable of supporting wet-rice agriculture, were characterised by a hierarchical ideology in which the ruler held auto-cratic power over his subordinates; while the societies of the highlands were torn between an egalitarian set of values based on reciprocity between kinsmen and a hierarchical set of values modelled on those of the lowlands:

> it is the culmination of *gumsa* ideals that the Kachin *duwa* [chief] should be treated as a *saohpa* [prince] by his Shan counterpart. Commoner Kachins on the other hand can only become Shan by ceasing to be Kachins. At commoner level the Kachin and Shan systems, although linked economically, are totally separated by barriers of kinship and religion. (ibid.: 222)

Kachin society is supposed to oscillate through time between the hierarchical model held by the Shan lowlanders and the egalitarian model held by certain Kachin highland communities.

Now, the Buid have also had demonstrable economic, political and military relations with neighbouring Christian and Muslim communi-ties for a very long time; they adhere to an egalitarian set of values in marked contrast to the hierarchical values held by their lowland neighbours, and for a Buid to become a Filipino means adopting the Christian religion and ceasing to be a Buid. Where the situation in Mindoro differs from that in highland Burma is that, in the first place, the Buid have always been regarded by, and have always regarded, their lowland neighbours as 'foreigners entirely beyond the pale of social recognition' and, in the second place, they have always been much weaker than their lowland neighbours. They have been treated historically only as a source of cheap labour, trade goods and, more recently, as a minor impediment to the occupation of free land. The Kachin, on the other hand, have often been able to impose their will on the Shan through superior military strength:

> the mountaineers are sometimes regarded as the political overlords of the valley, so that the valley people pay a feudal rent to the hill chieftains; sometimes the hill peoples merely exploit the fact that they control the cross-country communications between the valleys

and levy a toll on passing caravans; sometimes the valley peoples have been willing to pay 'blackmail' provided the hill men agree not to raid the valley crops; sometimes the valley chieftains have engaged the hill men as mercenaries on a large scale. (ibid.: 21)

It would be interesting to examine any parallels between this situation and that which obtained in northern Luzon during the seventeenth and eighteenth centuries (see Chapter 2). But as far as Mindoro is concerned, the lowlands have always been able to dictate the terms on which the inhabitants of the highlands could participate in the lowland polity and economy.

What was, I think, insufficiently emphasised by Leach was that in a complex cultural environment such as is found in much of Southeast Asia, the values held by the members of one society are as likely to be defined in opposition to the values held by the members of neighbouring societies as they are to be modelled on them. The Kachin were often strong enough to apply the maxim 'if you can't beat them, join them', while for the Buid the situation was that 'since you can't join them, run away'. What we find among the Buid and other insular shifting cultivators who have been subjected to slave raiding and other forms of coercion in the past is a systematic and wholesale rejection of the hierarchical political values of their predatory neighbours.

The peaceful and anarchic Subanun have long been prey to more strongly organised neighbours. Beginning before the Spanish conquest of the Philippines and continuing intermittantly until the twentieth century, Moslems from Sulu and Lanao raided the Subanun for slaves, collected tribute, and established a system of forced trade. (Frake, 1960: 52)

The extreme emphasis on egalitarian values I have been describing among the Buid is intelligible only as part of a larger structural system in which those values have been elaborated in opposition to the hierarchy and coercion practised by the surrounding lowland societies. The Buid political culture strongly condemns any display of violence and aggression, and any attempt to establish ties of dependency and domination within the society. I see this culture as having developed in response to the continuous pressures which have been exerted on it from the outside in the past few decades, if not centuries. Clearly, our historical knowledge is at the moment far too limited to demonstrate this hypothesis and, like Leach, I can offer it only as a plausible speculation not contradicted by the available evidence. Neither would I claim that Buid society represents the only possible outcome of such pressure: the social organisation of the neighbouring Hanunoo and Taubuid is certainly very different, despite the fact of their having undergone similar historical experiences. It may be that the surviving evidence on the ethno-history of Mindoro is too slight to take this argument much further, but it is possible that there are other areas in Southeast Asia in which it might be more convincingly substantiated. Further historical work, combined with meticulous fieldwork, is necessary.

It has not been my intention in this book to treat the Ayufay Buid as an example of a pristine tribal society, whose sole interest lies in the fact that they have preserved a set of exotic customs into modern times, but to understand their total social situation at a particular moment in time, 1979–81. That situation is not in equilibrium: it represents a great modification of the one that obtained five years before and in all likelihood it will have undergone a great modification five years from now. But, as I hope I have demonstrated, this has probably been true throughout Buid history. The Buid have always lived within sight of a very different form of economy and society in the lowlands of Mindoro, and have rejected them. The 'traditional' institutions I have been describing are themselves the products of previous social transformations, produced in part as a response to predatory neighbours. The historical creativity of the Buid was not extinguished when they finally decided to form large permanent settlements and pay taxes to the state. For convenience, I have taken as my base line the sort of economy and society which is at present in operation among the interior Buid communities of Fawa and Alid, and as my model of a possible future for the Ayufay Buid the form of economy and society that has developed in Batangan. It remains to be seen whether the Ayufay Buid will allow the substitution of Christian ideology for their own. In all the Christian sects I have observed in operation on Mindoro, Truth is defined by a hierarchy of religious specialists who have undergone a prolonged training at the hands not only of non-Buid, but of non-Filipinos. This hierarchical structure is in marked contrast to the egalitarian structure of Buid religion. The survival of the Ayufay Buid as an autonomous culture depends on the continued transformation of their received collective representations. I have no doubt that even if they do take on Christian ideology, they will try to make it their own in a manner impossible to predict.

Appendix I: The identity and distribution of the mountain tribes of Mindoro

In the first scientific survey of the mountain tribes of Mindoro, Conklin remarked that 'More than most other parts of the Philippines, Mindoro and Palawan had been neglected by ethnographic and linguistic research until 1947' (Conklin, 1949a: 268). This situation has been rectified to some extent over the last thirty-five years due to a series of publications, of which those by Conklin are the earliest and most significant. In his initial survey, Conklin showed that the 'Mangyan' of Mindoro were in reality composed of a number of distinct cultural groupings which had little contact with one another. He proposed a division into nine major groups and three sub-groups (see Map II). His identification of the two northernmost groups as Iraya and Alangan, and of the three southern most groups as the Hanunoo, Ratagnon and Buid has been accepted by all subsequent researchers, despite minor revisions in their proposed boundaries. The identity and distribution of the central groups has, however, been called into question. On the basis of his experience as a missionary in Mindoro between 1954 and 1957, and following consultations with other members of the Overseas Missionary Fellowship who worked there subsequently, Tweddell has proposed a reduction in the number of groups occupying the centre of the island from four to two (Tweddell, 1970: see Map III). These he calls Tadyawan, who are divided into four distinct residential and dialectical bands (ibid.: 195), and the Batangan, who occupy the very centre of the island. Pennoyer, who worked among the latter group, prefers to call them the Taubuid. He asserts that they are divided into an eastern and a western dialect group, who share about 65 per cent of the basic Swadesh word list between them, and who are linked by a chain of dialects (Pennoyer, 1977: 21). The existence of blurred linguistic boundaries is common throughout the island, with the exceptions of the clear-cut boundary between the Hanunoo and Buid, and the even clearer boundary between the Hanunoo and Ratagnon. The latter speak a dialect of Cuyonon unrelated to the other Mangyan languages (Tweddell, 1970: 190). Zorc has shown that there is a clear division between the northern Mangyan languages of Iraya, Alangan and Tadyawan on the one hand, and the southern Mangyan languages of Hanunoo and Buid, on the other (Zorc, 1974). To the latter group, Pennoyer adds Taubuid (1980a). The southern group shows clearer affinities to the Palawanic languages than it does to the northern group (Zorc, 1974: 585). In his 1975 thesis, Zorc classifies North Mangyan with Pampango and Zambal, which are spoken in central Luzon, while South Mangyan is assigned to the Meso-Philippine group of languages, along with Palawan and Kalamian (cited in Llamazon, 1978: 27). The projected time depth for the splitting of these language groups is very great and this fact should lead one to treat with caution the claim advanced by Lopez that the inhabitants of Mindoro constituted a homogeneous population before the arrival of the Spanish (Lopez, 1976: 8).

According to Zorc, the three northern languages themselves form a chain (1974: 562), and it is clear from Tweddell's account that dialectical variation within each of them is also very great (1970: 192, 195). A similar situation exists in the Buid and Taubuid areas according to my own observations and those of Pennoyer (1977, 1980a). It is difficult, in consequence, to make a clear-cut classification of Mangyan groups on linguistic grounds alone.

A further difficulty stems from the fact that most Mangyan groups classify themselves in terms of spatial and geographical criteria and not in terms of social or linguistic ones. It must be emphasised that, with the exception of the Buid and Taubuid (both of which mean simply 'high-lander'), none of the Mangyan groups refer to themselves by the terms for them current in the anthropological literature. *Hanunoo* means 'real, true', and is used by the group which bears that name as a prefix to Mangyan to distinguish themselves from other highland groups. Conklin decided to drop the term 'Mangyan' because of its pejorative local connotations. The Pula, Batangan, Nauhan, Tagaidan and Bangon mentioned by Conklin in his initial survey are all geographical terms, some of which are used in self-reference, others of which are only applied to neighbouring groups.

If we turn now to the area I know at first hand, the Buid refer to themselves as Buid. 'Buid' means simply 'uphill'. Used in its widest sense, 'Buid' may be used to refer to any highlander who possesses customs similar to one's own and distinct from those of the lowlanders. Thus my informants identified the individuals shown in photographs of the Ilongot, a highland tribe of northern Luzon, as *Buid yadi* 'also Buid'. It appears from Pennoyer's adoption of the term that all the Mangyan north of the Hanunoo and south of the Alangan use this term as their most general self-appellation. At a more restricted level, 'Buid' is used in opposition to *Bangun*, 'those living even further uphill', i.e. for the Ayufay Buid, the Taubuid of Pennoyer, and to *Mangyan patag* 'lowland Mangyan', i.e. the Hanunoo of Conklin. Now, as there is no ambiguity about the linguistic boundary between the Buid and the Hanunoo, there is no ambiguity for the Buid as to who is a *Mangyan patag*. The situation to the north is not so simple. *Bangun* is a term used by all Buid to refer to those other Buid living up-river whom they consider to be dirty, savage and disreputable, and to be possessed of inordinate mystical power. *Bangun* are thus looked down upon and feared. No one would apply the term to themselves. For example, the Ayufay Buid describe themselves as Buid, but are considered by the Batangan and Siangi Buid to be Bangun (see Map V). When an Ayufay Buid uses the phrase *Bangun arungan* 'true Bangun', he is referring to the inhabitants of Ginyang and beyond. There is a relatively sharp break in social interaction between those groups living up-river from Ginyang, and those living down-river. It may be taken as forming the real boundary between the Buid and the Taubuid (see Map IV).

The Buid proper have been variously subdivided. Tweddell classifies them according to outstanding features of material culture, viz. the 'script-writing Buid' on the Sumagui and Tangun rivers, the 'pipe-smoking Buid' along the middle Bongabon river and its tributaries from Ginyang to Siangi, the 'Beribi' from the headwaters of the Siangi west, and the 'cloth-making Buid' to the south of the Siangi and along the northern boundary of the Hanunoo (Tweddell, 1970: 197–8: see Map III). Pennoyer agrees with these divisions, but points out that the 'cloth-making Buid' are also familiar with the Hanunoo script (Pennoyer, 1975: 12). All four groups intersect on my Map IV. Ugun Liguma, where I conducted fieldwork, would then be part of the pipe-smoking group, Batangan part of the cloth-making group, those in the lower left of the map would be Beribi and those in the upper right would be script-writing Buid. The Ayufay Buid see matters somewhat differently. The outstanding features of material culture in their eyes are the weaving of baskets carried on in their region and the making of clay pots carried on by the groups living south of the Siangi. It is to this economic specialisation that they attribute the fact that the two groups are prohibited from intermarrying.

Similar confusions are apparent elsewhere in the Philippine literature. Relational terms such as 'Buid' and 'Bangun' are present, for example, in Panay:

I have accepted the term Sulod on the basis of what neighbours call their neighbours, rather than what individuals call themselves. . . . In fact it is difficult, if not impossible, to locate the Sulod by asking the people directly, for as one travels across the mountain region . . . one is successively directed to the next hill, settlement, or river bend as the home of the Sulod. (Jocano, 1968: 7)

Previous ethnography on the Mangyan

Conklin followed up his initial survey with intensive fieldwork among the Hanunoo of Yagaw in the years 1952–4 and in 1957. He defines his general methodological orientation as follows:

An adequate ethnography is here considered to include the culturally significant arrangement of productive statements about the relevant relationships obtaining among locally defined categories and contexts (of objects and events) within a given social matrix. (Conklin, 1964: 25)

His publications reflect this orientation, dealing with such themes as the analysis of categories applying to semantic segregates such as plant species (1955a), colours (1955b), swidden plant associations (1957), modified speech forms (1959), kin terms (1964) and landform categories (1976), a Hanunoo-English vocabulary (1953b) and detailed descriptions of technical procedures such as pottery making (1953a), shifting cultivation (1957) and betel-chewing (1958).

Much valuable material concerning the Hanunoo has also been collected by Father Antoon Postma SVD, who has run a mission in the Hanunoo settlement of Panaytayan since 1960 (Postma, 1981b: 2). His publications concern such topics as the traditional syllabic script (1968, 1971), ethno-history (1974, 1977b), and the traditional poetic form, the *ambahan* (1977a, 1981a, 1981b). He has also been host to a number of Filipino and foreign researchers, among whom the most notable is Miyamoto who has written on Hanunoo society and folk beliefs (1975, see also de la Paz, 1968).

The northern Mangyan groups are still almost untouched by anthropological investigation. To my knowledge the only published accounts are those of Maceda (1967) and those of Charles Macdonald (1971) and Nicole Revel-Macdonald (1971) on the Iraya and Alangan. The last two publications are based, however, on an initial trip of two weeks and a second trip of two months at the beginning of 1970 (Macdonald, 1970: 273). They offer little in the way of ethnographic data, except to confirm existing accounts of the general fear of out-siders which affects the interior Mangyan groups (ibid.: 273) and the presence of large communal houses among the Alangan, called *banwa* (ibid.: 275).

More substantial work has been done among the Taubuid by Pennoyer, who spent twelve months among them in 1973–4 (1978: 54). His thesis is devoted to the use of plants in ritual, but includes much information on social organisation as well (1975). The longest period he spent in one place seems to have been in a settlement on the Sumagui river which had been converted to Christianity by the fundamentalist O.M.F. (1975: 18). His attempts to work with a more traditional group in the interior were frustrated by the refusal of the Taubuid to cooperate (1978: 53). Pennoyer took fear to be a charac-teristic feature of the whole of Taubuid culture (1980b: 703, 1978), a culture ruled by 'megalomaniac big men' who control their followers through fear of withcraft (1975: 96).

The first ethnographic publication on the Buid was that by Conklin in 1953, on pottery techniques. This was followed by Miyamoto who made several short exploratory trips among them (1974). More re-cently, Lopez spent twelve months among the Batangan Buid (see Map V) in 1978–9, overlapping my own period in the field to some extent. Lopez has published previously on the ethno-history of Mindoro (1974, 1976). Her doctoral dissertation deals with the impact of the state and the market economy on the southern Buid, or what Tweddell calls the cloth-making Buid. Because of the presence of the phoneme 'h' in this area, this group calls itself and is called by Lopez, the Buhid. For the sake of simplicity, I use the northern form of Buid throughout this work to refer to both groups, qualifying it when necessary with the adjectives 'southern' or 'northern'.

Lopez was unable to observe much of the traditional Buid way of life in Batangan, so extensive have the changes in the economic, political and religious systems been in that area. She devotes about sixty pages of her thesis to the traditional system (1981: 120–38, 155–93). Similarities and differences between the northern and southern Buid are mentioned in the course of this book.

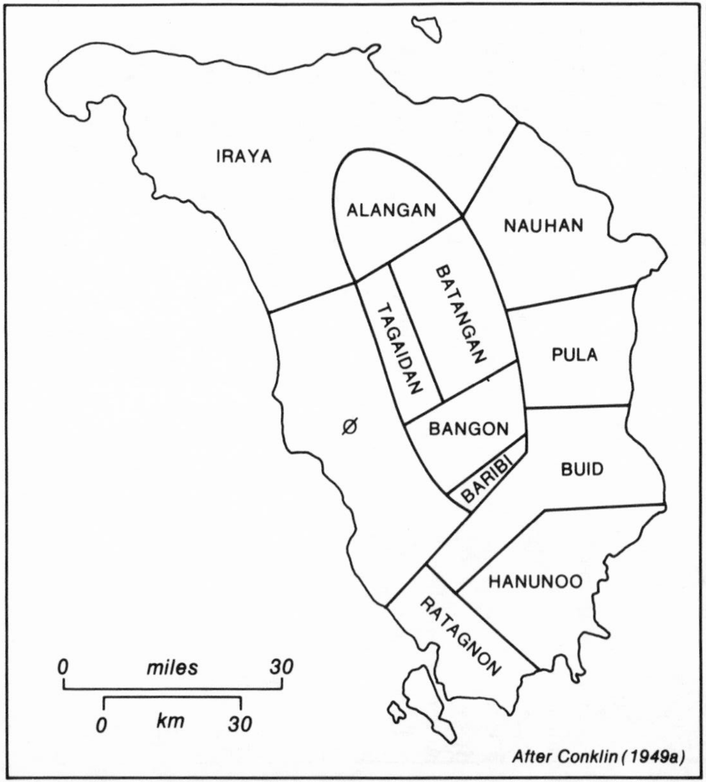

Map III Tribal Territorial Distribution in Mindoro (after Tweddell)

a 'script writing'
b 'pipe smoking'
c 'Baribi'
d 'cloth making'

After Tweddell (1970)

Map II Tribal Distribution in Mindoro (after Conklin)

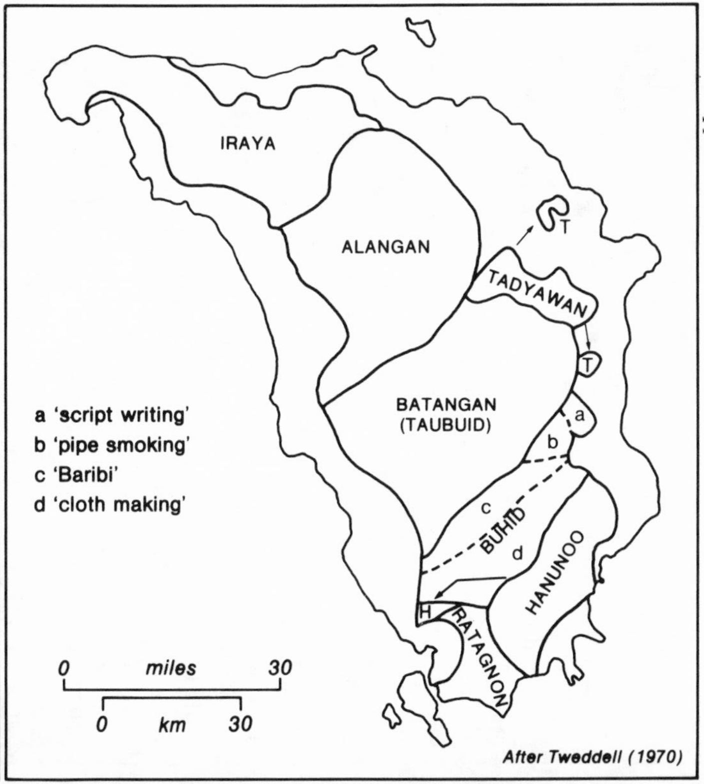

After Conklin (1949a)

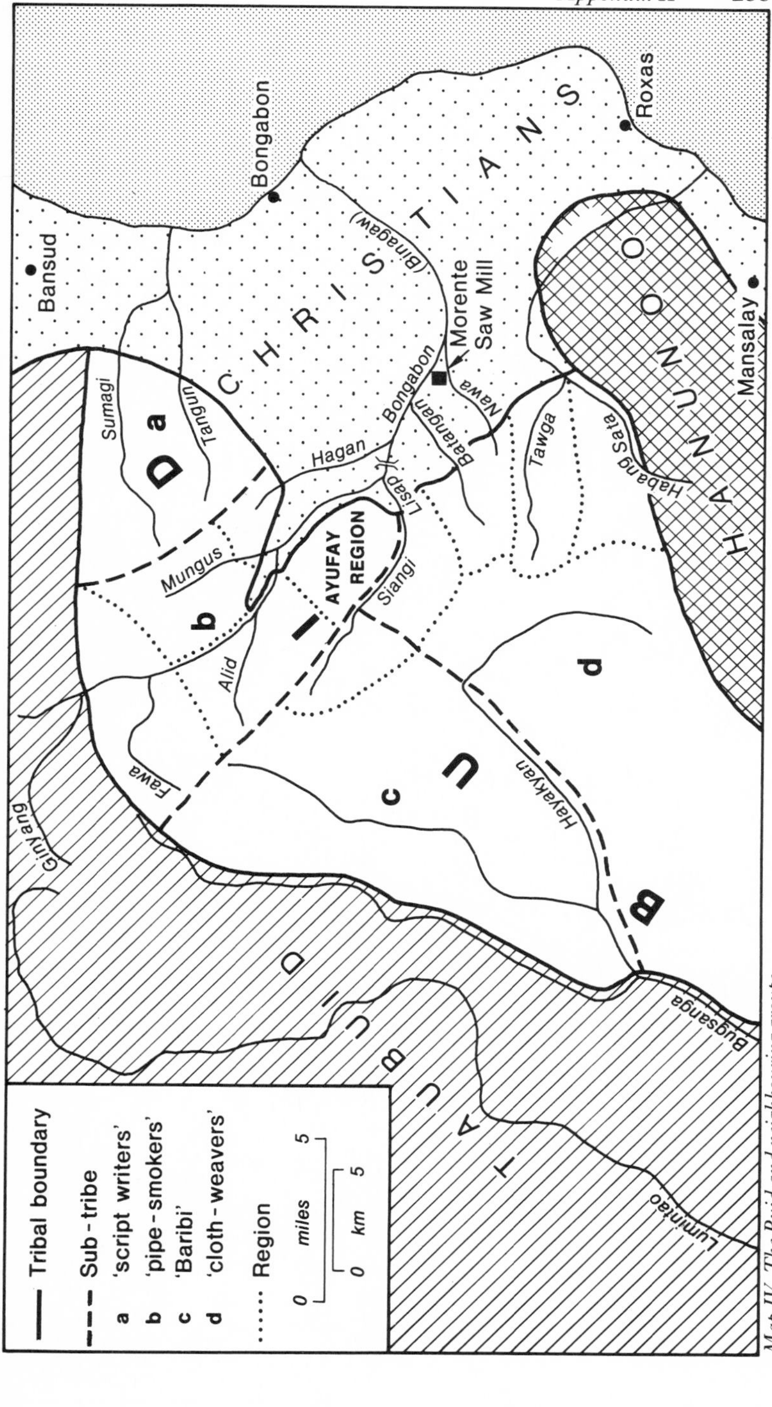

Map IV The Buid and neighbouring groups

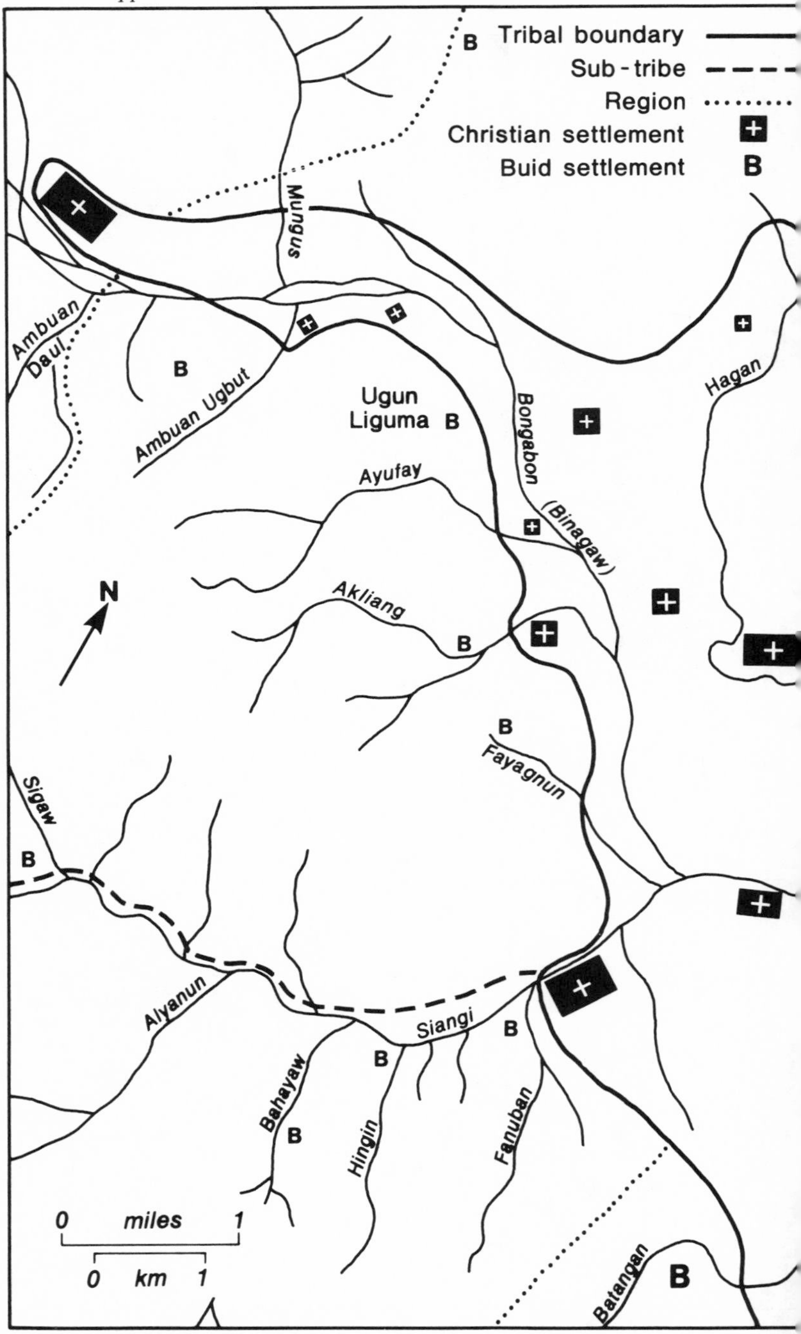

Map V The Ayufay region

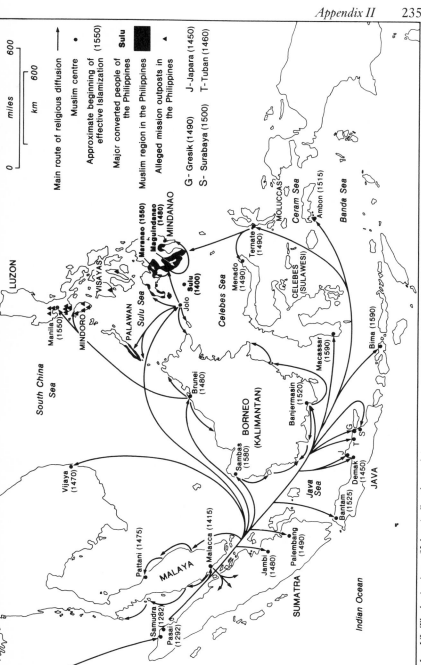

Map VI The beginnings of Islam in Southeast Asia

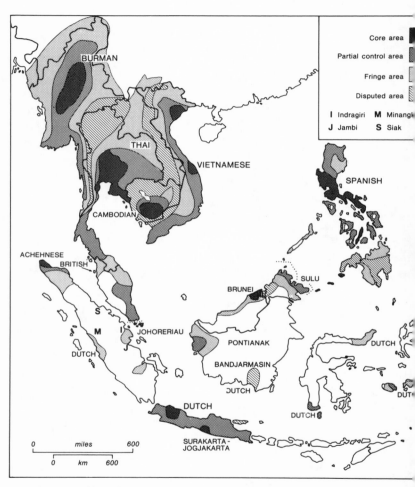

Map VII   Centres of power in Southeast Asia at the end of the eighteenth century

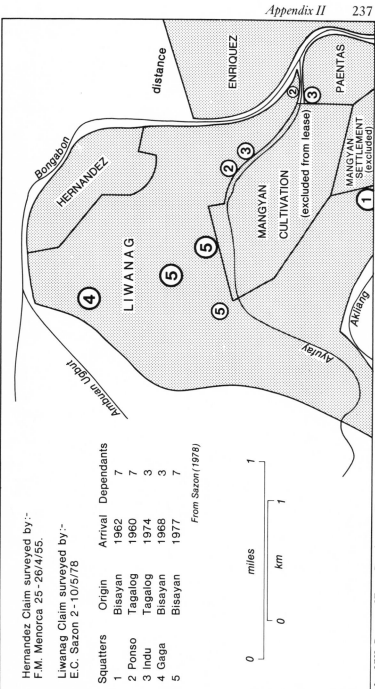

Hernandez Claim surveyed by:-
F.M. Menorca 25 - 26/4/55.

Liwanag Claim surveyed by:-
E.C. Sazon 2 - 10/5/78

Squatters	Origin	Arrival	Dependants
1	Bisayan	1962	7
2 Ponso	Tagalog	1960	7
3 Indu	Tagalog	1974	3
4 Gaga	Bisayan	1968	3
5	Bisayan	1977	7

From Sazon (1978)

Map VIII Bureau of Forest Development Pasture Lease Surveys in the Ayufay area, 1955–78

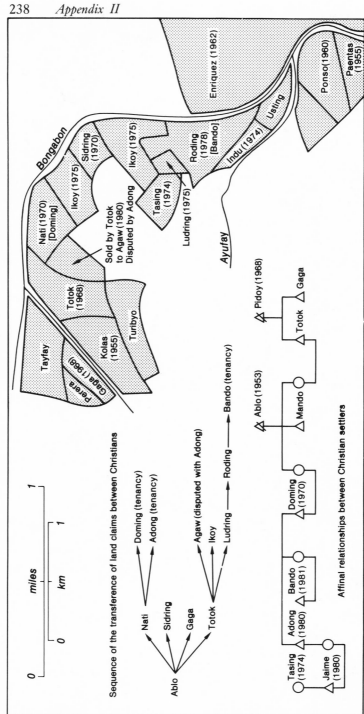

Map IX Actual Christian land holdings in Ayufay, 1981

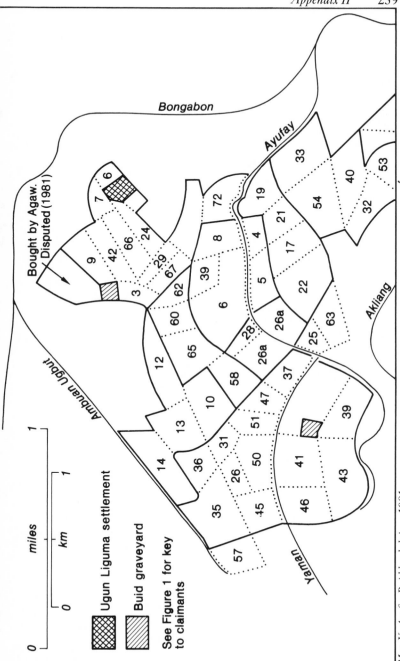

Map X Ayufay Buid land claims, 1981

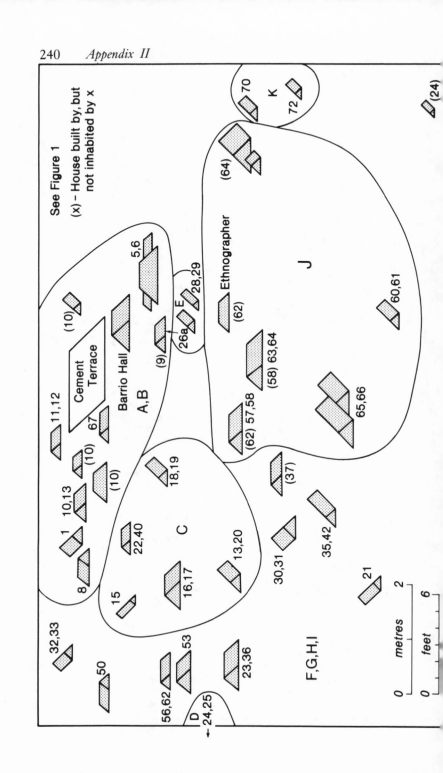

See Figure 1

(x) – House built by, but
    not inhabited by x

Notes

Chapter 3 Environment and economy

1 On the simultaneous cultivation of grain, root and tree crops elsewhere in Southeast Asia, see Conklin, 1957: 77; Schlegel, 1979: 39; M. Rosaldo, 1980: 110; Karim, 1981: 105, 119; Freeman, 1970: 190–2; Leach, 1954: 72. On the qualitative and ritual importance of rice, see Conklin, 1957: 30, 88; Schlegel, 1979: 41–7; M. Rosaldo, 1980: 111, 123–7; Freeman, 1970: 154, 203–18ff; Jocano, 1958: 250–7; Karim, 1981: 109; Manuel, 1973: 246, 363.

2 For hunter-gatherers, see Woodburn, 1968; Lee, 1979; Gardner, 1972; Turnbull, 1965; Morris, 1982; Roy, 1925. For hunter-cultivators, see M. Rosaldo, 1980: 119; Turner, 1957: 25.

3 There may be a more general pattern among the shifting cultivators of Northern Luzon in which agricultural cooperation between households is deliberately minimised. See, for example, the case of the Gaddang, who neighbour the Ilongot (Wallace, 1970: 61).

4 There is an interesting parallel here with the Zafimaniry of Madagascar, who also say that the planting of long-lived trees hastens their owner's death (M. Bloch, personal communication).

5 The Provincial Development Staff of Oriental Mindoro had this to say about the Mangyan Reservation on Buyayao Island: 'It is being developed as a tourist spot by PANAMIN Secretary Elisalde, who found in Bulalacao an echo of paradise. It is also the haven of the Hanunoo, the most civilized branch of stone age primitive Mangyan with colourful beadwork, baskets and mats.'

Chapter 4 Idioms of social organization

1 This statement anticipates Murdock's concept of the deme, a form of kinship grouping characteristic of the Austronesian culture area (cf. Bloch, 1971: 46). Its relevance to Buid social organisation is discussed below.

2 See Conklin, 1957: 12; Schlegel, 1970: 14; Frake, 1960: 54; Yengoyan, 1973: 166; R. Rosaldo, 1980: 9; Jocano, 1968: 237 for the Philippines and Morris, 1978: 47; Crain, 1978: 127; Appell, 1978: 145 for Borneo.

3 It may be that the lack of emphasis on defined rights and duties between specific kinsmen in the bilateral systems of Southeast Asia was a contributing factor in the development of the 'cognitive' approach of kinship by such writers as Conklin and Frake. As Conklin notes: 'After beginning a field investigation with kinship analysis one may find that political alignment, economic activities, or religious demands are determinant of

rights and duties among the members of a society far more often than are kin ties' (1964: 26).

4   The relative weakness of a society is mentioned because of the contrasting situation in Borneo, where a three-tier ranking system composed of a minority of aristocrats and slaves and a majority of commoners was not uncommon. A case can be made that the shifting cultivators of the Philippines, a prime target for Muslim slave raiders, often ended up being sold to the highland groups of Borneo (see Warren, 1981). This historical difference, of being at the supplying as opposed to the receiving end of slave raiding, may help to explain some of the differences between these two groups of societies.

5   According to Eggan, 'bilateral descent groups of some type exist in Ifugao and Sagada, and very probably in Kalinga and Bontoc as well' (1967: 198). These are the only Philippine examples of which I am aware, and they all involve wet-rice cultivators.

6   The importance of language in the differentiation of social groups has been noted by Morris among the Melanau: 'every village took a pride in its own distinctive accent and dialect words' (1978: 42).

7   The other communities in the Ayufay region contained the following number of households: Fayagnun, 15; Hagan, 15 (both of these communities have lost most of their land to the Christians); Ambuan, 20; Akliang, 40; Sigaw, 45. According to Lopez, the settlement of Batangan contains 96 households and 394 individuals (1981: 104). It is well on its way to including the entire population of its region in one settlement.

8   The same values are present among the Subanun, with the exception that among the latter it is possible for there to be more than one wife in a household. Otherwise, 'a Subanun family is strictly limited to two generations: parents and unmarried offspring' (Frake, 1960: 54).

9   C. Barton on the Ifugao: 'No promises are made by the contracting parties [to a marriage] to each other or to anyone else. Nor do the contracting parties take part in any religious ceremonials or in any marriage ceremonials of any kind. Marriage may be terminated at any time by mutual agreement. But that marriage is considered a contract is shown by the fact that if either party terminates the marriage against the will of the other the injured party has the right to assess and collect damages' (1919: 11). This account could be taken as an exact description of Buid marriage practices.

10   This belief appears to be widespread in the Philippines. It has been noted by Barton among the Ifugao (1919: 30) and among the Atta of Cagayan by Marques Guedes (personal communication).

11   Pennoyer claims that the first child is always killed among the Taubuid (1980b: 701).

12   Macdonald explains the existence of a special term for the relationship between brothers-in-law, but not between sisters-in-law, among the Palawan by the fact that marriage is predominantly uxorilocal. This means that the former are more likely to live in close proximity to one another than the latter (1977: 62).

13   Contrast this with the attitude of the Ilongot, among whom the notion of

tuydek, 'command', is the epitome of all speech, and is characteristic of the hierarchical relationships of age and sex in their society (M. Rosaldo, 1980: 72–6).

Chapter 5 Transformations in social organisation

1 To take the contrast between the Tausug and the Buid even further, it is interesting to note that Kiefer goes on to characterise the former as a 'dyad-centered society' (1972: 105).

Chapter 6 Spirit mediumship

1 According to Pennoyer, the Taubuid believe in the existence of two souls, which may leave the body temporarily without causing death (1975: 78; 1980: 700). The soul of the Hanunoo can also leave the body during illness and dreams without necessarily causing death (Conklin, 1955a: 228).

2 According to Lopez, the Batangan Buid hold that the soul of a dead person becomes like a pig, without a mind (*fangayufan*), shame (*kaya*), or honour (*kafiyan*) (1981: 183).

3 See Pennoyer, 1980b: 708 for an account of the elaborate devices constructed by the Taubuid to ward off evil spirits from their settlements.

4 The Buid are exceptional in not associating the power of spirit mediums with the possession of magical stones. They assert that only the Bangun shamans possess them. This belief is widespread in Southeast Asia (Conklin, 1955: 236; Jensen, 1974: 107; Atkinson, 1979: 3; Morris, 1967: 201). The Buid do believe that another class of healer, the *fangamlang*, who cure through the use of massage, do derive their power from certain black stones found in springs.

Chapter 7 Animal sacrifice

1 The Taubuid employ the swinging pit ritual to thank the head benevolent spirits for a good harvest; to ask for medical help; and to atone for a 'sin'. The pig is offered to the Taubuid equivalents of the spirits of the earth (Pennoyer, 1980b: 700). The Taubuid also employ a swinging dog ritual to exorcise evil spirits from an individual (ibid.).

2 In Batangan, the *andagaw* are known as *afu fungsu*, 'owners of mountain peaks' (Lopez, 1981: 179). There, the term *andagaw* is not associated with a specific type of spirit, but with the effects of breaking a taboo: earthquakes and floods. Among the Taubuid, the *andago* are a class of half-human, half-pig spirits, who punish people who laugh at animals with headaches (Pennoyer, 1975: 82). The Ayufay Buid were quite explicit in stating that offences against the *andagaw* were distinct from those against *ama dalugdug*, 'father thunder'. It is the latter who punishes offences such as incest, laughing at animals and mixing the wrong kinds of foods. In general, that which is thought to be taboo is more or less the

same among the Batangan Buid, the Ayufay Buid and the Taubuid, while the mystical agencies thought to be responsible for enforcing these taboos are highly variable, bearing to one another a complex of 'family re-semblances'. Cf. Endicott on the similar situation among the Negritos of Malaya (1979: 203–4).

3   See Pennoyer, 1980b: 696 for an account of a similar ritual among the Taubuid.

4   Compare this practice with the reference in myth presented in the last chapter about the trapping of *fangablang* beneath the roots of fig trees.

5   Compare this practice with that of the Cantonese, among whom the chief heir and mourner has to take on the bulk of the death pollution (Watson, 1982: 170).

6   The Ma'Betisek of Malaya believe that spirits see things in a reversed form to the way humans see them. 'Consequently, large portions of food will be seen as small, while small portions of food will be seen as large' (Karim, 1981: 185).

7   According to Lopez, the Batangan Buid believe that the *afu daga* are merely a subset of the *lai*, 'spirit familiars', and that all spirits with a human form are *lai*, and good. I have reservations about accepting this statement, as even the Hanunoo recognise the existence of evil spirits with a human form (Conklin, 1953: 155).

8   This belief appears to correspond with the Taubuid belief in two supreme eternal spirits, one male *funbalugu*, 'chief vine', and one female *fufuina*, 'grandmother'. They do not, however, appear to reside at the places of the rising and setting sun (Pennoyer, 1980b: 698). But see Fox on the belief among the Tagbanuwa of Palawan that the most sacred region of the universe is the area 'directly beyond the effulgence of the sunset, the *langut*, but still between the sky-cover and the earth. Here dwells the highest ranking deity and his entourage' (1954: 214).

Chapter 9 Summary and conclusions

1   Excepting the 'immediate-return' hunter-gatherer societies discussed by Woodburn (1982), who resemble the Buid in so many other ways as well.

Bibliography

APPELL, G. N., (ed.) 1976. *Studies in Borneo Societies*, Center for Southeast Asian Studies, Northern Illinois University, Special Report No. 12.

——, 1978. 'The Rungus Dusun', in *Essays in Borneo Societies* (ed.) V. T. King, Oxford University Press.

ATKINSON, J. M., 1979. 'Paths of the spirit familiars', unpublished thesis, Stanford University, California.

BARTON, R.F., 1919. *Ifugao Law*, University of California Publications in American Anthropology and Ethnology.

——, 1949. *The Kalingas: Their Institutions and Custom Law*, Chicago University Press.

BEYER, H. O., 1979. 'The Philippines before Magellan', reprinted in *Readings in Philippine Prehistory* (ed.) Mauro Garcia. Filipiniana Book Guild, Manila.

BLOCH, M., 1971. *Placing the Dead*, Seminar Press, London.

——, 1973. 'The long and the short term', in *The Character of Kinship* (ed.) J. Goody, Cambridge University Press.

——, 1975. 'Property and the end of affinity', in *Marxist Analyses in Social Anthropology* (ed.) M. Bloch, Malaby Press, London.

BLOCH, M. AND PARRY, J., (eds.) 1982. *Death and the Regeneration of Life*, Cambridge University Press.

BLOCK, E. AND LAWRENCE, H. L., 1927. *Digest of the Reports of the Supreme Court of the Philippines*, vol. 4, Lawyers' Cooperative Publishing Company, Rochester, N.Y.

BULMER, R., 1967. 'Why is the cassowary not a bird?' *Man* (NS) 2.

CONKLIN, H. C., 1949a. 'Preliminary report on field work on the islands of Mindoro and Palawan, Philippines', *American Anthropologist* 51.

——, 1949b. 'Bamboo literacy on Mindoro', *Pacific Discovery* 2.

——, 1953a. 'Buhid pottery', *University of Manila Journal of East Asiatic Studies* 3.

——, 1953b. *Hanunoo-English Vocabulary*, University of California Publications in Linguistics 9.

——, 1955a. 'The relation of Hanunoo culture to the plant world', unpublished thesis, Yale University.

——, 1955b. 'Hanunoo color categories', *Southwestern Journal of Anthropology* 11.

——, 1957. *Hanunoo Agriculture*, FAO, Rome.

——, 1958. 'Betel chewing among the Hanunoo', *Proceedings of the Fourth Far Eastern Prehistory Congress*.

——, 1959. 'Linguistic play in its cultural context', *Language* 35.

——, 1964. 'Ethnogenealogical method', in *Explorations in Cultural Anthropology* (ed.) W. H. Goodenough, McGraw-Hill, New York.

245

——, 1976. 'Ethnographic semantic analysis of Ifugao landform categories', in *Environmental Knowing* (eds.) G. T. Moore and R. G. Gollege, Dowden, Hutchinson Ross, Stroudsburg, Pa.

COSTA, H. DE LA, 1961. *The Jesuits in the Philippines*, Harvard University Press, Cambridge, Mass.

CRAIN, J. B., 1978. 'The Lun Dayeh', in *Essays on Borneo Societies* (ed.) V. T. King, Oxford University Press.

CUSHNER, N. P., 1971. *Spain in the Philippines*, Ateneo de Manila University Press, Quezon City.

DAVENPORT, W., 1959. 'Nonunilinear descent and descent groups', *American Anthropologist* 61.

DOUGLAS, M., 1963. *The Lele of the Kasai* Oxford University Press.

——, 1973. 'Self-evidence', *Proceedings of the Royal Anthropological Institute*.

DOZIER, E. P., 1966. *Mountain Arbiters*, University of Arizona Press.

DURKHEIM, E. AND MAUSS, M., 1963. *Primitive Classification*, Cohen & West, London.

EDER, J. F., 1975. 'Naming practices and the definition of affines among the Batak of the Philippines', *Ethnology* 14.

EGGAN, F., 1960. 'The Sagada Igorots of Northern Luzon', in *Social Structure in Southeast Asia* (ed.) G. P. Murdock, Quadrangle Books, Chicago.

——, 1967. 'Some aspects of bilateral social system in the northern Philippines', in *Studies in Philippine Anthropology* (ed.) M. D. Zamora, Phoenix Press, Quezon City.

——, 1972. 'Lewis Henry Morgan's *Systems*: a reevaluation', in *Kinship Studies in the Morgan Centennial Year* (ed.) P. Reining, Anthropological Society of Washington.

EMBREE, J. F., 1950. 'Thailand: a loosely structured social system', *American Anthropologist* 52.

ENDICOTT, K. M., 1970. *An Analysis of Malay Magic*, Clarendon Press, Oxford.

——, 1979. *Batek Negrito Religion*, Clarendon Press, Oxford.

EVANS, I. H. N., 1937. *The Negritos of Malaya*, Cambridge University Press.

——, 1953. *The Religion of the Tempasuk Dusuns of North Borneo*, Cambridge University Press.

EVANS-PRITCHARD, E. E., 1940. *The Nuer*, Oxford University Press.

——, 1956. *Nuer Religion*, Oxford University Press.

——, 1965. *Theories of Primitive Religion*, Oxford University Press.

EVERS, HANS-DIETER, 1969. *Loosely Structured Social Systems*, Yale University Southeast Asian Studies.

FAST, J. AND RICHARDSON, J., 1979. *Roots of Dependency*, Foundation for Nationalist Studies, Quezon City.

FINLEY, J. P., 1913. *The Subanu*, Carnegie Institute of Washington.

FIRTH, R. 1957. 'A note on descent groups in Polynesia'. *Man* 57.

——, 1963. 'Bilateral descent groups', in *Studies in Kinship and Marriage* (ed.) I. Schapera, Royal Anthropological Institute, London.

——, 1964. *Essays on Social Organization and Values*, Athlone Press, London.

——, 1967. 'Ritual and drama in Malay spirit mediumship'. *Comparative Studies in Society and History* 9.

FORGE, A., 1972. 'The golden fleece', *Man* (N.S.) 7: 4.

FORTES, M., 1959. 'Descent, filiation and affinity', *Man* 59.

——, 1966. 'Some reflections on ancestor worship in Africa', in *African Systems of Thought* (eds.) M. Fortes and G. Dieterlen, Oxford University Press.

FOX, R. B., 1954. 'Religion and society among the Tagbanuwa of Palawan Island, Philippines', unpublished thesis, University of Chicago.

FRAKE, C. O., 1960. 'The eastern Subanun of Mindanao', in *Social Structure in Southeast Asia* (ed.) G. P. Murdock, Quadrangle Books, Chicago.

——, 1980. *Language and Cultural Description*, Stanford University Press, California.

FRAKE, C. O. AND GOODENOUGH W. H., 1956. 'Malayo-Polynesian land tenure', *American Anthropologist* 58.

FRANCISCO, J. R., 1966. 'Palaeographic studies in the Philippines', *Sarawak Museum Journal* 13.

——, 1973. 'Philippine palaeography', *Philippine Journal of Linguistics*, Special Monograph No. 3.

FREEMAN, J. D., 1958. 'The family system of the Iban of Borneo', in *The Developmental Cycle in Domestic Groups* (ed.) J. Goody. Cambridge University Press.

——, 1961. 'On the concept of the kindred', *Journal of the Royal Anthropological Institute* 91.

——, 1970. *Report on the Iban*, Athlone Press, London.

GARDNER, F., 1940. *Indic Writings of the Mindoro-Palawan Axis* vol. 3, Witte Memorial Museum, San Antonio.

——, 1943. *Philippine Indic Studies*, Witte Memorial Museum, San Antonio.

GARDNER, F. AND MALIWANAG I., 1939. *Indic Writings of the Mindoro-Palawan Axis*, vols. 1–2, Witte Memorial Museum, San Antonio.

GARDNER, P. M., 1972. 'The Paliyans', in *Hunters and Gatherers Today* (ed.) M. G. Bicchieri, Holt, Rinehart & Winston, New York.

GEERTZ, C., 1963. *Agricultural Involution*, University of California Press.

GEERTZ, H. AND GEERTZ C., 1975. *Kinship in Bali*, Chicago University Press.

GOODENOUGH, W. H., 1955. 'A problem in Malayo-Polynesian social organization', *American Anthropologist* 57.

GOODY, J., 1961. 'The classification of double descent systems', *Current Anthropology* 2.

——, 1973. 'Bridewealth and dowry in Africa and Eurasia', in *Bridewealth and Dowry* (eds.) J. Goody and S. J. Tambiah, Cambridge University Press.

HOLLNSTEINER, M. R., 1973. 'Reciprocity in the lowland Philippines', in *Four Readings on Philippine Values* (eds.) F. Lynch and A. de Guzman, Institute of Philippine Culture, Ateneo de Manila University Press.

ICL RESEARCH TEAM, 1979. *A Report on Tribal Minorities in Mindanao*, Regal Printing Company, Manila.

JENSEN, E., 1974. *The Iban and Their Religion*, Oxford University Press.

JESUS, E. C. 1980. *The Tobacco Monopoly in the Philippines*, Ateneo de Manila University Press, Quezon City.

JOCANO, F. L., 1968. *Sulod Society*, University of the Philippines Press.

KARIM, W. J., 1981. *Ma'Betisek Concepts of Living Things*, Athlone Press, London.

KEESING, F. M., 1962. *The Ethnohistory of Northern Luzon*, Stanford University Press, California.

KERKVLIET, B. J., 1977. *The Huk Rebellion*, University of California Press.

KESSLER, C. S., 1977. 'Conflict and sovereignty in Kelantese Malay spirit seances', in *Case Studies in Spirit Possession* (eds.) V. Crapanzano and V. Garrison, John Wiley, New York.

KIEFER, T., 1972. *The Tausug*, Holt, Rinehart & Winston, New York.

KIKUCHI, Y., 1971. 'A preliminary consideration of the social structure of the Bayanan group of the Batangan, Mindoro, Philippines', *Chuo-Gakuin Daigu Ronso* 6.

KING, V., 1976. 'Cursing, special death and spirits in Embaloh society', *Bijdragen tot de Taal- Land- en Volkenkunde* 132

——, 1978. 'The Maloh', in *Essays on Borneo Societies* (ed.) V. King, Oxford University Press.

KIRSCH, A. T., 1969. 'Loose structure: theory or description', in *Loosely Structured Social Systems* (ed.) H. D. Evers, Yale University Southeast Asian Studies.

LEACH, E., 1954. *Political Systems of Highland Burma*, Athlone Press, London.

——, 1962. 'On certain unconsidered aspects of double descent systems', *Man* 62.

——, 1964. 'Anthropological aspects of language', in *New Directions in the Study of Language* (ed.) E. H. Lennenberg, MIT Press, Boston.

LEE, R. B., 1979. *The !Kung San*, Cambridge University Press.

LÉVI-STRAUSS, C., 1966. *The Savage Mind*, Weidenfeld & Nicolson, London.

——, 1969. *The Elementary Structures of Kinship*, Eyre & Spottiswoode, London.

LEWIS, I. M., 1971. *Ecstatic Religion*, Penguin Books, Harmondsworth.

LIEBAN, R. W., 1967. *Cebuano Sorcery*, University of California Press.

LIENHARDT, G., 1961. *Divinity and Experience*, Oxford University Press.

LLAMAZON, T. A., 1978. *Handbook of Philippine Language Groups*, Ateneo de Manila University Press, Quezon City.

LOPEZ, V. B., 1974. 'Culture contact and ethnogenesis in Mindoro up to the end of Spanish rule', *Asian Studies* 15.

——, 1976. *The Mangyans of Mindoro*, University of the Philippines Press.

——, 1981. Peasants in the hills: a study of the dynamics of social change among the Buid swidden cultivators in the Philippines, unpublished thesis, University of Toronto.

LUNA, S. N., 1975. *Born Primitive in the Philippines*, Southern Illinois University Press.

MACDONALD, C., 1971. 'Notes de terrain: Mindoro Philippines', in *Langues et Techniques: Nature et Société* (eds.) J. Thomas and L. Bernot, Paris.

——, 1973. 'De quelques manifestations chamanistiques à Palawan', *ASEMI* 4.

——, 1977. *Une Société Simple*, Institut d'Ethnologie, Paris.

——, 1981. 'Extase et esthétique', in *Orients pour Georges Condominas*, Sudestasie/Privat, Paris.

MACEDA, M., 1967. 'A brief report on some Mangyans in northern Oriental Mindoro', *Unitas* 40.

MAJUL, C. A., 1973. *Muslims in the Philippines*, Saint Mary's Publishing Company, Manila.

MANUEL, E. A., 1973. *Manuvu Social Organization*, University of the Philippines Press.

MARSHALL, L., 1961. 'Sharing, talking and giving: the relief of social tensions among !Kung Bushmen', *Africa* 31.

MIYAMOTO, M., 1974. 'Fieldtrips to Buid areas in Oriental Mindoro', *SHA* 7.

——, 1975. 'The society and folk beliefs of the Hanunoo-Mangyan in Southeast Mindoro, Philippine Islands', unpublished thesis, Tokyo Metropolitan University.

MORRIS, B., 1976. 'Whither the savage mind', *Man* (NS) 11.

——, 1982. *Forest Traders*, Athlone Press, London.

MORRIS, H. S., 1967. 'Shamanism among the Oya Melanau,' in *Social Organization* (ed.) M. Freedman, Frank Cass, London.

——, 1978. 'The coastal Melanau', in *Essays on Borneo Societies* (ed.) V. King, Oxford University Press.

MURDOCK, G. P. 1949. *Social Structure*, Macmillan, New York.

——, 1960. 'Cognatic forms of social organization', in *Social Structure in Southeast Asia* (ed.) G. P. Murdock. Quadrangle Books, Chicago.

NARRA, 1957. *National Resettlement and Reconstruction Agency Annual Report*, Manila.

NEEDHAM, R., 1966. 'Age category and descent', *Bijdragen tot de Taal- Land-en Volkenkunde* 122.

——, 1967. 'Percussion and transition', *Man* (NS) 2.

PAZ, E. DE LA, 1968. 'A survey of the Hanunoo Mangyan culture and barriers to change', *Unitas* 41.

PELZER, K. J., 1945. *Pioneer Settlement in the Asiatic Tropics*, American Geographical Society Special Publication No. 29, New York.

PENNOYER, F. D., 1975. 'Taubuid plants and ritual complexes', unpublished thesis, Washington State University.

——, 1977. 'The Taubuid of Mindoro, Philippines', *Philippine Quarterly of Culture and Society* 5.

——, 1978. 'Leadership and control in a Sumagui river Bangun settlement', *Philippine Sociological Review* 26.

——, 1979. 'Shifting cultivation and shifting subsistence patterns', in *Contributions to the Study of Philippine Shifting Cultivation* (ed.) H. Olofson, University of the Philippines Forestry Research Institute.

——, 1980a. 'Buid and Taubuid: a new subgrouping in Mindoro, Philippines', in *Papers from the Second Eastern Conference on Austronesian Languages* (ed.) P. B. Naylor, University of Michigan Press.

——, 1980b. 'Ritual in Taubuid life', *Anthropos* 75.

PHELAN, J. L., 1959. *The Hispanization of the Philippines*, University of Wisconsin Press.

POLANYI, K., 1944. *The Great Transformation*, Reinhart, New York.

——, 1957. 'The economy as instituted process', in *Trade and Markets in the Early Empires* (eds.) K. Polanyi, H. Pearson and C. Anderson, Free Press, Glencoe.

POSTMA, A., 1965. 'The *ambahan* of the Hanunoo Mangyan of southern Mindoro', *Anthropos* 60.

——, 1968. 'Contemporary Philippine syllabaries in Mindoro', *San Carlos Publications* Series E, No. 1, Cebu City.

——, 1971. 'Contemporary Mangyan scripts', *Philippine Journal of Linguistics* 2.

——, 1974. 'Development among the Mangyans of Mindoro', *Philippine Quarterly of Culture and Society* 2.

——, 1977a. 'Mangyan folklore', *Philippine Quarterly of Culture and Society* 5.

——, 1977b. 'Mindoro missions revisited', *Philippine Quarterly of Culture and Society* 5.

——, 1981a. *Treasure of a Minority*, Arnoldus Press, Manila.

——, 1981b. *Mindoro Mangyan Mission*, Arnoldus Press, Manila.

PROVINCIAL DEVELOPMENT STAFF, 1979. Briefing sheet: Typescript.

RADCLIFFE-BROWN, A. R., 1952. *Structure and Function in Primitive Society*, Cohen & West, London.

REED, R. R., 1978. *Colonial Manila*, University of California Press.

REVEL-MACDONALD, N., 1971. 'La collecte du miel', in *Langues et Techniques: Nature et Société* (eds.) J. Thomas and L. Bernot, Paris.

ROBERTSON-SMITH, W., 1907. *Lectures on the Religion of the Semites*, 3rd edn., A. & C. Black, London.

ROSALDO, M., 1980. *Knowledge and Passion*, Cambridge University Press.

ROSALDO, R., 1975. 'Where precision lies'. In *The Interpretation of Symbolism* (ed.) R. Willis, Malaby Press, London.

——, 1979. 'The social relations of Ilongot subsistence'. In *Contributions to the Study of Philippine Shifting Cultivation* (ed.) H. Olofson, University of the Philippines Forestry Research Institute.

——, 1980. *Ilongot Headhunting 1883–1974*. Stanford University Press.

ROTH, D. M., 1977. *The Friar Estates in the Philippines*, University of New Mexico Press.

ROY, S. C., 1925. *The Birhors*, GEL Mission Press, Ranchi, India.

SAHLINS, M., 1963. Review article: remarks on *Social Structure in Southeast Asia*, *Journal of the Polynesian Society* 72.

——, 1965. 'On the ideology and composition of descent groups', *Man* 65.

——, 1972. *Stone Age Economics*, Tavistock Publications, London.

SATHER, C., 1978. 'The Bajau Laut'. In *Essays on Borneo Societies* (ed.) V. King, Oxford University Press.

SCHARER, H., 1963. *Ngaju Religion*, Martinus Nijhoff, The Hague.

SCHEFFLER, H. W., 1965. *Choiseul Island Social Structure*, University of California Press.

——, 1966. 'Ancestor worship in anthropology', *Current Anthropology* 7.

SCHLEGEL, S., 1970. *Tiruray Justice*, University of California Press.

——, 1979. *Tiruray Subsistence*, Ateneo de Manila University Press, Quezon City.

SCHLIPPE, P. DE, 1956. *Shifting Cultivation in Africa*, Routledge & Kegan Paul, London.

SCHNEIDER, H., 1981. *Livestock and Equality in East Africa*, Indiana University Press.

STEINBERG, D. J., (ed.) 1971. *In Search of Southeast Asia*, Pall Mall Press, London.

STRATHERN, A., 1971. *The Rope of Moka*. Cambridge University Press.

STICKLEY, C., 1975. *Broken Snare*, OMF Press, Sevenoaks, Kent.

TAMBIAH, S. J., 1968. 'Animals are good to think and good to prohibit', *Ethnology* 8.

THIEL, E., 1954. Application for Mangyan reservation. Typescript in Bureau of Forest Development files (224/D-23 Land).

TURNBULL, C. M., 1965. *Wayward Servants*, Natural History Press, Garden City, NY.

TURNER, V. W., 1957. *Schism and Continuity in an African Society*, Manchester University Press.

TWEDDELL, C. E., 1970. 'The identity and distribution of the Mangyan tribes of Mindoro, Philippines', *Anthropological Linguistics* 12.

WALLACE, B. J., 1970. *Hill and Valley Farmers*, Schenkman, Cambridge, Mass.

WANG TEH-MING, 1964. 'Sino-Filipino historico-cultural relations', *Philippine Social Sciences and Humanities Review* 29.

WARREN, J. F., 1981. *The Sulu Zone 1768–1898*, Singapore University Press.

WATSON, J. L., 1982. 'Of flesh and bones', in *Death and the Regeneration of Life* (eds.) M. Bloch and J. Parry, Cambridge University Press.

WEBER, M., 1947. *The Theory of Social and Economic Organization*, Free Press, New York.

WERNSTEDT, F. L. AND SPENCER, T. E., 1967. *The Philippine Island World*, University of California Press.

WHITTIER, H. L., 1978. 'The Kenyah', in *Essays on Borneo Societies* (ed.) V. King, Oxford University Press.

WILSON, M., 1950. 'Nyakyusa kinship', in *African Systems of Kinship and Marriage* (eds.) A. R. Radcliffe-Brown and D. Forde, Oxford University Press.

WINSTEDT, R. O., 1925. *Shaman, Saiva and Sufi*, Constable, London.

WOODBURN, J., 1968. 'Stability and flexibility in Hadza residential groupings', in *Man the Hunter* (eds.) R. Lee and I. DeVore, Aldine Press, Chicago.

——, 1982. 'Egalitarian societies', *Man* (NS) 17.

WORCESTER, D. C., 1930. *The Philippines, Past and Present*, Macmillan, New York.

YENGOYAN, A. A., 1973. 'Kindreds and task groups in Mandaya social organization', *Ethnology* 12.

ZORC, D. R., 1974. 'Internal and external relationships of the Mangyan languages', *Oceanic Linguistics* 13.

ZUNIGA, J. M. DE, 1973. *Status of the Philippines in 1800*, Filipiniana Book Guild, Manila.

Combined Index and Glossary

Note: Unless otherwise indicated, all non-English words are in the Ayufay Buid dialect. Tagalog words are indicated by (T).

London School of Economics
Monographs on Social Anthropology

Published by The Athlone Press, 44 Bedford Row, London WC1R 4LY

Titles marked with an asterisk are now out of print. Those marked with a dagger have been reprinted in paperback editions and are only available in this form. A double dagger indicates availability in both hardcover and paperback editions.

†18 MAURICE FREEDMAN
Lineage Organization in Southeastern China, 1958.
†19 FREDRIK BARTH
Political Leadership among Swat Pathans, 1959.
†20 L. H. PALMIER
Social Status and Power in Java, 1960.
†21 JUDITH DJAMOUR
Malay Kinship and Marriage in Singapore, 1959.
‡22 E. R. LEACH
Rethinking Anthropology, 1961.
*23 S. M. SALIM
Marsh Dwellers of the Euphrates Delta, 1962.
†24 S. VAN DER SPRENKEL
Legal Institutions in Manchu China: A Sociological Analysis, 1962.
*25 CHANDRA JAYAWARDENA
Conflict and Solidarity in a Guianese Plantation, 1963.
*26 H. IAN HOGBIN
Kinship and Marriage in a New Guinea Village, 1963.
*27 JOAN METGE
A New Maori Migration: Rural and Urban Relations in Northern New Zealand, 1964.
†28 RAYMOND FIRTH
Essays on Social Organization and Values, 1964.
*29 M. G. SWIFT
Malay Peasant Society in Jelebu, 1965.
*30 JEREMY BOISSEVAIN
Saints and Fireworks: Religion and Politics in Rural Malta, 1965.
 31 JUDITH DJAMOUR
The Muslim Matrimonial Court in Singapore, 1966.
*32 CHIE NAKANE
Kinship and Economic Organization in Rural Japan, 1967.
†33 MAURICE FREEDMAN
Chinese Lineage and Society: Fukien and Kwantung, 1966.
 34 W. H. R. RIVERS
Kinship and Social Organization, 1914, Constable & Co. Reprinted with commentaries by Raymond Firth and David M. Schneider, 1968.
*35 ROBIN FOX
The Keresan Bridge: A Problem in Pueblo Ethnology, 1967.
*36 MARSHALL MURPHREE
Christianity and the Shona, 1969.
 37 G. K. NUKUNYA
Kinship and Marriage among the Anlo Ewe, 1969.
†38 LUCY MAIR
Anthropology and Social Change, 1969.
 39 SANDRA WALLMAN
Take Out Hunger: Two Case Studies of Rural Development in Basutoland, 1969.

40 MEYER FORTES
Time and Social Structure and Other Essays, 1970.
41 J. D. FREEMAN
Report on the Iban, 1970.
42 W. E. WILLMOTT
The Political Structure of the Chinese Community in Cambodia, 1970.
43 I. SCHAPERA
Tribal Innovators: Tswana Chiefs and Social Change 1795–1940, 1970.
†44 E. R. LEACH
Political Systems of Highland Burma: A Study of Kachin Social Structure,
1954, G. Bell & Sons. Reprinted 1970.
45 PHILIP STANIFORD
*Pioneers in the Tropics: The Political Organization of Japanese in an Immigrant
Community in Brazil*, 1973.
46 SUTTI REISSIG DE ORTIZ
Uncertainties in Peasant Farming: A Colombian Case, 1973.
47 STUART B. PHILPOTT
West Indian Migration: The Montserrat Case, 1973.
48 J. DAVIS
Land and Family in Pisticci, 1973.
49 LOUISE MORAUTA
Beyond the Village: Local Politics in Madang, Papua New Guinea, 1974.
50 J. DAVIS (ed.)
Choice and Change: Essays in Honour of Lucy Mair, 1974.
51 ALFRED GELL
Metamorphosis of the Cassowaries: Umeda Society, Language and Ritual,
1975.
52 GILBERT LEWIS
Knowledge of Illness in a Sepik Society: A Study of the Gnau, New Guinea,
1975.
53 ABBAS AHMED MOHAMED
White Nile Arabs: Political Leadership and Economic Change, 1980.
54 WAZIR-JAHAN KARIM
Ma'Betisék Concepts of Living Things, 1981.
55 BRIAN MORRIS
Forest Traders: A Socio-Economic Study of the Hill Pandaram, 1982.
56 WILLIAM D. WILDER
*Communication, Social Structure and Development in Rural Malaysia: A
Study of Kampung Kuala Bera*, 1982.
57 THOMAS GIBSON
*Sacrifice and Sharing in the Philippine Highlands: Religion and Society among
the Buid of Mindoro*, 1986.